EXECUTIVE COMPENSATION IN LARGE INDUSTRIAL CORPORATIONS

NATIONAL BUREAU OF ECONOMIC RESEARCH

FISCAL STUDIES

WILBUR G. LEWELLEN

Purdue University

EXECUTIVE COMPENSATION IN LARGE INDUSTRIAL CORPORATIONS

NATIONAL BUREAU OF ECONOMIC RESEARCH

NEW YORK 1968

Distributed by COLUMBIA UNIVERSITY PRESS

NEW YORK AND LONDON

Copyright © 1968 by National Bureau of Economic Research
All Rights Reserved
L.C. Card No. 67-29643

Printed in the United States of America

RELATION OF THE DIRECTORS TO THE WORK AND PUBLICATIONS OF THE NATIONAL BUREAU OF ECONOMIC RESEARCH

1. The object of the National Bureau of Economic Research is to ascertain and to present to the public important economic facts and their interpretation in a scientific and impartial manner. The Board of Directors is charged with the responsibility of ensuring that the work of the National Bureau is carried on in strict conformity with this object.

2. To this end the Board of Directors shall appoint one or more Directors of Research.

3. The Director or Directors of Research shall submit to the members of the Board, or to its Executive Committee, for their formal adoption, all specific proposals concerning researches to be instituted.

4. No report shall be published until the Director or Directors of Research shall have submitted to the Board a summary drawing attention to the character of the data and their utilization in the report, the nature and treatment of the problems involved, the main conclusions, and such other information as in their opinion would serve to determine the suitability of the report for publication in accordance with the principles of the National Bureau.

5. A copy of any manuscript proposed for publication shall also be submitted to each member of the Board. For each manuscript to be so submitted a special committee shall be appointed by the President, or at his designation by the Executive Director, consisting of three Directors selected as nearly as may be one from each general division of the Board. The names of the special manuscript committee shall be stated to each Director when the summary and report described in paragraph (4) are sent to him. It shall be the duty of each member of the committee to read the manuscript. If each member of the special committee signifies his approval within thirty days, the manuscript may be published. If each member of the special committee has not signified his approval within thirty days of the transmittal of the report and manuscript, the Director of Research shall then notify each member of the Board, requesting approval or disapproval of publication, and thirty additional days shall be granted for this purpose. The manuscript shall then not be published unless at least a majority of the entire Board and a two-thirds majority of those members of the Board who shall have voted on the proposal within the time fixed for the receipt of votes on the publication proposed shall have approved.

6. No manuscript may be published, though approved by each member of the special committee, until forty-five days have elapsed from the transmittal of the summary and report. The interval is allowed for the receipt of any memorandum of dissent or reservation, together with a brief statement of his reasons, that any member may wish to express; and such memorandum of dissent or reservation shall be published with the manuscript if he so desires. Publication does not, however, imply that each member of the Board has read the manuscript, or that either members of the Board in general, or of the special committee, have passed upon its validity in every detail.

7. A copy of this resolution shall, unless otherwise determined by the Board, be printed in each copy of every National Bureau book.

(Resolution adopted October 25, 1926,
as revised February 6, 1933, and February 24, 1941)

This report is one of a series of studies on tax structure and economic growth aided by grants from the Rockefeller Brothers Fund and the Life Insurance Association of America. These organizations, however, are not responsible for any of the statements made or views expressed.

TAX POLICIES FOR ECONOMIC GROWTH

ADVISORY COMMITTEE

The Advisory Committee on the Study of Tax Policies for Economic Growth has generously assisted in planning and reviewing the work of the staff. Their advice is gratefully acknowledged without, however, implying their concurrence with the views expressed in this report. The members of the committee are:

Carl S. Shoup, Chairman, *Columbia University*
Julian D. Anthony, *Hartford Life Insurance Company*
Walter J. Blum, *University of Chicago*
George T. Conklin, Jr., *Guardian Life Insurance Company of America*
John F. Due, *University of Illinois*
Richard B. Goode, *International Monetary Fund*
C. H. Greenewalt, *E. I. du Pont de Nemours and Company*
Albert J. Hettinger, Jr., *Lazard Frères and Company*
E. Gordon Keith, *University of Pennsylvania*
Wesley Lindow, *Irving Trust Company*
Stacy May, *Wellfleet, Massachusetts*
Maurice Moonitz, *University of California at Berkeley*
Richard A. Musgrave, *Harvard University*
James J. O'Leary, *Lionel D. Edie & Co., Inc.*
Joseph A. Pechman, *Brookings Institution*
Maurice E. Peloubet, *Price, Waterhouse & Company*
George B. Roberts, *Larchmont, New York*
Lawrence H. Seltzer, *formerly of Wayne State University*
Dan T. Smith, *Harvard University*
Stanley S. Surrey, *U.S. Treasury Department*
George Terborgh, *Machinery and Allied Products Institute*
William C. Warren, *Columbia University*
Laurence N. Woodworth, *Joint Committee on Internal Revenue Taxation*

CONTENTS

PART II
EMPIRICAL ANALYSIS

APPENDIXES

TABLES

CHARTS

PREFACE

This volume had its origins in a master's thesis completed by the author at the Massachusetts Institute of Technology in 1961. That study and a subsequent article prepared jointly with Daniel M. Holland [1] dealt in particular with a comparison between the value to corporate executives of their stock options and their annual salary plus bonus payments. The investigation reported on here, which also served as the basis for the author's doctoral dissertation at M.I.T., extends the conceptual framework developed for options to the remaining components of the compensation package. In that respect, it represents the latest in a series of analyses of the structure, evolution, and impact of executive rewards which have appeared in the literature of business and economics over the last thirty years or so. The classic works of Baker and of Washington and Rothschild are the landmarks in the field, but more recent studies by Hall, Roberts, Smyth, Patton, and Burgess [2] have contributed significantly to our knowledge and understanding of the process of managerial remuneration. The Burgess book, which appeared while the present investigation was in progress, is perhaps its closest intellectual antecedent with respect to concepts and objectives, in that both are concerned with measuring what may be termed the "current income equivalent" of non-current rewards. While there are rather substantial differences in the

---

[1] Daniel M. Holland and Wilbur G. Lewellen, "Probing the Record of Stock Options," *Harvard Business Review,* March-April 1962.

[2] John C. Baker, *Executive Salaries and Bonus Plans,* New York, 1938; George T. Washington and V. Henry Rothschild, *Corporate Executives' Compensation,* New York, 1942 (title changed to *Compensating the Corporate Executive* for the second and third editions, 1951 and 1962); Challis A. Hall, *Effects of Taxation on Executive Compensation and Retirement Plans,* Cambridge, 1951; David R. Roberts, *Executive Compensation,* Glencoe, Ill., 1959; Richard C. Smyth, *Financial Incentives for Management,* New York, 1960; Arch Patton, *Men, Money, and Motivation,* New York, 1961; and Leonard R. Burgess, *Top Executive Pay Package,* New York, 1963.

valuation methodology employed in the two studies, many of the findings reported here are, where comparable, consistent with those of Burgess.

Because this study has been several years in preparation and has required a considerable amount of data collecting and processing at various stages, more than the usual number of individuals became involved in its execution. The contributions of the staff of the National Bureau were invaluable. Norman Ture, who has directed the Bureau's project on Tax Policies for Economic Growth, supplied encouragement when encouragement was needed, paved the way for additional research support and, most importantly, enforced the kind of discipline in concept and presentation which—although I did not always appreciate it at the time—was essential to the preparation of a cohesive document. The Bureau's staff reading committee, composed of Gerhard Bry, Ralph Nelson, and Thomas Juster, provided the perspective and critical judgment which, I trust, kept my more blatant preconceptions from finding their way into the finished version. Joan Tron's editing skills smoothed out most of the remaining rough spots. I am most grateful also to Theodore Yntema of the Board of Directors of the National Bureau for incisive comments on the manuscript. The reading committee of the National Bureau's Board of Directors, Thomas D. Flynn, Charles G. Mortimer, and Gus Tyler, made many helpful comments, which I gratefully acknowledge. Throughout, Geoffrey Moore kept the whole effort moving toward fruition.

The study owes much to the advice and counsel of Douglass V. Brown and Paul Cootner of the Alfred P. Sloan School of Management at the Massachusetts Institute of Technology, who gave generously of their time on numerous occasions during the past few years. My research assistants—Jack Brown, Peter Grant, William Mihaltse, Abraham Setnick, Peter Thurston, and William Ryan of the Sloan School, and Franz Giguere, Charles Holt, Juie-Min Cheng, and Stanley Lipstadt of the Herman C. Krannert Graduate School of Industrial Administration at Purdue University—aided significantly in the collection of the data and in programming the computations.

Winthrop T. Lewis of the John Hancock Mutual Life Insurance Company in Boston provided important help in the crucial early stages of the investigation in connection with the conceptual framework and the relevant actuarial mathematics. Albert E. Whiton of The Travelers

Insurance Company and Hugh Dolby of the Connecticut General Life
Insurance Company, both in Hartford, supplied needed historical information on individual annuity premium rates. John E. Steele, Placement Director at the Harvard University Graduate School of Business
Administration, did the same for the starting salaries of MBA graduates.
In all four cases, these men took time out of busy schedules to respond
cheerfully to my requests for assistance.

In addition to the support provided by the Rockefeller Brothers Fund
and the Life Insurance Association of America to the National Bureau's
project of which this study is a part, I wish to acknowledge the assistance
given by the Standard Oil Company of Indiana and the Ford Foundation. The former, through the Standard Oil Foundation, granted the
author a fellowship which financed the final year of his doctoral studies,
during which time the research represented herein was begun. The Ford
Foundation's grant to the Sloan School of Management for research in
business finance was drawn on over a period of several years to provide
funds for computer time and for salaries of research assistants. The
computations themselves were performed at the Computer Centers of
M.I.T. and Purdue University and at the computer facility of the Sloan
School of Management.

Special mention should also be made of the debts owed John S. Day,
Associate Dean of the Krannert School at Purdue, and Mrs. Jean Stanton
of M.I.T. Dean Day's moral and financial support—and patience—
during the last two years materially aided completion of the study. So
did his friendly but firm admonitions to "Get on with it." Jean Stanton's
role was the delicate one of typing the final manuscript. Her forbearance
under that always difficult circumstance was as welcome as her skill and
speed in performing the work.

There is, however, no way to measure or even reasonably suggest
the magnitude of the contributions of the two persons most responsible
for there being a document to present at all: my wife, Jean, and Daniel
M. Holland of the Sloan School of Management, who shepherded me
through my doctoral studies at M.I.T. It is in no sense an exaggeration
to say that the end product is as much a result of their energies as of
my own.

W. G. L.

FOREWORD

This study is one of a series undertaken by the National Bureau of Economic Research to add to our understanding of the influence of federal tax policies on economic growth. This broad endeavor, directed by Norman B. Ture, falls into two parts: one concerned with the effects of the corporate income tax on business decisions, and the other with the effects of the personal income tax on individual effort.

The present volume belongs to the second group and is concerned with questions such as the following: What happens to the net returns from effort when a heavy personal income tax is imposed as it was in the United States twenty-five years ago? What changes take place in the level of compensation, in the structure of compensation among various occupations, and in the form in which it is arranged? What effect do these changes have on the supply of effort, i.e., the number of people available for productive work, the pace at which they labor, and the tasks they choose to do?

Answers to these questions are the links in a chain that runs from taxation at one end to economic growth at the other via an effect on personal effort. Lewellen's analysis comprises the basis for the answers that make up the first several links in that chain. Two other studies—one that analyzes tax return data to determine the income and tax characteristics of high-salaried persons, and the other that draws on a series of interviews, are designed to get at the remaining links.

That these are important questions is not open to dispute. That we should not expect a general answer, applicable to all kinds and conditions of effort, should also be clear. For the Bureau's project we have sought the answer to these questions in the specific context of a particular category of "workers"—business executives.

The decision to focus the study in this manner reflects the judgment that very little in the way of interesting, important, and valid findings on the effect of taxation on effort is possible for "workers in general."

Numerous factors enter into the decision to work, and this decision is made in the context of a particular market for labor and specific conditions of work that importantly interact with other determinants of the decision. Having surveyed the relevant economic theory and previous empirical work, we concluded that the questions we posed could be meaningfully answered only in the complex reality of a well-defined category of personal effort.

For the choice of business executives as the initial [1] group of "workers" on which to concentrate, there were a number of compelling reasons. Executives have an importance in the economy that far transcends their numbers, their return from effort, or their personal resources. The decisions they make significantly affect the employment and allocation of a major portion of the community's resources. They are, therefore, an efficient group for our purposes; with a small sample we can learn something about a sizeable fraction of the economy. Moreover, top executives as a group receive among the highest labor incomes, and they should, other things equal, be among those workers most noticeably affected by a high and progressive personal income tax. Indeed, their compensation arrangements give clear evidence of tax-induced transformations. Finally, for the highest-paid executives, at least, more information on compensation is publicly available than for any other class of workers. From published sources—primarily the proxy statements sent to stockholders—a record can be developed of the amount of their compensation and its distribution among the various forms of current, deferred, or contingent arrangements that it can assume. This is the focus of Lewellen's study.

Income taxation could affect how hard executives work most directly by lowering their net return from effort. Very little is known, but much has been conjectured, about the effect of income taxation at the level and degree of progressivity we have experienced over the last twenty-five years on the economic rewards of business executives. Some have contended that there is no question that the effect must be a deterioration in their earnings and a decline in their economic standing.[2] As Dan T.

---

[1] Initial because, although this is the only group the resources available for the present project permitted us to study, we felt that procedures developed in this effort could be used at a later date by other investigators.

[2] Dan Throop Smith, "Taxation and Executives," *National Tax Association: Proceedings of the Forty-Fourth Annual Conference,* 1951.

Smith explains: "Based on 1952 individual income tax rates and the 1951 consumer price index, it would take an income of over $75,000 to yield the same net real income as a 1929 income of $25,000 before taxes. It would now require about $200,000 to give the same net real income as that provided by a 1929 gross income of $50,000 and about $1,000,000 to provide the equivalent of $100,000. No statistical study is needed to show that increases of corporate salaries and bonuses, substantial though they have been, have fallen far short of what would have been necessary to permit executives to maintain earlier standards of consumption and savings.[3] Quite the opposite kind of result, however, has been suggested as likely by Musgrave and Richman, who state that high marginal rates of tax "at the executive level . . . are bypassed to a considerable degree by various payment arrangements. Also, it may well be that high rates are shifted in considerable degree, i.e., compensated for by higher executive salaries." [4]

These conjectures cover the spectrum of possible outcomes. Other students, of course, have expressed opinions or judgments that fall within this range. Most discussions of executive compensation, however, have failed to take systematic account of all forms of compensation. In particular, with the notable exception of the recent pioneering effort by Leonard R. Burgess,[5] they have not attempted to incorporate in the total "compensation package" the deferred and/or contingent arrangements that have grown so important in recent years. Indeed, a major reason for the abundance of conjecture and paucity of fact on how top executive compensation has fared over the period of high income taxation lies in the major transformation of the pay structure away from currently taxable salaries and bonuses to pension benefits, profit-sharing arrangements, deferred compensation contracts, stock options, stock purchase arrangements, etc., which, because of deferral or capital gains treatment, are subject to lower tax rates. The proliferation of such arrangements suggests that they have meant substantial rewards for their recipients.

[3] *Ibid.,* p. 234.
[4] Richard A. Musgrave and Peggy Brewer Richman, "Allocation Aspects, Domestic and International" in *The Role of Direct and Indirect Taxes in the Federal Revenue System,* A Conference Report of the National Bureau of Economic Research and the Brookings Institution, Princeton University Press, 1964, p. 84.
[5] *Top Executive Pay Package,* New York, 1963. See also comments in the author's Preface to this volume.

Lewellen's work provides a soundly conceived and well-supported basis for judging how much.

By developing a methodology for measuring the value of all the major nonsalary forms of compensation received by executives, Lewellen has been able to: (a) trace the history of total compensation between 1940 and 1963 for a large sample of top executives; (b) assess the relative importance of the various components of their compensation packages; and (c) undertake a comparison of executive compensation with that of other groups in the labor force. It is fitting, of course, that he, himself, tell us what he did, what he found, and what it signifies. But I would like very briefly here to indicate how his findings, by providing the basic background, constitute the first several links of the "chain of explanation" that our studies in this area are seeking to forge.

He finds that the salary and currently taxable bonus of top executives has increased somewhat in money terms, so that, by the end of the period, it averaged one-third higher after taxes than in 1940. When adjusted for changes in purchasing power, however, after-tax salaries turn out to be only about half as large in recent years as they were just before the sharp wartime increase in personal income tax rates. On this evidence of salaries, then, top executives have "failed to keep up."

But to increase salary, after all, is a hard and unimaginative way of providing additional compensation in the face of a progressive income tax. Other arrangements, subject to lower tax rates, were made use of to a significant degree. Deferred compensation and stock options combined, for example, were worth more than salary over the years 1955–63. In all, after-tax compensation (in money terms) more than doubled over the period. In terms of purchasing power, however, top executives appear to have been just about as well off in recent years as in 1940. Whether or not this can be adduced as evidence of tax shifting requires that we know much more about the determinants of executive compensation and related factors than we now do. This constancy of total after-tax compensation does indicate at least that top corporate executives have managed to live with the tax.

They have not, on the other hand, fared as well as certain other segments of the labor force—doctors, lawyers, dentists, general production workers, and new business school graduates. For all these groups, real after-tax income from effort grew significantly. Consequently, over time the after-tax compensation of top executives has declined relative to that of other "workers," and the effect of taxation on the effort of executives would seem not to be an idle question despite the sharp increase in deferred and contingent forms of compensation. Moreover, Lewellen's findings suggest that an important area to investigate is the effect of this transformation in compensation on the motivation and decisions of executives.

There is also a hint of a purposeful response to taxation in the design of compensation packages. Over the period studied by Lewellen, the differentials in after-tax compensation among the five most highly compensated officers in each company have remained remarkably stable. Constancy in the face of a growing reliance on forms of reward other than salary—and the different proportions of each nonsalary item in total compensation at each compensation rank—suggests a policy designed to maintain differentials.

Stock options, which inevitably involve the executive in ownership, have grown tremendously in importance since 1940, as have stock-based bonuses and deferred compensation and profit-sharing plans. In addition, the top officers frequently hold amounts of company stock that are large relative to their total portfolios.[6] All this implies that top business executives should not be viewed simply as employees, professional managers, or civil servants. Their motivation could very well be closer to that attributed to classical entrepreneurs, i.e., owner-managers, than most current discussions would indicate. Many students point to the small fraction of stock outstanding owned by top management and conclude that there is a real danger that they will have goals and interests at variance with those of stockholders. But at least as likely is the possibility that the self-interest of top management *coincides* with that of stockholders because of the important fraction of his personal wealth represented by the top executive's ownership stake in his company.

DANIEL M. HOLLAND

[6] I interviewed, among others, eighteen top executives whose holdings of company stocks could be found in proxy statements. They averaged $1,140,000, with a range from $49,000 to just under $5 million. Moreover, I have the impression from these and other interviews that substantial holdings of the employing company's stock are quite common if for no other reason than the fact that executives, as all other investors, like to invest with knowledge, and of course they know more about their own company than any other.

1

INTRODUCTION

In recent years, economists and public officials have become increasingly interested in the nature and causes of economic growth. As a reflection of this concern, scholarly attention has been directed toward those individuals in our society who occupy positions such that their activities and decisions are felt to be closely related to the generation of an expansion in the output of goods and services. Among such individuals, corporate executives have been recognized as a group whose behavior is particularly important. Not only do they, in their capacity as stewards of shareholder interests, determine the uses to which large aggregations of scarce resources are put, but their remuneration for that stewardship enables them to acquire substantial personal wealth whose form and disposition are of concern as well. Any attempt to understand the mechanisms by which economic growth is generated—or, more broadly, to appraise the character of the process of resource allocation within the community—should, therefore, include an investigation of the contributions made and the rewards enjoyed by this strategic group of decision makers.

If, for example, one assumes that the several markets in which factors of production are offered for sale are operating reasonably efficiently, it will be the case that the prices of these factors will be approximately equal to their respective marginal revenue products. Under such circumstances, an accurate and comprehensive measure of the compensation received by executives permits us to determine directly the magnitude of their contributions to output. On the other hand, if—as seems more likely—there are reasons to suspect that certain imperfections may exist in the relevant factor markets, the amounts of executives' remuneration are still of interest, since both the extent and the cause of the differences between those amounts and the actual value of the services

1

rendered are important matters for public consideration in the context of a general concern with effective resource allocation.

Similarly, questions as to the appropriate degree of progression in the personal income tax structure and the logic of the prevailing pattern of income distribution in the community are often raised in connection with executives' earnings. Because top executives are highly paid individuals, much of their remuneration has been subject to the upper end of the steeply graduated marginal tax rate schedules which have been in effect in this country during the last quarter century. At the same time, however, a number of compensation arrangements have become available which generate income that not only is taxed on more favorable terms but also is almost invisible to those of us outside the corporations which provide it. Since there has thus far been only limited empirical evidence as to the net impact of these two phenomena, it has not really been possible where the professional manager is concerned to examine meaningfully either the question of "equity" in the tax structure or the problem of the possible disincentive effects of high marginal rates.

A further issue involves the mobility of the labor force. It has been asserted that labor mobility is impeded by the increasing importance of items of remuneration such as pension plans which stipulate that the individual who stands to receive benefits thereunder relinquishes his right to do so if he changes employers prior to retirement. Persons in executive positions, of course, are likely to be precisely those who have been with their present firms for a considerable period of time and who consequently could lose substantial amounts of accumulated benefits should they resign to accept positions elsewhere. The relative importance, in the scheme of executive rewards, of compensation arrangements which incorporate such penalties is therefore of particular interest in appraising the job mobility of this key segment of the working population.

Finally, comparisons of the performance and attributes of our economy with those of other countries are being made with increasing frequency. The patterns of growth in national product, price levels, wage rates, personal income, and other economic indicators have become criteria around which discussions of efficiency of resource use are centered. In that context, the size and form of the remuneration of executives in different countries has begun to receive attention. While some casual observations—and a good many opinions—have been offered, there is little that can confidently be said about international compensation relationships until more is known of the American experience. Accordingly, the present study seeks not only to provide a thorough treatment of what seems an important topic in its own right, but also to generate a body of data which can be used as raw material by subsequent investigators.

Orientation

As the preceding paragraphs suggest, the often-used term "compensation package" is especially appropriate for executives. In response to a growing concern on their part with such goals as economic security in retirement, comprehensive life and health insurance protection for their families, and more extensive participation in the ownership of the firms which employ them, executives have come to be the beneficiaries of a wide variety of indirect, deferred, and contingent compensation arrangements over the years. This trend has been accelerated by the advent of high progressive personal income tax rates on salary and bonus receipts and the concomitant enactment of legislation which quite specifically accorded much less severe treatment to other forms of reward. Descriptions of the legislation itself, surveys of the relative popularity of particular instruments of remuneration, and judgments as to the evils inherent in the "tax loopholes" thus created continue to abound, but it remains true that the surface has only begun to be scratched with respect to the most elementary—as well as most important—piece of evidence in the area of managerial rewards. We do not yet have, very simply, sufficient information as to how much in total those rewards are worth to their recipients. Until we do, it clearly is not very fruitful to undertake to assess either the impact or the efficacy of the pay package. It is the task of the exposition that follows to first develop a rigorous conceptual framework in which the monetary value of all the various supplements to individuals' salaries and bonuses can be measured and compared and then to apply that framework empirically to the experience of a large and diverse sample of corporate executives. The goal is to determine how business firms in this country have, in fact, reshaped their compensation practices in response to changes over time in the tax laws and in the economic environment.

Conceptual Framework

The approach which is taken here in attempting to achieve these objectives utilizes the executive's traditional rewards—salary and bonus—as both standards of value and bases of comparison. Since salary and bonus are the most familiar and least complicated arrangements currently in use, the analysis which results is not only clearest if organized around them but the mechanics of translating the various disparate components of the compensation package into a common denominator are also most easily developed.

The magnitude of the remuneration accruing to executives from their salary and bonus payments is readily determined merely by applying to the observed pretax figures the relevant personal income tax schedules and an estimate of the probable amount of deductions and exemptions claimed. The compensation embodied in instruments which have more complex timing, taxation, and contingency features is rather less obvious, but can be ascertained by the following procedure: for each deferred and contingent form of reward, there can be constructed a "current income equivalent," defined as the amount of additional current income—additional salary and bonus—which is as valuable to the executive in question as the particular reward being examined. In effect, the proposition is that the most appropriate way to measure on a common basis the worth of the numerous supplements to direct current remuneration is simply to calculate the size of the salary increments which, if substituted for those supplements, would leave the individuals involved as well off.

In the case of a pension plan, for example, the question is asked: "How much of an increase in annual after-tax salary would the prospective pension recipient require in order to be able to purchase therewith an individual retirement annuity from an insurance company similar in form and equal in value to the pension promised him under his company's retirement plan?" In the view here, the indicated series of annual premium payments comprise the "after-tax current income equivalent" of that pension. Corresponding indexes can be developed for other compensation arrangements and, once established, provide a vehicle for convenient and accurate statements as to the absolute value and relative importance in the pay package of originally quite dissimilar rewards.

In developing the appropriate indexes (the particulars of which are presented in Part I of the study) two principles are followed throughout and are worth noting at the outset. First, equivalence between a series of increments to salary on the one hand and the benefits anticipated from a given supplement thereto on the other is defined in every instance in terms of the after-tax *present values* of the two sets of payments. Second, all "current income equivalents" so created are intended not only to measure the compensation inherent in particular instruments but are also designed to represent feasible alternatives to those instruments in an actual scheme of executive rewards. In short, the concept of discounted cash flows and a persistent effort to be practical will both play an important role in the analysis.

Focus

Within the analysis, answers are sought to questions of the following sort:

1. How much, after taxes, is the corporate executive's total compensation package worth to him?

2. How rapidly has the value of that package grown over time?

3. How does this pattern compare wtih the rate of growth of the company he works for, with the earnings of other occupational groups, and with increases in the price level?

4. Which components of the pay package are the most important currently?

5. Has that emphasis changed since the appearance of high progressive personal tax rates?

6. Have there been changes over the years in the compensation differentials between particular executive positions within the same corporation?

7. Do deferred and contingent rewards become more or less important at successively higher levels in the corporate hierarchy?

8. How significantly do stock market conditions affect the amount and form of executives' compensation?

9. Do salary and bonus levels provide a reliable indication of the relative size of individuals' *total* remuneration?

In each case an attempt is made to develop an explanation for, as well as a description of, the relevant phenomena, special attention being paid to the influence of taxes on the patterns observed. In the process, information will be obtained and techniques devised which are useful in connection with some related issues that are examined only in passing here. One of these is the tax revenue consequences of various compensation arrangements from the standpoint of the federal government. Since the tax treatment of particular instruments is often an important factor in their adoption by the employer corporation, the Internal Revenue Service is likely also to have an interest in those decisions. A second area is the nature of the career profile of the corporate executive. The data required for the empirical portion of the study include executives' ages and a substantial amount of evidence concerning their employment histories. Brief digressions are made to discuss these topics as they arise. More generally, the analysis necessarily provides a format by which the individual employee can assess the value to him of the reward structure in effect at his company and it will sketch some guidelines for the firm which seeks better measures of the relative costs and desirability of a wide range of compensation devices.

The Sample

The proxy statements issued by corporations in conjunction with their annual shareholders' meetings are the one consistent and systematic source of information about the remuneration received by executives. Because the Securities and Exchange Commission requires that these documents contain tabulations of the rewards enjoyed by only the most senior officers of the firm, the sample on which an empirical investigation of compensation may be based must be restricted to such individuals. The analysis here is directed in particular to the experience of those men who, in the 1940–63 period, occupied the five highest-paid positions in each of a group of fifty of the nation's largest manufacturing corporations—a sample which turns out to include data on some 550 different executives and encompass approximately 8,000 man-years' worth of compensation history.

This sample should afford a basis not only for examining the compensation of the individuals covered thereby but also for drawing some general conclusions about the size and structure of managerial rewards. For one thing, the remuneration of the senior officers of a firm is likely to set the pattern for payments to individuals at lower levels in the organization as well. Top executives are therefore an appropriate group on which to concentrate if the objective is to observe the formulation of policy in this area. Similarly, the corporations included in the sample are among the most important and most influential in the economy. The compensation norms they establish can be expected to be emulated by a number of other firms. Finally, because these are large companies, the amounts of remuneration associated with their top positions are sufficiently great that if tax considerations play any role at all in the design of executives' pay packages, the effects should show up in their experience.

Scope of the Study

Since proxy statements provide the basic data for the study, their characteristics and availability necessarily define its boundaries. In practice, this means that 1940 is just about as far back in time as an historical record can be constructed. Formal proxy information was required of all firms listed on an organized stock exchange by the then newly created Securities and Exchange Commission in the late 1930's, but the initial rules for reporting compensation figures were not rigorous enough to bring about uniform and comprehensive disclosure of the necessary data until several years thereafter. From 1940 on, however, a very good record can be assembled for most listed companies. Fortunately, that year is a sensible starting point for a study of executive rewards because it just precedes the era of high progressive personal tax rates and thus allows meaningful historical comparisons to be made.

The particular set of compensation arrangements which may be included in the analysis is similarly limited by the proxy statements. Salaries and bonuses, pensions, stock options, deferred-pay agreements, and profit-sharing plans are the instruments whose features are reported on in sufficient detail to permit proper application of the valuation techniques which will be developed. Since these are by far the most important components of the pay package and together almost certainly account for all but a small percentage of executives' total remuneration, they should provide a solid foundation on which to base conclusions about the various patterns of reward. A methodology for measuring the compensation implicit in such items as employee life and health insurance programs, expense account privileges, and savings plans is presented even though those arrangements cannot be treated empirically.

For simplicity and computational convenience, only federal income and estate tax liabilities are considered in the analysis. The amounts involved in connection with social security tax assessments and state or local income taxes have been small enough in relation to top executives' aggregate remuneration during the period studied that little in the way of accuracy is sacrificed by ignoring them entirely. Estate taxes are relevant in the case of instruments such as pension plans which incorporate provisions for certain payments upon the death of the executive as part of the benefit package.

Organization

Part I of the study, Chapters 2 through 6, is concerned with the development of techniques by which to measure on a common scale the compensation provided by each of the individual executive's deferred and contingent rewards. It describes in detail the construction of what are termed here the "current income equivalents" of those rewards. Part II, Chapters 7 through 13, presents and evaluates the results obtained by applying the conceptual framework to the compensation experience of the indicated sample of senior corporate officers.

The Findings

Among the more significant conclusions which emerge from the empirical analysis are the following:

1. The annual before-tax salaries and bonuses received by senior corporate executives increased by approximately 80 per cent between 1940 and 1963.

2. After taxes, on the other hand, the increase amounted to only 33 per cent of the 1940 figure.

3. Executives' *total* after-tax compensation, including the value of the various supplements to salary and bonus, just about doubled during the same interval.

4. All this growth occurred in the ten years immediately following World War II. From 1940 to 1945 top executives' aggregate remuneration declined steadily and has not increased appreciably since 1955.

5. Deferred and contingent rewards now comprise approximately half the value of the total pay package and have therefore accounted for

the major portion of the observed growth in compensation over the last quarter century.

6. Stock options in particular have become an important item. Nearly one-third of the after-tax remuneration received by senior executives in recent years has been attributable to options.

7. Because many of the now popular supplements to salary and bonus utilize shares of the employer corporation's common stock as the compensation medium—stock options being perhaps the best example— the volatility of the value of the pay package has increased substantially over time.

8. The rate of growth in executives' total after-tax compensation since 1940 has been less, by a wide margin, than that of the after-tax earnings of physicians, lawyers, dentists, or manufacturing production workers.

9. The companies the executives worked for grew more rapidly than their compensation in every important respect.

10. In terms of *real* after-tax income, executives are no better off nowadays than they were before World War II.

11. The salary differentials between the top five executive positions in the fifty corporations studied have narrowed since 1940, but the total compensation differentials have remained quite stable.

12. Deferred and contingent rewards comprise a larger percentage of the individual's pay package the higher the position in his firm he holds. For the same reason, his aggregate remuneration also becomes more volatile as he is promoted.

13. The executives who are the five highest-paid in their companies currently are, on average, approximately five years older than were their counterparts in 1940.

14. Top executive compensation policies vary much less widely among firms than do any of the measurable attributes of the firms themselves.

Each of these findings will be analyzed and their implications appraised in the chapters that follow. Those readers whose main concern is with the results of the study rather than with the methodology employed may find it most efficient to begin with Chapter 7, referring to the earlier chapters primarily for clarification of questions as they arise.

PART I
METHODOLOGY

2

EXECUTIVE SALARIES, BONUSES, AND PENSIONS

Salary and bonus—aggregate direct current remuneration—are the executive's traditional rewards and represent in many instances the largest proportion of his total compensation. For our purposes, it is as important that they also admit readily to measurement, are prominently and fully reported on in corporate proxy statements, and provide a convenient standard around which an examination of the other components of the pay package may be oriented.

While the term "salary" should require no elaboration, it is necessary to spell out what is included in the category of "bonus" payments in the discussions that follow. The definition here encompasses not only those awards made in a given year as remuneration for that same year's services but also the arrangements frequently referred to as "incentive compensation." Under the latter, a specified total amount is promised the executive but is paid to him in a series of cash installments "earned out" over several years rather than in a single lump sum. Since all such payments are taxable to the individual at ordinary personal income tax rates when received, they will be grouped with salary throughout the study.[1]

Tax Liabilities

All income recipients can and do take advantage of the numerous provisions of the tax law permitting both personal exemptions and either a standard or an itemized deduction from taxable income for such outlays as personal interest payments, state and local taxes, medical expenses,

[1] As are directors' fees to executives who serve on their respective boards.

13

charitable contributions, and so on. The senior corporate executives examined here almost certainly fall among the group of taxpayers who itemize. In order to provide a sensible measure of the after-tax value of their direct current remuneration, therefore, it is necessary to estimate the amount of the deductions and exemptions they claim.

The relationship between gross income and taxable income for all taxpayers can be obtained from the annual tax return tabulations provided by the Internal Revenue Service.[2] If it is assumed that each executive acts in the same manner as does the "typical" individual in his income bracket, it turns out that he would have had, on average during the period 1940 to 1950, deductions and exemptions together amounting to approximately 10 per cent of his annual gross income. From 1951 through 1963 the corresponding figure was about 15 per cent.[3] In computing the executive's tax liability here, then, each dollar of his before-tax salary and bonus is translated into either 85 or 90 cents of taxable income—depending on the calendar year involved.

A second aspect of a man's personal situation which is relevant to the tax treatment of his rewards is his marital status. Because of the major impact of the income-splitting privilege on average and marginal rates, an attempt is made in each case to determine whether or not the executive whose compensation is being examined is married. If no positive evidence can be uncovered, the assumption will be that he is— since the probabilities seem to point strongly in that direction. Personal exemptions for himself and the members of his family are, as noted, included in the percentage figure above.

A third factor involves income the executive may receive from sources other than his corporate employer. If he does enjoy some "outside income" of this sort, he will be in a higher tax bracket than that suggested by salary and bonus alone, and the tax liabilities imputed to him should be adjusted accordingly. Unfortunately, the probable size of such income is difficult to establish. Certainly, the senior executive's familiarity with the profit potential of various security instruments and business ventures can be expected to lead him to undertake a substantial amount of investment activity on personal account. His high income status,

[2] U.S. Treasury Department, Internal Revenue Service, *Statistics of Income, Individual Tax Returns,* Washington, D.C.
[3] See Appendix A for the derivation of these values.

which supplies a reservoir of funds for that purpose, reinforces this expectation. It seems reasonable, therefore, to believe that his outside income will be sizeable.

An estimate which is taken here to be a suitable one is 15 per cent of direct current remuneration. Thus a man having a net worth three to four times his annual salary and bonus, and earning 4 or 5 per cent thereon before taxes, is considered representative. While that may perhaps seem a low investment yield to assume in view of postwar stock market conditions, it must be emphasized that only items taxable as ordinary income at the regular statutory rates are pertinent in this connection. To the extent that a significant portion of the executive's return on his portfolio consists of capital appreciation, that return will not affect the tax liabilities applicable to his salary and bonus. Dividend and interest income is therefore the appropriate concern, and the indicated yield does not seem unduly pessimistic in those terms. A complete analysis would, of course, also recognize the influence of such factors as a man's age, his past earnings history, his propensity to save, his investment skill and preferences, any inherited wealth, changes in external economic conditions, and so on. Clearly, information of this nature is not only hard to come by but would require for its full assimilation the development of a model for predicting investment results that exceeds the legitimate needs of the present study. The real objective in acknowledging the existence of so-called "outside income" is very simply the removal of what would otherwise be a persistent bias toward attributing too low a tax rate to the executive's salary and bonus. For that purpose, the estimate described should suffice.[4]

After-Tax Salary and Bonus

Given these assumptions, the executive's gross income, taxable income, personal tax liability, and, therefore, after-tax current income each year are easily computed. The final step is to specify the share of this last figure that should be credited to salary and bonus. In order to avoid arbitrarily designating one kind of receipt as "basic" and the others as

---

[4] The effect on the empirical results of choosing some alternative assumptions, both for outside income and for deductions and exemptions, is explored in Chapter 12.

marginal, the allocation will be made according to the proportion of total before-tax income each item represents. Thus, if in a particular year an executive has a salary of $80,000 plus $20,000 in bonus awards, he is assumed also to have outside income amounting to $15,000. With the relevant percentage of deductions and exemptions and the statutory personal tax schedule for that year, his after-tax income can be calculated. Of that figure, 80/115 is taken to be the after-tax counterpart of his salary and 20/115 the contribution of his bonus.[5] In effect, current income is regarded as homogeneous, with deductions and exemptions—and taxes—applying uniformly to all its components.

Pensions

The central characteristic of a pension arrangement is the right of the executive to receive a series of yearly or monthly payments of a given size beginning at a specified future retirement date and continuing thereafter during his lifetime. A pension may, therefore, be termed a "deferred contingent" form of reward.

ORIENTATION

Retirement plans may be classified according to a number of criteria, depending on one's purpose. If interest lay in the pattern of asset accumulation and in the investment policies associated with different methods of providing for pensions, plans would be separated into categories related to degree of funding and funding medium, such as "insured," "trusteed," and "pay-as-you-go." If personnel administration were of major concern, the breakdown might be on the basis of the benefit formula into "career average," "final pay," and "flat benefit" plans. While these are important distinctions for many decisions, they are not particularly relevant to the valuation of executive rewards. For that purpose it is necessary to know only the promised benefit and how much, if anything, the executive must contribute toward the financing of the arrangement—i.e., whether the plan is "contributory" or "noncontributory." Under a contributory plan, both the corporation and the executive set aside certain amounts each year during the latter's active

---

[5] A more detailed illustration is provided in the numerical example contained in Chapter 6.

working life to provide for a specified retirement benefit. In the case of a noncontributory plan, the full cost of the prospective pension is borne by the corporation.

CONCEPTUAL FRAMEWORK

The worth of a pension to its potential recipient will be assessed here by asking the question: How large would the annual premiums be if the executive were to purchase from an insurance company a retirement annuity equal in value and similar in form to his pension promise? Those premiums are taken to constitute the "after-tax current equivalent" of the pension. Since they measure the annual expenditure out of after-tax income that would be required for an individual to provide the same retirement benefits on his own, it is possible to compare them with the after-tax income generated by salary and bonus payments and to make statements about compensatory value on that basis. We may then take the further step of calculating the increase in *before-tax* salary and bonus that would raise the executive's take-home pay by an amount equal to the pension's after-tax current equivalent, thereby defining a "before-tax current equivalent" which represents the alternative of actually rewarding the man via salary instead. A "what if" computation of this sort is particularly useful in discussing the impact of taxes on the level and form of compensation—as will be seen later.

RATIONALE

It is, of course, true that a number of avenues exist through which an executive could provide on his own for economic security in retirement if he were not eligible to receive pension benefits. Selection of the individual annuity contract as the most appropriate alternative to—and, hence, index of the worth of—a pension was dictated by several considerations.

First, there is the matter of precision. The terms on which annuities are available are extremely well defined. The quoted premiums reflect guaranteed rates of return, established mortality experience, and specific charges for administrative expenses. Most other instruments are necessarily less definite, especially with regard to return on investment.

Secondly, it seems important to take full account of the risks borne by the executive. Since a corporate pension plan removes virtually all financial uncertainty about the eventual receipt of a given retirement benefit,[6] the alternative suggested should provide the same degree of assurance. An annuity fulfills this requirement. It represents a contractual obligation of the issuing insurance company and is backed by a governmentally regulated investment policy and reserve system. Even though the potential return offered by other investment media may be greater, few, if any, will guarantee a particular outcome. Perhaps a more significant kind of risk for the executive involved, however, is that of living *too long* after retirement and exhausting the funds he has set aside. Pension plans and insured individual annuities are the only arrangements which insulate their beneficiaries against that contingency.

Finally, there are the costs of managing the individual's funds. Retirement annuity premiums contain complete allowances for such expenses, whereas most other investment possibilities do not. Certainly, the energies which a highly paid executive would have to devote to managing his own portfolio represent a sizeable cost to him, but one which both the pension and the annuity obviate.

The premiums on an individual retirement annuity, then, are considered here to be the best measure of the after-tax current income equivalent of a pension because the two devices are similarly precise, certain, and comprehensive. If there are other arrangements which offer many or even all of these advantages, it can be assumed that competitive pressures in the financial markets will eliminate any significant differences in their prices and render the present choice no less desirable than any other. To the extent that the retirement annuity *is* singularly possessed of the requisite virtues, it should be preferred.[7]

THE NOTION OF EQUIVALENCE

Even with the above approach, the determination of the worth of a pension promise is not quite as simple as it might initially appear. Because of the nature of the benefits afforded by the typical corporate pension plan, it is not possible for an individual to purchase for himself

[6] Except insofar as that benefit is not completely "vested," however. See the discussion below, pp. 25–26.

[7] The issue of whether, given complete freedom of choice, every executive would in fact choose to purchase an individual annuity with the salary payments provided him in lieu of his pension is not critical to this argument. Our interest is only in guaranteeing that he *could* achieve an exactly equivalent position if he so desired.

exactly the same arrangement from an insurance company. Noncontributory pensions ordinarily provide no benefits if the employee should die prior to retirement. Contributory plans contain only a small death benefit feature. In addition, there is the matter of vesting and the contingencies it introduces. An individual annuity contract, on the other hand, will specify that, in the event of the policyholder's death before attaining the age at which the annuity is to begin, his estate shall receive the full amount of the net premiums [8] he has paid together with the interest accumulated thereon. And, of course, an individual annuity is "fully vested" in the sense that the purchaser can alter or cancel it at will and lay claim to the prescribed cash surrender value at any time. The executive cannot, therefore, obtain an individual annuity whose benefits correspond in all respects to those of his pension.

Another problem is the different tax treatment of the two arrangements. The benefits eventually accruing to an executive are subject to one set of taxes if he purchases an annuity himself and another if that annuity is provided by a corporate pension plan.[9] It is not correct to say, for example, that the after-tax current equivalent of a $20,000 per year pension promise is equal to the annual premium on a $20,000 per year individual retirement annuity.

As a result, "equivalence" must be established by first measuring the after-tax *present value* of the pension and then finding the individual annuity which has the same present value. The annual premiums quoted for *that* annuity comprise the pension's after-tax current income equivalent. Since the nature and degree of deferral and contingency involved in both arrangements have been given formal expression within the framework of actuarial science, methods by which the necessary calculations can be made fortunately are readily available.

TIME SPAN OF THE CURRENT EQUIVALENT

The size of the premiums on a particular annuity policy depend, of course, on the time period over which they are spread. Since the annuity, for our purposes, represents the executive's pension alternative, it seems appropriate that this period coincide with the years when he is performing the services that give rise to the pension. Thus, a man who

---

[8] Gross premiums minus the charges for sales and administrative expenses.
[9] See below, pp. 30–32, for the details.

comes under a pension plan at age 40 and who expects to retire at age 65 is credited here with an after-tax current equivalent consisting of twenty-five annual premiums. The magnitude of each year's premium is determined by the initial pension promise and the pattern of changes in benefits which occur.

BENEFIT CHANGES

Because the pension promised an executive is ordinarily adjusted over time to reflect his performance and increased experience, our analysis must be equipped to deal with such changes. Consistent with the general approach outlined above, each increase—or decrease—in benefits will be regarded as a separate pension award whose current equivalent begins at the time that award is made and continues thereafter up to the man's anticipated retirement age. For example, an executive who is first covered by a pension plan at age 50 and promised $20,000 per year upon retirement at age 65 will have attributed to him an initial after-tax current equivalent made up of the fifteen equal annual premiums which would purchase an individual retirement annuity having the same present value as that pension. If, at age 55, his prospective benefit is raised to $25,000 per year, a second current equivalent is calculated—the ten equal annual premiums required for an *additional* individual annuity which is as valuable to him as the additional $5,000 pension promise. The sum of this new annual premium plus the original one represents the total after-tax current equivalent for the years from age 55 through age 64.[10] Whenever a benefit change occurs, the procedure is repeated. In effect, the complete current equivalent finally generated for the executive's pension will be comprised of a series of "layers" of annuity premiums, each one corresponding to an increment in the benefits promised him and extending over successively shorter periods of time.

THE ANNUITY PREMIUM SCHEDULE

One of the advantages of choosing the individual retirement annuity as a measure of the value of a pension was taken to be the precision it

---

[10] Had the pension benefit instead been reduced by $5,000, the *difference* between the two premiums would be the current equivalent for the last ten years.

offered. This contention is valid, however, only in the case of a particular annuity contract—the "nonparticipating" policy.

Most large insurance companies are organized on a "mutual" basis, returning to their policyholders as dividends the fruits of investment, mortality, or administrative experience more favorable than was contemplated in the premium rates quoted. In effect, the policyholder is guaranteed some minimum result and then has the right to "participate" through lower premiums or larger benefits if the company's projections are pessimistic. Since the ultimate cost of retirement annuities of this sort is ambiguous, such arrangements are not suited to our purposes here.

"Stock" insurance companies and many "mutual" ones do, however, make available nonparticipating annuities on which the terms are completely fixed. The insurance company assumes the risk of adverse developments, while the policyholder foregoes the right to share in any unexpected gains. The premiums on a nonparticipating individual retirement annuity are therefore the appropriate index of the current income equivalent of a pension.[11]

THE POSTRETIREMENT ECONOMIC CONTEXT

The value of a pension and its individual annuity counterpart to an executive depends to a large extent upon the circumstances which will accompany the receipt of the promised benefits. Anticipated "outside income," deductions and exemptions, and future tax rates are the major parameters involved.

It was mentioned earlier that an accurate appraisal of the personal tax liability on salary and bonus payments should include the effect of income from outside sources. The executive can expect to receive such income after retirement as well. Since he will be able to accumulate wealth in the intervening period, it might be reasonable to project a larger amount than he presently enjoys. On the other hand, he may have to draw upon his capital when his salary ceases in order to main-

---

[11] In the long run, of course, the exigencies of competition should cause the costs of participating and nonparticipating policies to be approximately equal. If properly handled, either type could be a useful standard of pension value. Because only the nonparticipating annuity is precise from an entirely ex ante standpoint, however, it is more convenient to use here.

tain an accustomed standard of living or to take advantage of the vacation and travel opportunities previously denied him. A number of additional factors could be considered, but any statement made must be highly tentative—and it is by no means certain that the estimate made here of the size of the executive's *current* outside income is correct. For lack of a better hypothesis, therefore, the assumption will be that such income is just about as important after retirement as it is before, and that the amount being received at the time the present value of a pension or a benefit change is assessed will also occur in retirement.[12]

A case can similarly be made for either higher or lower deductions and exemptions during the postretirement years. Medical expenses are likely to increase and the personal exemption doubles at age 65, but charitable contributions and various employment-connected outlays may well decline. Because the relevant influences are again complex and probably countervailing, the executive will simply be assumed to claim in retirement the same proportion of deductions and exemptions that is indicated by Internal Revenue Service data for his current income: either 10 or 15 per cent of each receipt, depending on the calendar year involved.[13]

Finally, tax rates must be projected forward. Since it seems that taxes were, over the period studied, as prone to increase as they were to fall, the tax schedule which might reasonably have been anticipated in the future could, at each point in time, have been fairly well approximated by that of the moment. The result of all these assumptions is perhaps best described by an example. In 1945 an executive is promised a $20,000 per year pension which is to begin when he retires in 1960. His outside income in 1945 is $10,000. Expected annual postretirement income is therefore taken to be $30,000 before taxes, 90 per cent of which is assumed taxable [14] at the rates prevailing in 1945. Following the procedure adopted in the case of salary payments, two-thirds of the calculated after-tax remainder is attributed to the pension.[15]

[12] Any Social Security benefits the executive may expect to receive are irrelevant in this connection, since they are tax-free and will not affect the tax liability on prospective pension receipts.

[13] See above, p. 14, and Appendix A.

[14] As noted, deductions and exemptions are specified to be 10 per cent of gross income during the period 1940–50.

[15] See above, p. 16.

ACTUARIAL CONCEPTS

The present value of a pension arrangement or an individual retirement annuity is a function of the opportunity cost involved in having to wait for the promised benefits and the probability that the potential recipient will live to claim them. Our concern, then, is with the specification of two discount factors, one for time deferral and one for mortality.[16] Actuarial science provides the necessary analytical framework.

Information pertaining to the likelihood of death is compiled by insurance companies from their historical policy-underwriting experience and presented in what is known as a mortality table. From this table the numerical probability that an "average" individual of any age will attain any other age can be computed.[17] Multiplying that figure by the time-discounted dollar amount of the prospective after-tax benefit for the year in question, we obtain the expected present value of the benefit. The aggregate present value of the pension or annuity from the viewpoint of the executive is determined by repeating this procedure for each year and totaling the results.[18]

DISCOUNT RATE

The particular interest rate chosen as a measure of the executive's opportunity cost should, in general, reflect the characteristics of the investment activity he might engage in to meet his postretirement financial needs if he were not promised a pension nor able to purchase an individual annuity. Perhaps more to the point, it should reflect the returns available from investments whose outcomes are no less certain than those of these instruments. Since time deposits in commercial banks, deposits in mutual savings banks, and federal government debt instruments, if held to maturity, involve essentially no risk, a portfolio comprised of one or more of these elements may be regarded as a logical vehicle. Taking into account the taxability of interest earnings, a discount rate of 2½ per cent per annum after taxes appears to be consistent with the history of such investments. Once again, it is either

[16] And also, perhaps, one for any vesting provisions that apply. See the section on "vesting" below.

[17] For a description of the mortality table and a summary of the relevant probability measures, see Appendix B.

[18] Appendix D offers an illustrative example.

impractical or impossible to identify and include in this estimate the many factors that would enable differences over time and among individuals to be fully recognized.[19] However, by using the same figure to calculate the present value of both the pension and its annuity counterpart, whatever errors might otherwise cause concern should be largely neutralized. Certainly, the order of magnitude assumed is not out of line—and the effect of some alternative assumptions is tested in Chapter 12.[20]

MORTALITY TABLE

An appropriate mortality table is also important to the analysis. The 1951 Group Annuity Table for Males [21] was adopted for use throughout in the belief that it provides an adequate representation of the longevity characteristics of executives during the period with which the study is concerned. The assumption is that executives, many of whom were included in the compilation of data for this table, are not significantly different from the typical employee covered by a corporate pension plan—i.e., a "group annuity" contract—in terms of physical well-being.[22] The gradual improvement in individual life expectancies over time does render the table, which extrapolates that trend to a certain extent, a better description of the mortality experience of the later years of the study, and its use may be open to some question on that basis. However, since the major part of the empirical effort—as measured both by number of executives and by dollar magnitude of pension promises—is necessarily concerned with these later years, the improvement in accuracy that might be achieved by using several mortality tables does not appear to justify the additional effort involved.

---

[19] Even settling on a given before-tax rate of return on investment and recognizing differences among the sample executives' tax rates each year quickly becomes a very complicated and computationally inconvenient process.

[20] It must also be confessed that precisely 2½ per cent rather than, say, 2¼ or 2¾ per cent after taxes was chosen because the mortality table adopted for the study incorporated that figure in its tabulation of certain shorthand actuarial symbols which greatly facilitate the calculation of the relevant present values.

[21] A portion of this table was utilized in Appendix B. It is reproduced in its entirety in Appendix C.

[22] While no conclusive evidence on this question is available, a related discussion can be found in Robert J. Lampman, *The Share of Top Wealth-Holders in National Wealth, 1922–56*, Princeton University Press for National Bureau of Economic Research, 1962. On pp. 42–48 and in annotated references, he considers the relationship between mortality and income class.

Furthermore, as in the case of a discount-rate choice, the use of the same mortality table to appraise both the executive's pension and its posited individual annuity alternative means that any errors offset rather than reinforce each other.

VESTING

One aspect of the imperfect correspondence between a corporate pension arrangement and an individual retirement annuity is the matter of vesting. An employee who decides to change jobs at some time during his working life usually forfeits all rights under the pension plan of his original employer unless he has worked for a specified number of years or attained a particular age, or both. To the extent that he can claim a portion of the promised benefits if he leaves, his pension is termed "vested." In order to assess the present value of a pension, therefore, the likelihood and consequences of the executive's resignation should be considered.

Although almost everyone can point to an example of a corporate officer who was either lured away from or forced out of his job, the conclusion suggested by an examination of proxy statements is that such occurrences are quite infrequent when viewed in relation to the entire senior managerial group.[23] Thus, if it were possible to compute for each age the probability that an executive might resign, the contention is that the indicated discount would be very small and the resulting pension present values would be only slightly different from those obtained by assuming that vesting is complete.[24] This argument is re-

[23] For example, out of the some 550 executives in 50 companies whose compensation experience is analyzed below, there were only 29 instances of resignations to take another job in the twenty-four-year period examined and, of these, nine occurred in just two firms. Further support comes from the information which is available on labor force turnover in general, which shows high mobility primarily among younger and newer employees. As the worker ages and accumulates job seniority, the likelihood of his departure diminishes steadily. Executives at the level the empirical effort here is concerned with clearly fit the latter description. See James A. Hamilton and Dorrance C. Bronson, *Pensions,* New York, 1958, pp. 212–216.

[24] Obviously, one of the *reasons* for low job turnover among executives and other long-time employees may well be the threat of cancellation of accumulated pension rights, and there is no intention here to downgrade the possible influence of that threat. Indeed, one might look at the pension values obtained in the subsequent empirical analysis under the assumption of complete vesting as in some sense an index of the *degree* of pressure on the individual not to change jobs. At the moment, however, only the fact of low turnover, not its source, is at issue.

inforced by the recognition that the senior executives included in the current sample almost certainly meet whatever age and job tenure requirements their respective employers' retirement plans specify for vesting and, hence, are not likely to be subject to full forfeiture of their pension rights in any event. There will, of course, be a small bias in the direction of overstating the worth of a pension if the possibility of forfeiture is ignored, but that bias should not be significant.

It should also be pointed out that a compensating error is built into the pension's current equivalent. No upward adjustment is made in those figures for the likelihood that the executive may not remain with his company until the designated retirement age and actually "collect" the full series of salary increments which are cast up as the substitute for his pension. To the extent that executives do change jobs, therefore, the after-tax current equivalents as calculated are also less valuable than they are credited with being here, and since this is the same sort of error as that associated with the present value of the pension itself, the two should cancel.[25]

BENEFIT TIMING

The usual pension plan provides for a specified payment each month following retirement, as do most individual annuity contracts. For several reasons, however, it seems appropriate to calculate the value of both arrangements as if benefits were paid only once a year.

First of all, the mathematics are much simpler, substantially reducing the effort involved in programming the computations. If both instruments are treated under the same assumption, little accuracy is sacrificed in comparing them.

Secondly, the techniques involved in constructing a monthly valuation framework are not really completely satisfactory. Mortality tables, for example, do not provide an intrayear tabulation of the pattern of demise, and some arbitrary assumption would therefore be necessary.

---

[25] It is also worth noting that insofar as the current equivalent outlined is offered as an operational alternative to a pension, it carries with it similar pressures on the executive not to leave his job. Thus, if he does leave and his pension is not fully vested, he gives up some of his benefit rights. If he were instead being paid its "current income equivalent," the same consequence would follow, i.e., he would not receive the remainder of the annual payments due him under that arrangement.

A similar problem arises with respect to discounting to obtain present values. There are several "correct" ways to convert from an annual to a monthly interest rate, the choice among them being largely a matter of taste.

Finally, our tax laws do not provide any reason for undertaking the complications. An individual is taxed according to his economic performance over a full year's time. Month-to-month variations in his income are quite irrelevant. The same aggregate tax liabilities on pension and annuity receipts therefore pertain whether they are assumed payable only once or in twelve installments over the year.

THE BENEFIT STRUCTURE OF THE PENSION

In order to generate a precise statement of the present value of a pension, it is necessary to speak of some sort of "typical" plan. Since there are a wide variety of benefit provisions that a retirement package may contain, any choice of a particular combination cannot be entirely comprehensive. It is neither practical nor very fruitful to explore in detail here all the options which are available, however. Attention will be concentrated instead on the most popular form of both the contributory and noncontributory pension. That analysis should be sufficient to establish the soundness—or lack thereof—of the approach chosen and also to illustrate the manner in which other benefit structures could be valued.

The usual noncontributory pension plan is a fairly simple device. There is no death benefit feature of any sort, and the only promise made is for a specified monthly payment beginning at retirement and continuing thereafter for as long as the employee lives.

A contributory pension is somewhat more complicated because of the participation by the employee in its financing. The most common arrangement provides certain death benefits as well as the same sort of basic monthly retirement award offered by a noncontributory plan. If the employee involved should die prior to attaining the designated retirement age, his estate receives the total amount of the contributions he has made up to that time, together with the interest accumulated thereon, at a rate specified by the plan. Alternatively, if the employee dies after retiring but before receiving in monthly benefits an amount equal to the interest-accumulated value of his contributions as of the date he retired, a death benefit equal to the difference between that amount and the monthly payments received is paid to his estate. These provisions guarantee, in effect, that the employee or his family will at least recover the "investment value" of his own contributions to the plan.

OTHER BENEFIT FORMULAS

The consequences of choosing the above arrangements as typical should be considered briefly. If the pension present value calculations can be expected to vary significantly depending on the benefit pattern assumed, the usefulness of the findings here will be limited. Fortunately, conditions exist which prevent this from being a problem.

From the standpoint of the medium through which the corporation finances its pension plan—whether it is an insurance company, a bank, or its own trusteed fund—the present value of all benefit packages offered the executive must be the same, given the amount of his and his employer's contributions. The executive may, for example, have the option of trading off a large annual retirement benefit, payable only during his lifetime, for a smaller yearly amount accompanied by "period certain" or "survivorship" features.[26] However, when the relevant deferral and contingency aspects of each device are assessed, they all must be equal in terms of present value to the pension plan's administering agent. As a result, the benefits associated with a given pension promise may be restructured only within quite definite bounds.

The extent to which the several present values will be the same from the executive's point of view depends on the personal tax treatment of the various benefit alternatives and on the difference between the executive's opportunity cost and the earnings rate assumed by the pension plan in establishing those alternatives. Tax variations are not pronounced, especially in the initial retirement years which weigh most heavily in present value calculations. Moreover, the interest rates used to estimate probable pension fund portfolio yields have been close to the 2½ per cent figure chosen above as appropriate for the executive.

[26] A "period certain" arrangement provides that a specified minimum number of years' benefits be paid to either the retired employee or his beneficiary. The "survivorship" agreement makes benefits payable to the employee while he lives and then to a designated heir for the rest of that person's lifetime. In most cases neither option contains any postretirement death benefit provisions of the sort described above for the "typical" contributory plan.

Accordingly, certain benefit options will give rise to larger and some to smaller present values than the one assumed here, but it seems that the discrepancies are not likely to be great and that, on average, a reasonable approximation of the value of the pension will be obtained.

BENEFIT STRUCTURE OF THE INDIVIDUAL ANNUITY

Although individual annuity contracts which exactly duplicate corporate pension benefits are not offered by insurance companies, it is possible to choose an arrangement to use as a standard of comparison which at least looks very much like the "typical" pension plans described above.

Individual annuity policies have for some time contained a "return-of-premiums" provision to the effect that, if the purchaser should die before reaching the age at which the annuity is to begin, his estate will receive a death benefit equal to either the total dollar amount of the gross premiums or the interest-accumulated value of the net premiums paid up to that time, whichever is greater.[27] This feature must, therefore, be a part of any annuity proposed. On the other hand, a number of postretirement benefit options are made available. The one that seems most suitable is the "straight life" annuity: a series of monthly payments (aggregated to yearly here) beginning at the man's retirement age and continuing until he dies. A package consisting of the indicated preretirement death benefit and this simple straight life annuity will be taken to be an appropriate alternative to both the contributory and noncontributory pension. A "current equivalent" therefore will consist of the series of annual premiums necessary to purchase an individual annuity of that form which has a present value equal to the present value of the particular pension being considered.[28]

---

[27] The "return-of-contributions" aspect of the contributory pension is very similar to this. However, because the full cost of an individual annuity is borne by the policyholder through his premium payments, while only a portion of his pension is financed by his contributions, the preretirement death benefit represents a larger share of the present value of an annuity than of a pension. In the case of a noncontributory pension, of course, the difference is even more marked.

[28] The question might again be raised about the probable sensitivity of the empirical results to the choice of other benefit patterns for the annuity. As was true of the pension, the changes that may be expected to arise should be quite small, since the differences in the tax treatment of various annuity arrangements and between individual and insurance company investment opportunity costs are not great.

TAX TREATMENT OF PENSIONS

Employees participating in "qualified" corporate retirement plans—i.e., those which, as do the ones we will be concerned with, satisfy certain conditions relating to labor force coverage and nondiscrimination—need not include in their taxable income amounts representing the share of pension costs borne by their employers.[29] Tax liability to the employee or his estate results only when benefits are actually received. The contributions, if any, made to such plans by the employee, however, are not tax-deductible.

Retirement benefits provided by noncontributory pension plans are, when received, taxable in full at ordinary personal income tax rates. Benefits paid under most contributory plans are subject to the "life expectancy" rule. According to this formula, a portion of each monthly receipt is excluded from taxation, that portion determined by the ratio of the aggregate contributions made by the employee during his working life to the total monthly benefits which are anticipated on the basis of his life expectancy. To illustrate: An employee who contributed $300 per year for thirty years and then retired on a monthly pension of $200 would, assuming he had a life expectancy of fifteen years at the time of his retirement, pay taxes on only $150 of each month's receipt. Thus $200 times 12 times 15 is equal to $36,000 of expected benefits, and contributions amount to $300 times 30, or $9,000. Dividing $9,000 by $36,000, we get one-fourth. One-fourth of $200 is $50, which is the tax-free portion of each receipt.[30] In effect, his own pension contributions are taxed to the individual while he is working, and he obtains in return a deduction that he can claim after retiring. The Internal Revenue Service specifies the appropriate life expectancies, designating fifteen years as the figure for a man who retires at age 65.[31]

[29] Appendix E summarizes the requirements for status as a "qualified" retirement plan and the tax consequences of not meeting those standards.

[30] Actually, the IRS requires that a slight reduction be made in the value of the employee's total contributions used in calculating this tax-free portion to reflect the fact that those contributions also give rise to a postretirement death benefit right. Since the necessary adjustment is not large for the pension promises that will be dealt with here, the general nature of the computation is as indicated. In the development and programming of the present value formulae, however, that adjustment was taken into account, and the particulars are spelled out in Appendix D.

[31] *Internal Revenue Code,* Sections 72 and 402.

A special provision applies to a contributory pension plan when the benefits to be received in the first three years following retirement equal or exceed the employee's total contributions. In that event, the employee excludes from taxable income the entire amount of each receipt until he has "recovered" those contributions free of taxes. Payments received thereafter are taxable in full.[32] Thus, in the example above, if the man's benefit were $250 per month, he would pay no income tax on his pension until the fourth year of his retirement.

Death benefits payable under a pension plan are considered by the tax law to represent in part a return of the employee's contributions and in part an interest accumulation resulting from investment by the plan's managers. The first portion is simply included in the man's estate and taxed according to the regular estate tax schedule.[33] The interest earned component is not included in the estate as such, but is taxed separately as if it were a gain from the sale of a capital asset.[34] The details of these procedures are contained in Appendix D, where the complete pension present value expressions are derived.

One problem that arises in this connection is the specification of an estate tax rate to use in the computations. As was true in the case of "outside income," the pertinent information for obtaining an accurate estimate is absent. Given that no evidence as to either the size or the form of the estates of top corporate executives is currently available, and the fact that the estate tax is not really of major importance here, a choice that is computationally convenient might just as well be made. Since matters in several formulas [35] are greatly simplified if the over-all effective tax rate on executives' estates is taken to be roughly equal to the 25 per cent capital gains rate, that figure is adopted throughout.

TAX TREATMENT OF RETIREMENT ANNUITIES

Because annuity premiums have generally the same function and characteristics as do pension contributions by an employee, the tax provisions applicable to individual retirement annuities are similar to those associated with contributory pension plan benefits. Premium pay-

[32] *Ibid.,* Section 72.
[33] *Ibid.,* Section 2039.
[34] *Ibid.,* Sections 71, 401, and 501.
[35] Particularly for stock options.

ments are not tax-deductible when made, but a fraction of the annuity later received by the policyholder is deductible—specified, in this case, by the "life expectancy" rule to be the ratio of total *premiums paid* to total benefits anticipated at retirement.[36]

Annuity policy death benefits are also divided into two parts for tax purposes, but the levies are computed in a slightly different manner from those for the corresponding pension plan payments. The full amount of the benefit is taxed in the man's estate, and, in addition, the segment representing an interest accumulation is subject to a capital gains tax. As a partial offset to this combined assessment, the estate tax on the interest accumulation is first deducted from that figure before the capital gains tax is applied.[37] Appendix D provides a complete description.

THE PRESENT VALUE EXPRESSIONS

Given the benefit structures of the two pension plans and their individual retirement annuity counterpart, and given the relevant tax liabilities, a comprehensive present value formula can be developed for each arrangement. The present value to an executive of a single prospective benefit payment is obtained by subtracting from its total dollar amount the required taxes, multiplying the remainder by the probability that it will actually be received—as determined from a mortality table—and, finally, discounting that result back to the present at a specified interest rate. The aggregate present value of a pension or an annuity is then simply the sum of the present values of all the separate benefits it provides. This expression is derived for noncontributory pension plans, contributory plans, and for the individual annuity alternative in Appendix D.

EARLY AND LATE RETIREMENT

While almost all corporate pension plans now provide for retirement at age 65, it is not uncommon for an important executive to stay on for several years past that point or—especially in more recent years—to take advantage of an early-retirement provision in his company's plan. The procedures described above, however, are geared to evaluate

---

[36] *Internal Revenue Code*, Section 72.
[37] *Ibid.*, Sections 72 and 2039(c), and IRS Regulation 1.72.

the experience of a man who retires at the "normal" time. The question must therefore be raised as to whether a "current equivalent" constructed on the expectation of retirement at one age is a legitimate index of the worth of an executive's pension if he ultimately retires at a different one.

Take first the case of a man who works past age 65. In the vast majority of instances, the applicable pension plan will specify that benefits do not continue to accrue for years of service beyond the designated retirement date. The executive therefore acquires nothing additional in the way of pension during his last years on the job, and a current equivalent set up to run only through age 64 *is* a complete alternative to that pension. From age 65 on, the current equivalent is by definition equal to zero, and there is no problem.[38]

If instead an executive should retire early and accept a lower retirement benefit from his company, the situation is less clear. If the current equivalent is terminated at that point and no further adjustment made, it must be assumed that the individual retirement annuity which the now-attenuated series of premium payments will provide will have the same after-tax present value as the reduced pension benefit. Whether such an assumption is valid depends, of course, on the specific schedule of early-retirement benefits under the plan in question and on the nature of the adjustment by the insurance company to a shorter stream of premium receipts. In the empirical work that follows, the convention will be that the two reductions in benefits are likely to be close enough in size to permit the view that simply terminating the current equivalent in the event of premature retirement does not distort the measurements. Apart from the fact that the available data rarely spell out the extent of the executive's sacrifice and thus provide any basis for a different procedure, there are good reasons to believe that the "truth," if known, *would* be very much like the assumption made. Both corporate pension trustees and the insurance companies selling individual annuity policies

[38] The exception to this would be the case in which the entire pension plan is revised. When that happens, even employees who were not entitled to accumulate additional benefits under the previous plan because they were overage are frequently included in a *general* benefit increase. If so, we confront a one-shot increment in our man's pension expectation which can be handled by determining the single-premium payment to an insurance company that will provide him with a straight life annuity policy having the same after-tax present value as his pension benefit increase—both evaluated as if they were to begin immediately.

must necessarily manage their affairs according to the same actuarial principles and will appraise their alternatives using similar mortality tables and opportunity costs. For a particular executive, therefore, those computations should not yield very different answers.

THE BEFORE-TAX CURRENT EQUIVALENT

Once the after-tax present value of an executive's pension has been determined, the premiums required for the purchase of an individual annuity having the same present value define its "after-tax current equivalent." A logical extension of this approach is the definition of a "before-tax current equivalent": the increase in actual gross salary and bonus receipts from the employer corporation that would be necessary to raise the man's current after-tax remuneration by the amount of his pension's after-tax current equivalent. Since that salary increase would enable the executive to do as well for himself as is done for him by his pension, he should be indifferent between the two arrangements. The concept of a "before-tax equivalent" therefore describes an operational alternative to the pension which makes use of direct current payments rather than promises of future benefits.

Several applications of this instrument are suggested by a general interest in appraising the characteristics of the compensation transaction. A comparison in before-tax terms of the relative importance of salary, bonus, and pension in the pay package can be drawn. The "efficiency" of a particular pension from the viewpoint of the employer can be determined by calculating the cost of financing the actual retirement income promise and contrasting it with the cost of its before-tax current equivalent. Finally, we may compare the federal tax revenue consequences of the two arrangements, taking into account both personal and corporate tax differences. Within the confines of the present study, however, company costs and governmental tax yields are not directly at issue, and are considered only briefly below.[39]

SUMMARY

Because the pension benefits promised corporate executives differ in timing and in likelihood of receipt from the other components of the pay package, it is necessary to develop a procedure for their valuation

[39] See Appendix M, for example, for a discussion of the relative costs.

which permits meaningful comparison as well as measurement. The before-tax and after-tax "current income equivalents" described seem appropriate to that purpose. Conceptually, the most important element in the analysis is the designation of the individual retirement annuity policy as the best index of the worth of a pension—in effect, its closest market substitute.[40] While the assumptions required in connection with executives' outside income, deductions and exemptions, opportunity costs, marital status, and mortality experience cannot be as accurate as one might wish, the parameters finally chosen should constitute a reasonable representation of actual experience.

[40] The difference between the pension valuation methodology followed by Leonard R. Burgess in *Top Executive Pay Package* and that outlined above is especially marked. For some comments on the procedures employed by Burgess, see Daniel M. Holland's review in the *Political Science Quarterly,* March 1964, pp. 129–133.

3

DEFERRED COMPENSATION

Deferred compensation is defined here to include all arrangements—other than the corporation's comprehensive employee pension plan—under which an executive is promised a series of cash payments after retirement in return for services performed currently. In almost every case these instruments take the form of contractual agreements between the corporation and individual executives and, as such, may contain a variety of provisions specifying the rights and duties of both parties. While their pronounced individuality makes it necessary to evaluate each contract according to its own peculiarities, the deferral and contingency aspects of most devices resemble those of pensions and a similar analysis can be applied.

Focus

The graduated personal income tax provides the most generally accepted—if not most frequently avowed—rationale for the use of a deferred payment contract. The executive's annual income and, hence, his marginal tax bracket are typically lower in retirement than during his active working life. By receiving a portion of his rewards in the later period, he incurs a smaller tax liability. Such objectives as the retention of a particular individual's services, the liberalization of executive retirement benefits in the absence of an increase in the pension rights of all employees, and the assurance that a key officer's knowledge and experience will continue to be available—as well as confidential—after he retires are more commonly claimed. Even so, the various arrangements devised are economically justified chiefly on the basis of their tax-ameliorating properties, and the question of whether and under what circumstances the other arguments advanced are valid will not be considered here.

36

Typical Arrangements

A deferred compensation contract may conform to any one of a number of patterns. While in each case a given amount becomes payable to the executive upon retirement, the period over which such payments are to continue varies considerably. A few of the arrangements are much like pensions in that payments are promised for the duration of the executive's life and then, perhaps, to a designated heir until he or she dies as well. The majority of contracts, however, guarantee the executive a fixed aggregate sum, the difference between that figure and any payments received prior to his death being payable to his estate, either in a lump sum or in installments to a particular heir.

In return for such promises, certain restrictions are usually imposed on the executive's activities. He may, for example, be required to:

1. Remain in the corporation's employ—at its discretion—until his normal retirement age.

2. Make himself available, in retirement, for consulting or advisory services.

3. Refrain from competing against the corporation or providing information to its competitors after he retires.

If the executive fails to keep his part of the bargain, except for reasons of health, he automatically forfeits his rights to the payments due him. The particular combination of rewards and obligations contained in each agreement is reported in the proxy statement of the corporation in the year in which it is made.

Tax Treatment

Because of their heterogeneity, deferred compensation arrangements have been taxed rather unsystematically over the years. The major difficulty lay in identifying the time at which the "true" receipt of income by the executive occurred, i.e., the date when the contract was entered into or the years when the payments thereunder eventually were made. In many instances the wording of an agreement was such that both its intent and practical effect were open to interpretation. Since no specific legislation similar to that defining the taxability of employee pensions has ever been enacted in this area, a degree of confusion was the inevitable result, and the courts have been confronted with a disproportionate number of individual cases for settlement. A 1960 ruling by the Internal Revenue Service, however, more or less standardized the favorable tax treatment of these devices along the lines of the developing pattern of court decisions.[1] Its import was that, as long as restrictive covenants of the sort described above were part of the contract, thus introducing the possibility of forfeiture by the executive, the postretirement payments specified were to be regarded as income taxable only *when received*. The deferred compensation arrangements adopted by the companies included in the present study qualify either for this ruling or, in prior years, for the generally equivalent position taken by the courts.[2]

The tax treatment of any death benefits or survivorship income rights provided under the agreement depends on their form. A single lump-sum cash settlement is taxed simply as a part of the man's estate.[3] Where a prescribed heir becomes eligible for a continuation of the executive's annual payments, a twofold tax assessment formula applies.[4] The aggregate dollar amount of the payments still due is taxed as part of the estate in the same manner as a lump-sum settlement. In addition, when those payments are eventually received by the designated beneficiary, they are taxed again as ordinary income. The beneficiary may, however, deduct from taxable income the proportionate share of the estate tax attributable to each such payment. To illustrate: If an executive who was to be paid $10,000 a year for ten years following his retirement under a deferred compensation contract which specified his wife as beneficiary died after receiving only two payments, there would be an estate tax assessed on the remaining $80,000. Were that tax to amount to, say, $20,000, then 20/80, or one-fourth of each $10,000 payment received by the man's wife in subsequent years, would be tax-free to her.

[1] Revenue Ruling 60-31, *Standard Federal Tax Reporter,* Commerce Clearing House, Inc., 1960, Vol. 6, pp. 6296–6298.

[2] A more extensive discussion of the tax history of deferred compensation is contained in an unpublished Master's thesis at the Massachusetts Institute of Technology by Kenneth R. Hootnick entitled "Deferred Compensation Agreements: A Study of Their Use and Effectiveness," June 1963, pp. 10–23.

[3] *Internal Revenue Code,* Section 2039.

[4] *Ibid.,* Section 691.

The Services Rewarded

There are two possible interpretations of the nature of a deferred compensation arrangement. One holds that the payments received by the retired executive should properly be regarded as remuneration for services he is performing at that time. The other contends that the timing of such payments is simply a matter of compensation administration and tax planning and that the rewards really apply to the man's active working life. The latter view is accepted here.

Evidence to support the first position is allegedly found both in the method by which the executive's taxes are assessed (the law assumes that the receipt of income does not occur until retirement) and in the structure of the deferred pay contract itself—the executive is obliged after retiring to be available for consultation and to refrain from assisting any of the firm's competitors. However, the tax doctrine is based not on a judgment about the corporation's motives or logic in designing its compensation package, but solely on an appraisal of the time at which the individual executive actually acquires and is able to freely dispose of a particular kind of income. As to the second point, the man's consulting chores are, in practice, almost invariably quite nominal and hardly represent a realistic quid pro quo for the payments he is receiving. Finally, the restriction that he not compete against his old firm is also more appropriately viewed as a precondition for the receipt of pay for certain earlier services rather than as an action being rewarded in and of itself. Indeed, one could well argue that both of these requirements are made a part of the contract in most instances chiefly to bring the arrangement under the cover of a favorable tax formula and are not considered the basis of an affirmative postretirement relationship.

A similar conclusion is reached if the intentions expressed by the corporation in setting up its deferred compensation plan are examined. Whether the reason given is the retention of an executive, the supplementing of his pension benefits, or some related purpose, the implication clearly is that his services *prior* to retirement are the focus of the arrangement. In the situation where, as sometimes happens, the man's salary is reduced—or not increased along with those of other executives—at the time a deferred compensation contract is entered into with him, the nature of the transaction is most obvious. By way of analogy, there is never any claim advanced that a pension, with its vesting provisions, is a reward for services performed *after* retirement. Accordingly, a deferred compensation agreement will be considered here as a device that represents, as does a pension promise, remuneration to the executive for the period from the time it is instituted up to the time he retires.

The Valuation Procedures

In order to assess the worth of a deferred pay plan in a manner that will permit comparison with other forms of reward, the concept of a "current equivalent" is once again adopted. Since the characteristics of such plans differ to some extent from those of pensions, however, their current equivalents will necessarily have a slightly different cast.

Given the size and timing of the various payments anticipated, the contingencies associated with them, and the applicable tax liabilities, the after-tax present value of any arrangement can be calculated. Its current equivalent is then determined by asking the question: "If the executive involved were to receive instead—beginning in the year when the deferred compensation agreement is made and continuing until his retirement—an annual after-tax salary increase having the same present value, how large would that increase have to be?" In effect, it is hypothesized that the most appropriate practical alternative to a deferred pay contract is simply an addition to the man's salary which, in terms of its after-tax present value, is as attractive to him—and that this alternative is therefore a good measure of the after-tax current income counterpart of such a contract for the purpose of relating it to other, similarly translated rewards.

Rationale

The current equivalent of a pension promise was taken to be the stream of annual premiums which—given an after-tax salary increase of the same magnitude—would enable the executive to purchase an individual retirement annuity having a present value equal to that of his pension. In the case of a deferred compensation arrangement, however, it is the after-tax salary increase *itself* whose present value is regarded as the relevant "equivalence" criterion. This difference in approach is a product of two considerations.

First, the benefit structures of pension plans are, as indicated, more standardized than those of deferred compensation agreements. It is therefore possible to propose a single, fairly representative market alternative to the two types of pensions, the price of which can be used as a common index of their worth. Deferred pay plans are not so readily characterized, and the computational effort involved in seeking out a close substitute for each of the various arrangements encourages the adoption of a simpler, more direct procedure.

Secondly, there are some fundamental differences in the characteristics of the two devices. Pensions are, by definition, oriented around the probable length of the executive's life. The benefits promised consist of a series of assured annual payments which terminate only upon his death. An individual annuity policy has similar features. Through its purchase an executive can guarantee himself the same lifelong income that the pension provides. Since this guarantee is viewed here as essential to a truly equivalent position and since he cannot self-insure the particular "risk" involved—i.e., the chance that he may live too long and exhaust his funds—he must bargain with the only institution that is set up to provide that service for him. Hence, an individual retirement annuity is a singularly appropriate personal alternative to the pension.

Deferred compensation arrangements, on the other hand, are centered much less on mortality considerations. While a few resemble pensions, with the length of the actual postretirement payment period being determined by the date of the employee's death, the large majority provide in some way for a *fixed* total reward instead. Mortality is taken into account in those terms of the agreement which specify the relevant death benefits, but the aggregate payout of the contract is not thereby affected. Consequently, there is no reason to propose here as a substitute an instrument whose most prominent characteristic is the guarantee of a lifetime, and therefore indeterminate, income stream. While insurance companies do offer other contracts which resemble many of the common deferred compensation arrangements, the special advantages they have where a pension is concerned are absent in this case; there are a number of investment media that can be regarded as sensible alternatives when mortality is not a key issue. Rather than attempt to specify a particular one, it seems more desirable to adopt a valuation procedure which is consistent with as many different choices as possible, i.e., simply calculating the after-tax salary increase which is as valuable in itself as the deferred compensation agreement in question.

Contingencies

The uncertainties associated with the eventual receipt of benefits under a deferred pay contract can be separated into two categories: those over which the executive has control and those he cannot influence. The former are introduced by the forfeiture provisions written into most agreements. Thus, the executive may be required to remain with his company until normal retirement age, keep his knowledge of its operations confidential, and be available to it for consultation after retirement—or else give up his rights under the contract. Because of the severity of this penalty and because it seems likely that a highly placed executive would be willing to fulfill at least the last two obligations without an overt threat of economic reprisal, the assumption here will be that all prospective deferred payments may be considered certain insofar as these factors affect them. The possibility that the executive might resign to take another job is probably the only real concern, and it has been argued previously that turnover is negligibly small. The prospect of losing substantial amounts of deferred pay should reduce it even further.

The second type of contingency is, of course, that of mortality. Although the total before-tax payout of a deferred compensation arrangement is typically not dependent upon the length of the executive's life, its after-tax present value is. If the man should die before receiving all the payments he is entitled to, the settlement made with his estate will result in a different tax liability and perhaps in a different pattern of benefits than would have been the case had he continued to live. Some appraisal of the anticipated mortality experience of executives is therefore necessary. For the reasons given in connection with pension valuation, the 1951 Group Annuity Table seems an appropriate estimate.

Discount Rate

Another form of uncertainty relevant to a determination of the worth of a deferred pay contract is that surrounding the ability of the employer corporation to meet its commitments. Not all arrangements are funded, as pensions are, and there may be some question about the degree of confidence it is proper to have in the ultimate payment of the stipulated rewards. The problem arises particularly in the case of small and new firms or those otherwise in a difficult financial position. However, since the present study focuses on large, well-established enterprises with favorable long-range prospects, it should be possible to regard their deferred compensation agreements as no less sound than their pension plans. Accordingly, if the executive were to seek to provide on his own for postretirement income having the same "risk" characteristics, a generally conservative investment policy similar to that suggested as an alternative to the pension would seem in order. A discount rate of 2½ per cent per annum after taxes will therefore be used to determine the present value of each deferred payment, and to calculate the after-tax salary increase that comprises its "current equivalent."

The Tax Environment

Once more, various factors external to the compensation transaction must be taken into account in computing tax liabilities. Following the convention adopted earlier, the executive will be credited with income after retirement in addition to his deferred pay equal to that which he is estimated to be receiving at the time the contract is entered into, i.e., 15 per cent of his then-current aggregate direct remuneration. Anticipated nontaxable deductions and exemptions are assumed again to be 10 per cent of total income for agreements concluded during the period 1940 to 1950 and 15 per cent for all subsequent ones. The tax rates used will be those in force on the date of the present value computations. Thus, an executive who was paid $60,000 in salary and bonus in 1955 and who was in that year promised, under a deferred compensation contract, $20,000 annually for ten years upon retirement would—if he had no pension in prospect—be expected to enjoy a total annual post-retirement income of $29,000. Of that amount 85 per cent would be regarded as taxable at the rates prevailing in 1955, and 20/29 of the resultant after-tax figure would be attributed to the deferred pay arrangement. The effect of a concurrent pension will be considered later.[5]

Present Value Analysis

The present value to an executive of each payment foreseen under a deferred compensation contract is equal to the product of its after-tax dollar amount and the probability of its receipt—discounted at the prescribed 2½ per cent rate of interest to the year the contract is entered into. The sum of all such quantities represents the aggregate present value of the arrangement. As in the case of pensions, benefits will be assumed payable yearly rather than monthly in order to facilitate computation.

The after-tax current equivalent of the device is then taken to be the annual after-tax salary increase which, if begun in the year the deferred pay agreement is made and promised the executive thereafter up to his retirement, would have the same present value. Since the individual in question might not live to receive all the indicated salary payments, a discount must be incorporated in the computations for mortality as well as for time deferral.[6] In Appendix F, formal mathematical expressions for the present value of a typical deferred compensation arrangement and for the determination of its after-tax current income equivalent are developed.

The Before-Tax Current Equivalent

Having made these calculations, we can readily derive a "before-tax current equivalent." If it should turn out, for example, that a man age

[5] In Chapter 6.

[6] It could be argued that an after-tax current equivalent more in keeping with the nature of the deferred pay plan would be one which provided for an annual salary increase plus either a lump-sum award or a continuance of payments to the man's estate if he should die prior to retirement. While it is true that this scheme would resemble more closely the provisions contained in most contracts, it would not represent a truly "current" equivalent. Direct payments to the executive would constitute only a portion of such an arrangement, and it would be incorrect, therefore, to describe it simply as a series of increments to salary, i.e., to current income.

55 is awarded a deferred compensation contract which has as its after-tax equivalent an increase in take-home pay of $10,000 per year for the next ten years, its before-tax equivalent may be defined simply as the sequence of additions to actual before-tax salary and bonus paid during each of those years which would generate an extra $10,000 annually after taxes. The magnitude of the requisite streams of both before-tax and after-tax increments may then be compared with the corresponding salary and bonus figures to measure the relative importance of deferred pay in the compensation package. Insofar as the "efficiency" of that package was also of interest, a further comparison could be made between the cost to the company of the contrived before-tax current equivalent, on the one hand, and the cost of the observed deferred pay arrangement on the other.

Summary

Deferred compensation, as defined here, refers to the contractual agreements between corporations and certain of their executives under which a specified series of annual payments is to be made to an executive after his retirement. Such rewards are taxed at ordinary personal income tax rates when received. A deferred compensation scheme differs from a pension in that it pertains only to a single employee and generally has an aggregate dollar value which is not dependent upon mortality considerations. As with pensions, however, the relevant deferral and contingency factors are quantifiable. A "current income equivalent" can therefore be developed which enables the remunerative capacity of a deferred pay arrangement to be assessed and then compared with that of other forms of managerial compensation.

4

STOCK OPTIONS

A stock option granted by a corporation to one of its executives stipulates that he may purchase from the firm, at any time within a stated period, a given number of shares of its stock at a price fixed on the date of granting. Since the economic benefit the executive ultimately derives from such an arrangement depends directly on the future price behavior of his company's stock, the option has associated with it a high degree of uncertainty and is, for that reason, particularly difficult to analyze. A "current equivalent" can once again be developed, but it necessarily will differ in several major respects from those created for forms of reward whose contingencies are more readily treated.

Orientation

For the moment, attention is directed solely toward the remunerative aspects of the stock option, i.e., its actual monetary value to the executive and a translation of that value into current income figures. The proclaimed ability of the device to elicit a certain kind of effort from executives and to induce them to acquire a more substantial ownership interest in their companies will be considered here only to the extent that such factors bear upon the worth of the option and upon the appropriateness of the alternative suggested for it. A comparison of the costs of a stock option and its "current equivalent" will also be postponed to a later discussion.[1] While these matters are important in a number of connections, an appraisal of the purely financial attributes of the option is an essential first step.

[1] Appendix M.

Tax Treatment

Stock options have, in one form or another, been used to reward executives for a good many years. Their real popularity, however, dates from 1950 when legislation was enacted providing them with favorable—and assured—tax treatment and establishing definite ground rules for their design.[2] Since then, virtually all option agreements have conformed to those guidelines.

The law specified that, as long as the option price set was at least 95 per cent of the market price of the stock on the day the option was granted, any income accruing to the executive as a result of the purchase and later resale of such stock would be considered a gain on the sale of a capital asset and taxed at the rates applicable thereto.[3] In order to qualify for this treatment, the option also had to be nontransferable and of no more than ten years' duration. In addition, any stock acquired could not be resold by the optionee until two years after the date of granting nor until six months after the date of exercise. Since these were relatively mild requirements, however, the capital gains tax feature made stock options especially attractive to executives in view of the high marginal rates on their salary and bonus earnings.

Typical Instruments

Within the general framework indicated, an option plan could be designed quite flexibly to fit the needs of both the individual executive and his firm. In most cases the maximum period permitted under the law

[2] Revenue Act of 1950, Section 218. A discussion of the checkered tax history and utilization of stock options prior to 1950 is contained in George T. Washington and V. Henry Rothschild, *Compensating the Corporate Executive,* New York, 1951, pp. 121–135.

[3] Options with prices as low as 85 per cent of market price were sanctioned, but their tax treatment was less sympathetic and they were granted infrequently. In Appendix G a full description of the relevant statutes is presented, including the changes made by the Revenue Act of 1964. Since the empirical portion of this study will include data on executives only through the end of 1963, the pre-1964 tax law is the relevant one. The valuation procedures to be developed can be adapted to the features of the new statutes, however, as Appendix G indicates. That discussion is most profitably referred to after reading the present chapter in its entirety.

was taken advantage of and the option stipulated to be exercisable, at the optionee's discretion, any time up to ten years from the date it was granted, either in a single bloc or in several installments. Depending on the corporation's objectives, a shorter time limit was occasionally adopted, and provision was sometimes made for a fixed sequence of exercises. For example, one-tenth of the total number of optioned shares might be eligible for purchase by the executive during the first year of the agreement, a second one-tenth during the following year, and so on. The large majority of plans, however, simply specified the maximum allowable ten-year term and did not insist on any particular pattern of exercise.

Option prices were seldom set at less than the tax-encouraged 95 per cent of market. That figure and full market price on the date of granting were by far the predominant choices, with 95 per cent being somewhat the more common.

The other elements of option plans were not as uniformly designed. The number of executives receiving options, the proportionate ownership share of the firm earmarked for option grants, the formula by which those grants were made to individual executives, the restrictions, either express or implied, placed on the resale of stock acquired under option, the disposition of unexercised options upon the death, retirement, or resignation of the executive, and the extent of any reciprocal obligation on the part of the optionee to remain in the employ of the issuing corporation varied, and still vary, substantially from plan to plan. Fortunately, most of these characteristics are important primarily from the viewpoint of the internal compensation administrator and need not be examined in great detail in order to determine the worth of a stock option and to develop a current equivalent for it. The duration of the option and its price are the significant factors for that interest.

The Reward Obtained from an Option

The essence of a stock option is, of course, the opportunity it provides for its recipient to purchase marketable securities at a discount. He is placed in a position where he can do something other investors cannot and is thereby able to employ his investible funds in a superior manner.

There are, however, two possible conceptual approaches to measuring the extent of the advantage which he enjoys.

The first is to treat the option as, in effect, a long-term "call" option and therefore to fix its value to the executive as of the date it is granted. The argument would be that the right to purchase shares of stock at an established price anytime within a period of up to ten years is clearly worth something in and of itself at the time it is created regardless of the actual results subsequently obtained from its exercise. Put another way, it would be possible in terms of the objectives of the current study to conceive of the executive involved being able to specify in advance the magnitude of the salary increase he would be willing to accept as a substitute for any given option, i.e., as its current income equivalent. While conceptually this line of reasoning is persuasive, it does have some important drawbacks.

For one thing, the computational problems it raises are severe. Even though there is an active market in call options which provides some prices that could be used as general guides to the ex ante value of executives' stock options, the contracts which are sold in that market are of no more than a year in duration, whereas every stock option issued by the fifty firms in the present sample had a term of at least three years. Actual prices cannot therefore be observed for the relevant arrangements, and it would be necessary to rely instead on a theoretical model of option valuation. While such models exist,[4] they not only require that a substantial amount of historical stock price information be collected and summarized each time an estimate of the worth of a new option is desired, but the discussions surrounding them have thus far left open some key issues concerning their implementation: the length of the time period over which historical data should be compiled, the relative weights to be given different portions of that data, whether the behavior of external economic indicators can be used to improve the models' predictive ability, and so on. In short, a fairly sizeable security

[4] See, for example: A. James Boness, "Elements of a Theory of Stock Option Value," *Journal of Political Economy,* No. 2, April 1964, pp. 163–175; G. Giguere, "Warrants: A Mathematical Method of Evaluation," *Analysts Journal,* No. 14, 1958, pp. 17–25; Paul A. Samuelson, "Rational Theory of Warrant Pricing," *Industrial Management Review,* Vol. 6, No. 2, Spring 1965, pp. 13–32. A comprehensive general reference in this area is Paul H. Cootner, ed., *The Random Character of Stock Market Prices,* Cambridge, Mass., 1964.

valuation effort would be called for if this approach were adopted. A commitment to that sort of an undertaking does not seem appropriate within the framework of the present study, especially since it would—if properly executed—almost certainly overwhelm the original concern with the compensation package itself.[5]

A second point concerns the applicability of such a procedure to actual compensation situations—an issue which has been stressed in connection with the current income equivalents of other rewards. Given the difficulties involved in estimating future stock prices, it seems unlikely that any predictive formula adopted here would be widely accepted by businessmen or, even where accepted, that its parameters could be agreed upon in practice by both parties to particular compensation transactions. Thus, one can imagine the difficulty that would be encountered by a corporate compensation administrator in attempting to reach agreement with his company's executives on the ex ante value of their proposed stock options. Now, it is true that the current equivalents developed above for pension and deferred compensation arrangements have some ex ante elements—the use of a discount for mortality in determining present values, for example. But it is also true that the relevant contingencies have been analyzed so extensively with the aid of large amounts of data that the necessary conceptual framework (actuarial science) and its empirical implementation (the mortality table) are no longer subjects of controversy. Whenever an appraisal of such contingencies is called for, then, it can be made with both confidence and precision. A similar claim is not yet possible for ex ante stock price estimates.

If these strictures are accepted, the clear alternative is to value the option according to the events which, in fact, follow from its employment. This can easily be done by considering the cost to the executive of purchasing his firm's stock if he were not the beneficiary of an option grant,

---

[5] It should also be noted that the question of the shape of executives' wealth-utility functions would be raised by an ex ante stock option valuation procedure. Thus, in order to determine what salary increase the executive would be willing to accept in place of an option before knowing what will happen to the price of his firm's stock, the strength of his aversion to "gambling" on the option as compared with receiving a guaranteed series of salary payments would have to be considered. This again is an issue which requires for its resolution more of an analytical digression than seems desirable in the present circumstances.

i.e., he would have to pay the full market price for the shares in question. On that basis, the difference between the option price to which he is entitled and the actual market price of the shares as of the date the option is *exercised* measures the extent of the advantage vis-à-vis other investors which he ultimately turns out to enjoy. That difference is taken here to be the most practicable index of the worth of a stock option to its recipient. It removes any need for speculation about future stock prices and renders our measurements independent of the attitudes of the executive and the company at the time the option is granted.[6] It also implies that the resulting current income equivalent will embody the same sort of incentive features as the option itself.

Thus, it is often claimed that stock options are designed to encourage behavior on the part of executives which will bring about an increase in the price of their firms' stock.[7] While an appraisal of such arguments is not our main concern here, there is some merit in developing a valuation procedure which—as does that proposed—gives rise to a current equivalent whose magnitude depends on *actual* stock price movements subsequent to the date the option is granted. If, then, there is any truth in the claims advanced, a stream of salary payments having this characteristic would, as a substitute for the option, provide a similar degree of encouragement to its recipient to identify himself with the position of his firm's shareholders. An entirely ex ante approach to stock option valuation would have none of that flavor.

It would be wrong, however, to carry this line of reasoning to the conclusion that the compensation provided by an option ought to be measured on the day the optionee eventually disposes of his stock and thereby realizes his profits. That procedure would fail to draw the necessary distinction between the option transaction, on the one hand, and the investment decision which follows, on the other. The day the executive exercises his right to purchase certain shares of stock at a discount, the action which was singularly open to him because he was granted a stock option is formally completed. At that time his advantage over the market is claimed, and he stands thereafter on the same basis with regard to in-

---

[6] We cannot, of course, be sure that any valuation procedure when applied empirically to executives' past option experiences will furnish a reliable guide to future developments. See especially the discussion in Chapter 8.

[7] See, for example: Henry Ford II, "Stock Options Are in the Public Interest," *Harvard Business Review*, July–August, 1961.

creases and decreases in the value of his asset holdings as does the rest of the investment community.[8] The worth of an option is therefore correctly determined, ex post, by market events, but only up to that event which signifies the exhaustion of the special privileges it confers.[9] The mechanics of translating the value thus obtained into a stream of current income equivalent payments are outlined below.

After-Tax Rewards

While not so labeled, the foregoing discussion has, in fact, been concerned with identifying and measuring before-tax remuneration. When the executive ultimately resells stock acquired under option, of course, he is assessed a capital gains tax on the difference between its value at that time and its original cost to him. Since whatever the magnitude of that difference, one of its components is the discount from market price which was obtained on the day the option was exercised, this discount should be considered a before-tax reward and the amount of tax attributable thereto subtracted in order to convert it to an after-tax measure. The executives with whom we shall be concerned (those for whom data are available from proxy statements) had incomes large enough to make it advantageous for them to choose to be taxed at the 25 per cent flat capital gains rate on any profits realized. Therefore, as a first approximation, the stock option's after-tax reward can be defined simply as 75 per cent of the difference between option price and market price on the date of exercise.

[8] Including the necessity of waiting six months before selling any shares in order to qualify for capital gains tax treatment. The reader is reminded again that the pre-1964 tax law is the relevant one for the present discussion.

[9] Of course, along with those "special privileges" may also go some special constraints. Because of pressures exerted on them either formally or informally by their companies, for instance, most executives are likely to be reluctant to resell shares acquired through the exercise of stock options even when market conditions would ordinarily lead them to do so. Such sales may be interpreted as an expression of lack of confidence in the company's prospects and be frowned on—and effectively deterred—for that reason. As a result, the executive might be induced by a stock option to hold a larger proportion of his personal investment portfolio in the form of the common stock of his employer than considerations of efficient diversification would dictate. In some sense, then, the option is really worth less in such situations than the discount from market price it provides would suggest. However, since both the extent of that loss and the frequency of its occurrence are almost impossible to quantify, they will necessarily be ignored here.

This procedure might, however, be open to criticism on several counts. First, the optionee may retain possession of his stock until he dies and thereby avoid entirely the payment of taxes on its appreciation in value. To the extent that this occurs, and it is probably not uncommon, a 25 per cent tax rate assumption will overstate the true average liability and understate the over-all after-tax compensation generated by options. Even though there is no information currently available which indicates how often this situation arises, a bias will clearly exist unless some offset is provided. Accordingly the convention here will be that a tax rate of 20 per cent is a more appropriate figure to use. While arbitrary—and quite unverifiable—the resulting adjustment does at least operate to change the imputed tax liabilities in the proper direction. It is certain that, on average, 25 per cent is incorrect and the lower rate should be regarded simply as an approximation of the "right" figure.

A second point concerns the deferral rather than the complete elimination of the capital gains tax. Even if optioned stock is actually resold by the optionee, there is a time lag between its purchase and that sale, which suggests that the amount of the associated tax payment should be diminished in present value terms to reflect its postponement relative to the date the option is exercised. For simplicity—and once again for lack of pertinent data—the assumption will be that the necessary adjustment for this factor is also included in the reduction of the applicable tax rate to 20 per cent.

Finally, there is the matter of the deductions from taxable income which may be generated by option profits. If the optionee is induced to increase his charitable contributions or, perhaps, is forced to borrow and incur deductible interest charges in order to obtain funds to exercise his options, his taxable income will be lowered. Since capital gains are taxed at a flat rate, any additional deductions so created will be subtracted by him from income which is taxable at "ordinary income" rates. The question, therefore, is whether stock option profits, some of which may exist only on paper, have a significant influence on deductible expenditures. Certainly, there should be some impact as long as the optionee is not completely insensitive to the fact that he has become a wealthier man. On the other hand, the timing of such expenditures is uncertain. They may occur even before exercise, as potential option profits accumulate; they may coincide with exercise; or they may follow later. In effect, the same problem is confronted as in the case of executives who may hold their optioned stock until they die and thus avoid the capital gains tax: some adjustment is necessary, but there is really no way of knowing just how large it should be.[10] For that reason, a similar solution will be adopted. The effective tax rate assumed on stock option income will be lowered another 5 per cent to 15 per cent. This reduction is intended to approximate, or at least have the same qualitative effect as, the tax saving on current income which might ensue from the extra deductions encouraged by a profitable stock option. Again, the intent of the assumption is simply to remove in a convenient way some part of what would otherwise be a persistent understatement of the value of an option.[11]

The After-Tax Current Equivalent

Having decided upon a method by which to measure the after-tax reward provided by an option, we may now consider the design of a technique to compare it with the other components of the pay package. To that end, the approach taken previously in connection with pensions and deferred compensation plans, whereby an "after-tax current equivalent" was constructed, can be repeated. Accordingly, the question will be posed: How much of an increase in the optionee's annual after-tax salary would be necessary were he to be as well rewarded by that increase as he is by his stock option?

There are, of course, several dimensions to a full description of such a device. One is the standard by which equality of reward is to be judged.

---

[10] There is, however, some evidence to indicate that the tax savings may be quite substantial—as much as one-half the 25 per cent capital gains tax—if the deductions associated with capital gains are proportionately the same as those pertaining to ordinary income. See D. M. Holland and W. G. Lewellen, "Probing the Record of Stock Options," *Harvard Business Review*, March–April 1962.

[11] In principle, the correct procedure would be to estimate the additional deductions at some percentage of option profits, to allocate those amounts to the various years in which they are considered likely to be claimed by the executive, and then to calculate the resulting tax savings according to the actual salary, bonus, and "outside income" received by him during those years. Obviously, this would become a rather demanding process, but because of the necessity to make a number of assumptions without much supporting evidence, it would not yield the compensating benefit of a great improvement in the accuracy of the results obtained.

Consistent with the principle established earlier, the after-tax present value of each current equivalent will be matched with that of the option whose substitute it is intended to represent. A second element is the period over which the current equivalent should be spread. In the absence of any support for a different convention, it seems reasonable to specify the same term of years that is provided in the option agreement. Thus, if the option is exercisable at any time within ten years from the day it is granted, its replacement will consist of a stream of ten annual salary payments.[12]

Even if these propositions are accepted, however, the features of what might be a sensible current equivalent are not as evident in the case of a stock option as they are for other forms of compensation. The difficulty lies in the peculiar nature of the device which led above to the view that its remunerative achievements can be properly assessed only after some action is taken by the optionee. The contingencies associated with a pension plan were seen to be well defined, and an almost identical instrument is available to the executive elsewhere on an individual basis. These conditions, which gave rise to a very clear "anticipatory" current income counterpart of the pension, are not met by a stock option. The ex post character of the reward in question causes a real problem in constructing a current equivalent which will (1) span the full term of the option it replaces, (2) be as valuable without perfect foresight, and (3) have some operational possibilities—and attractions—for the corporation. Unless the current equivalent exhibits all three qualities, it is not, in the view here, a truly satisfactory vehicle for expressing the relationship between the option and the remainder of the executive's compensation.

By that standard, the following procedure seems to accomplish, as well as any of the wide range of available alternatives, the objective desired. At the end of each calendar year after an option is granted, its prospective after-tax worth is estimated—by assuming it to be 85 per

---

[12] Despite the fact that a stock option is necessarily exercised at a particular point in time, it would be misleading to attribute the entire financial gain which results to the day—or even the year—of exercise. That gain is realized because of a history of stock price changes and the wide discretion enjoyed by the executive in choosing when to take advantage of his rights. Thus, while the exercise of an option is a discrete event, the benefits it confers depend on and accrue because of developments and decisions which are related to some *interval* of time.

cent of the difference between the option price and the stock's market price at that time. Beginning in the succeeding year and continuing through the final year of the option's term, the optionee's annual after-tax salary is increased by an amount such that the resulting series of payments has a present value equal to the estimate obtained. This process is repeated annually until the end of the calendar year in which the executive exercises his option—and therefore determines the actual magnitude of his reward. Thus, in each year an *additional* stream of salary payments is begun whose after-tax present value is equal to the *change* in the estimated after-tax value of the option during the year. The outcome of all this is a current equivalent which resembles that described for a pension arrangement: a series of "layers" of salary increases, each one corresponding to an increment in the (expected) value of the executive's compensation. At the end of the year of exercise, the interest-accumulated total of the salary payments made in anticipation of the now-measurable option gain is subtracted from that gain, and the difference is adjusted for by awarding the optionee a final series of additions to salary—these to replace all others and have a present value equal to the difference indicated. In effect, the current equivalent varies in size according to the developing experience under the option— i.e., the pattern of stock price changes—up to the point when the option is exercised, at which time its remaining components are fixed.

Consider the following example: On August 1, 1952, an executive is granted an option to purchase, at any time within the next four years, ten thousand shares of his company's stock at a price of $95 per share. On the day of granting, the market price of the stock is $100, and by December 31, 1952, it has risen to $105 per share. The option would therefore be worth, after taxes, 85 per cent of (10,000)($105 − $95), or $85,000 if it were exercised at that time. In the expectation of an eventual exercise, a series of four annual increments to the optionee's salary is initiated. For convenience, let us suppose that the promise of an extra $24,000 after taxes per year in each of the years 1953 through 1956 would have a present value equal to $85,000.[13] Accordingly, $24,000 is attributed to the executive, as the first portion of his current equivalent, in 1953. On December 31 of that year, a second appraisal

---

[13] The question of an appropriate interest rate and the mechanics of its use are discussed below.

of the situation is made. If the market price of the stock involved has climbed to $125 per share, an additional $170,000 in potential after-tax reward will have been generated. To reflect this change, an increase in the man's current equivalent is necessary. Again for the sake of numerical simplicity, let us assume that three annual payments, in this case for 1954, 1955, and 1956, of $60,000 each have a $170,000 total present value. The optionee is therefore credited with $84,000 worth of current equivalent in 1954. On October 1 he exercises his option in full. At that time, the market price of the stock purchased is $119 per share, resulting in an after-tax reward equal to $204,000 by the definition above.[14] Now, installments totaling $108,000 have been "paid" in anticipation of this event. With interest, they would have accumulated to approximately $110,000 by October 1, 1954.[15] Thus, a net of $94,000 is still "due" the executive, and two payments of, say, $50,000 each in 1955 and 1956 complete his current equivalent.[16]

With this approach it is possible to reconcile the apparent conflict between the desire for a current equivalent which extends over a period of time—beginning when the option is granted—and the principle that the actual compensation afforded by that device can be determined accurately only in retrospect. Having done so, we can perhaps claim to combine the virtues of both ex ante and ex post techniques. The choice of the end of the calendar year as the day on which to perform the periodic assessments of the prospective value of an option is merely for convenience; any date would do. The most obvious alternative is the anniversary of the option grant itself, but for the purpose of calculating current equivalents for a large number of executives, it is easier to specify one common date and collect stock price data only for it.[17] In any event, the general format of the after-tax current equivalent is fairly simple, and it is offered here not only as a useful instrument by which to compare the option with other rewards, but also as a workable substitute that should be brought to the attention of corporations in

[14] That is, 85 per cent of (10,000)($119 − $95).

[15] For the procedure involved, see the section on "present and cumulative values" below.

[16] Its final form is: 1953—$24,000; 1954—$84,000; 1955—$50,000; 1956—$50,000. The reason for the variation in annual amounts is, of course, the change in stock prices observed, particularly the drop in 1954 prior to exercise.

[17] And, of course, assessments could be made at more frequent intervals such as every six months or every quarter.

designing their executive compensation packages. Thus a firm might issue "shadow" stock options to its managerial group and use the current equivalent described as the *actual* means of payment. For instance, the executive could be told, "We will compensate you as well as if you had such-and-such an option, but you will be given instead an increase in your salary each year which depends on the price of our stock just as the value of that option would have. Let us know when you eventually would have exercised the option, and we'll settle up then with a final series of salary increments." In effect, the proposal is for a variable component of salary which will act as a proxy for the changing potential value of the option it replaces.

Mortality Considerations

In the development of current income equivalents for pensions and deferred compensation arrangements, it was deemed necessary to take into account the possibility that the executive in question might not live to receive some or all of the payments promised. The present value of both rewards was therefore computed using a discount for mortality as well as for time deferral. In the case of a stock option this additional discount is not required. The optionee's estate is permitted by law to exercise his option if he should die and, it may be assumed, will do so if that instrument has a positive value. While the relevant statutes sanction such an exercise up to the end of the original term of the option, all but a few companies specify a foreshortening of this period in the event of the optionee's death. In the large majority of plans, exercise must take place within a year thereafter. By making regular appraisals of the worth of the option in the manner described above, we therefore ensure that the actual financial gain it provides, if exercised by the executive's heirs, will—even though that gain is impossible to determine from any published source—be reasonably close to the most recent estimate made. Thus, if a series of salary payments is constructed which varies with changes in this estimate, those payments should represent an appropriate alternative to the option regardless of whether its initial recipient or his descendants exercise it.

Tax considerations are neutral in this respect also.[18] According to

---

[18] Internal Revenue Code, Section 421(d)(6)(C).

the law, an estate tax is payable on the difference between the market price of the stock on the date of the optionee's death and its designated option price. Under the same rule, however, the basis for calculating any capital gains achieved through the resale of stock acquired by exercising an *inherited* option is correspondingly increased. For example, if an executive should die holding an option to purchase shares of his company's stock for $20 at a time when the market price of that stock is $50, an estate tax would be assessed on the $30 difference. Were the option to be exercised subsequently and the stock resold for $90, only $40 of that amount would be subject to a capital gains tax. If, then, it is assumed, as was done previously, that the over-all effective tax rate levied on the estates of executives is likely to be close to the 25 per cent capital gains rate payable on any stock option profits they themselves might obtain, there is no need to make an adjustment in tax liabilities for the possibility that the executives may not live to exercise their options. There is, in short, no *additional* tax due, and approximately the same *rate* applies to the stock price differential which defines the executive's reward if he lives and which is taken to be the best estimate of the benefit claimed by his estate if he does not.

Mortality *is* a factor on the other side of the compensation "equation," however. It was asserted earlier that a current equivalent must be composed entirely of direct payments to the executive if it is to be, as advertised, a true current income alternative. Hence any scheme that requires a continuation of payments to the man's estate following his death is unsuitable. The salary increments which comprise the stock option's current equivalent must therefore be large enough to generate the necessary present values when they are discounted for both futurity and mortality. The promise of an annual salary increase extending some years into the future can only be made contingent upon its intended recipient's remaining alive. Since this is the sort of promise advocated here as a possible substitute for the stock option—or, at least, as a useful restatement of its compensatory value—the computations must take into account the fact that the executive's survival is not certain. In the illustration above, for example, the first series of four salary payments might have to be, say, $25,000 per year instead of $24,000 in order for them to represent the required $85,000 present value. Similar upward revisions in the other figures originally obtained are also necessary. The ultimate impact of these changes on the "typical" current equivalent will probably not be very great, but they are correct in principle and, for that reason, should be undertaken.[19] Moreover, the ready availability of mortality data makes the task of doing so quite simple.[20] If, then, an executive should die holding an unexercised option or before having received all the salary payments due him under the current equivalent of an option he *has* exercised, there is no need for any adjustment on that account—and no basis for a concern that the attenuated series of payments which results somehow understates his reward.

Discount Rate

The opportunity cost used to transform the financial gain provided by a stock option into a series of annual payments spread over a period of years should, by definition, indicate the return available from the investment activity in which the optionee might engage if his option actually were substituted for in the manner described. For two reasons it seems sensible to consider investment in common stocks his most appropriate choice. First of all, much has been made of the point that the reward obtained from a stock option should be measured by the net advantage it confers when compared with its closest market alternative. That alternative was taken to be the purchase of the shares acquired under option at their market price on the date of exercise. From that view followed also the notion that stock price developments thereafter were irrelevant, since they represented occurrences to which *all* investors were subject regardless of the circumstances surrounding their original stock purchases. In short, the value of an option is determined by the differences and the similarities between it and the opportunities open to the ordinary common stock investor.

Secondly, the role which an option can be thought of as playing in the

---

[19] In the absence of mortality considerations and assuming a discount rate of 5 per cent per annum, a series of ten annual payments of $12,330 each made at the beginning of every year would have a present value equal to $100,000. If those payments were to constitute part of a current equivalent for a man aged 50, the additional discount for mortality would require that the payments be $12,760 each in order to generate the same present value.

[20] As was true in the case of pensions and deferred compensation arrangements, the 1951 Group Annuity Table for Males will be used.

executive's personal financial planning is one which could logically be filled by a portfolio of equities. It was decided above that the current equivalent designed for a pension plan should provide the same sort of basic postretirement economic security. By similar reasoning, both the uncertainty and the profit potential associated with the stock option suggest that the executive should be inclined to pursue an investment policy having the same characteristics with any funds offered him as its replacement. Thus, an option—in effect and by intent—makes its recipient a stock market investor, and its current equivalent should be calculated using a discount rate which reflects that condition.

It remains then to choose a specific figure that reconciles the various pieces of evidence and opinion that exist about the likely outcome of employing capital in the purchase of common stocks. A substantial amount of information on the returns that could have been achieved through the ownership of a diversified portfolio of equities over the last three or four decades has been made available in a study conducted at the University of Chicago.[21] The conclusion reached was that after-tax yields from dividends plus capital appreciation would have ranged generally between 5 and 10 per cent per annum, depending on the particular time period involved and on the individual's personal income tax bracket. Executives might be expected to have done somewhat better on average than the typical investor because of their business experience and their access to both information and opportunities. On the other hand, they are subject to the upper end of the income tax rate schedule—which serves to constrain their net profits—and it must be remembered that the returns described were calculated in retrospect. The men who comprise the sample for this study would have been conditioned in their investment behavior by the unhappy financial events of the late 1920's and the 1930's. While it may today be generally believed, with some justification, that business indexes and stock prices move inevitably upward, many current investors have been exposed to a different sort of learning process and operate within a different sort of economic environment than those executives who appear in proxy statements covering the years of our empirical interest. A belief that the latter would lean toward a fairly conservative common stock portfolio and would

[21] L. Fisher and J. H. Lorie, "Rates of Return on Investments in Common Stocks," *Journal of Business*, January 1964, pp. 1–21.

project a fairly modest investment rate of return will therefore be the basis of the discount rate choice. Five per cent per annum seems to be a reasonable characterization of the probable result of that kind of attitude. Objections to this particular figure may then be answered in two ways: Alternatives of the same general order of magnitude will not produce significant differences in the calculations; [22] and 5 per cent at least bears a sensible relationship to the discount rate chosen earlier for debt portfolios.

Present and Cumulative Values

The size of each component "layer" of annual salary payments in the current equivalent is determined by requiring that its interest-and-mortality-discounted present value be equal to the corresponding yearly estimate of the change in value of the stock option. In order to facilitate computation, it will once again be assumed that such payments are made on an annual rather than on a monthly basis. Following the executive's exercise of his option, the payments credited to him in anticipation of the reward he thereupon obtains will be cumulated—by compounding annually at 5 per cent—to the *end* of the year of exercise, the convention being that all those payments occurred at the beginning of their respective years. Accordingly, the salary increment already specified for the year of exercise will be compounded to 1.05 times its original amount; the increment applying to the previous year to $(1.05)^2$ times its original value, and so on. The option exercise itself will also be considered to have occurred at the beginning of the year and therefore be cumulated to 1.05 times its measured value in order to compare it with its counterpart salary payments.[23] By adopting this rule, we preserve—but in a more convenient form—the same *relative* sequence of timing between the option gain and the current equivalent that would, on average, be observed if a detailed month-by-month analysis were undertaken. Thus, the futurity or retroactivity of a series of twelve monthly salary increments can be summarized fairly satisfactorily by assuming the payment of their total amount halfway through the year. Similarly,

---

[22] See Chapter 12 for confirmation.

[23] The only question involved here, it should be stressed, is timing. The amount of the option gain is still to be determined by the market price of the stock in question on the day the option is exercised.

option exercises are likely to be distributed evenly over the year, and the mean interest adjustment necessary for them should also be one-half the annual rate. If, instead, both transactions are treated as having taken place at the beginning of the calendar year, they are in effect moved ahead in time an average of six months apiece, and their relationship is not distorted. The final stream of payments in the current equivalent—the first element of which is scheduled by convention for the first day of the year *after* exercise occurs—is then established by setting its present value equal to the difference between the after-tax option gain and the indicated cumulative value of the "anticipatory" salary payments.

Retirement

Among the executives who receive stock options are some who contemplate retirement prior to the formal terminal date of their option grants. For example, ten-year options are often issued to a group which contains executives age 55 and over, who must retire at age 65 under the provisions of their company's pension plan. The tax law stipulates, however, that the right to exercise any option expires three months following the termination of the optionee's employment—and retirement is regarded as a "termination." Since the effective life of the option in such a situation is therefore abbreviated, it would be improper to attribute to it a current equivalent which would extend over the full ten-year period nominally prescribed. Rather, the years between granting and retirement will be considered the relevant interval. Except for this change, the procedures outlined above for calculating the option's "replacement" in the general case will be adhered to.

Resignation

Another eventuality that may require some adjustment in the current equivalent is the resignation—voluntary or otherwise—of the optionee. Obviously, any salary increments being credited to a particular executive should stop at the time his firm's proxy statements tell us he leaves his job. Unlike retirement, however, resignation is not a predictable factor, and the current equivalent cannot be constructed as though the instances in which it does occur could have been foreseen. In principle, another discount like that for mortality should be adopted. This would serve to reduce the present value of any given stream of annual salary increments—to reflect the possibility that the executive might decide to change jobs before receiving them all—and would therefore raise the amount of salary needed to replace the stock option.

On the other hand, it was concluded earlier that executive job changes, at least with respect to individuals at the level of the present sample, were both infrequent and very difficult to quantify. Recourse will once more be had to that argument, and the assumption here will be that any realistic discount for turnover is likely to be small enough to be ignored. As a result, the computations may slightly understate the stock option's "true" current equivalent.

It is not necessary even in theory to discount the prospective value of the option itself, however. As indicated above, that instrument is legally exercisable for three months after the termination of employment. We may reasonably expect the optionee to claim this privilege if his unexercised option is at all valuable. If it is not—and he does not—the corresponding current equivalent would almost surely be negligible anyway. In cases where an option is automatically revoked upon the resignation of the optionee, he can simply exercise it before quitting.[24] In short, an option is effectively "vested" insofar as resignation is concerned.

Partial Exercises

The executives who exercise their option rights in full with one transaction are a minority. In most cases, especially those involving very large option grants, the optionee will purchase his shares in several installments over a period of years. A ten-year option for ten thousand shares granted in 1952 may, for example, be exercised for three thousand shares in 1954, another three thousand in 1956, and a final four thousand in 1959.[25] A procedure must therefore be established for the current equivalent which allows this sort of behavior to be analyzed as well as the single-exercise case.

[24] The law permits but does not require a corporation to provide a three-month grace period. See the comparable discussion of exercises by an optionee's estate, p. 58.

[25] As was noted earlier, some option plans require a certain pattern of partial exercises.

The most appropriate solution would seem to be to treat the various partial exercises as definitive statements of the reward derived from their respective fractions of the option, and to construct for each one a separate stream of salary payments. Thus, in the situation described, an estimate of the potential worth of the entire option would be made at the close of both 1952 and 1953, and the regular series of "anticipatory" annual salary increments begun accordingly. At the end of 1954, the after-tax reward achieved from the exercise of three thousand shares would be measured, three-tenths of the accumulated value of the prior salary payments subtracted from that reward, and a series of payments running through 1962 and having a present value equal to the difference then calculated. This would complete the portion of the current equivalent attributable to the 1954 option exercise. Appraisals of the potential worth of the remaining seven thousand shares would continue to be made and the normal procedure for setting up further anticipatory salary increments for them carried out. Consequently, the total current equivalent during 1955 and 1956 would consist of a fixed and a variable component. By the end of 1956, however, another segment of the option's reward will have been established and a final stream of salary payments stretching from 1957 to 1962 computed for it. Ultimately, all ten thousand shares will be acquired and the full amount of the current equivalent fixed. In effect, an option is treated as a unit until some portion of it is exercised, after which time each bloc of shares purchased has attributed to it a separate series of salary increments.

Multiple Option Grants

Not only do most executives take advantage of their stock options in a piecemeal fashion, but many of them also receive several different option grants which have overlapping terms. In the illustration above the optionee might have been awarded an option for another five thousand shares in 1958, its term to coincide with that of the original grant up to 1962 and to continue thereafter for an additional six years. Situations of this kind can be handled in the same way partial exercises are—by keeping track of every option separately and constructing for each its own alternative reward. The complete current equivalent for an executive will therefore be comprised of a number of salary increment "vectors," the aggregate amount in any one year being the sum of all the various payments calculated for that year as a result of every option granted. These figures can be so added because there is no real interaction between them. The 25 per cent capital gains tax rate applicable to stock option profits is a ceiling rate that does not vary with either the pattern or the size of those profits. Thus, the after-tax current equivalent of each option is independent of all others, and they may simply be superimposed.[26]

Declining Stock Prices

Once an executive has purchased shares under option, subsequent changes in the price of the stock involved are asserted to be irrelevant— as, in fact, is his decision whether and when to resell the shares acquired. His reward is fixed by the discount from market price which he claims on the date of exercise. Prior to that time, of course, we are very much concerned with price fluctuations as a determinant of his current equivalent. A continual increase in stock prices during this interval is not only a happy circumstance for the optionee but is especially manageable from our point of view. The requisite current equivalent simply increases each year accordingly. Price declines imply a matching decrease. In the vast majority of cases, that is *all* that will be implied, i.e., the successive annual salary increments become smaller but remain positive. An example of such a pattern was seen in the illustration used to supplement the initial description of the current equivalent. Variations in the relevant payments are automatically smoothed by spreading out over a period of years the "salary substitute" for each year's change in the executive's prospective after-tax option reward and by establishing equivalence on a present value basis. If, instead, the procedure of awarding a lump-sum cash bonus equal to the annual change in option value were adopted, negative payments would be necessary quite often. In the example cited, the current equivalent would have consisted of an $85,000 bonus in 1953, a $170,000 bonus in 1954, and then—apart from any adjustments for interest accumulation—a $51,000 levy against salary in

---

[26] The same conclusion holds for the flat 15 per cent rate assumed here as an approximation to the impact of tax deferral, tax avoidance at death, and additional tax deductions due to option profits.

1955.[27] In the interest of offering a sensible alternative to the stock option, it seems important to minimize the likelihood of having to appropriate a portion of the optionee's salary if stock prices should ever fall. Under the method advocated here a decline in price will, with few exceptions, merely cause the optionee to forego receipt of some of the later installments of the salary increases promised when prices were high. If, for instance, the potential worth of an unexercised ten-year option should decrease by $100,000 during its fifth year, the counterpart of that change would be a reduction of about $25,000 per year for the next five years in the previously scheduled salary increments.[28]

This method does not, however, eliminate entirely the possibility that a negative current equivalent may at times be called for. While an actual loss by the executive on his option is ruled out—he simply need not exercise when the option price exceeds market price—a sharp increase in stock prices during the early years of the grant followed by a sharp drop can create a situation where the employer firm should "take back" part or all of the initial salary increments awarded. Thus, although the aggregate interest-adjusted current equivalent will at worst just cancel itself out over the term of the option, one segment of it may have to be negative.

Either of two responses can be made if such a situation should occur: We can adhere to the "theory" of the current equivalent and include in it the necessary negative values, or we can specify that zero be the smallest permissible annual salary "increment." The latter is almost certainly preferable from an operational standpoint. It seems improbable that a corporation would propose to its executives a scheme that might require them to "indemnify" it if early stock option forecasts turn out to have been too optimistic—even if a corollary of that optimism was a generous temporary salary increase. One somehow finds it difficult to conceive of a policy of that sort being carried out in practice and, if practicality is to be claimed here, this consideration is not irrelevant.

The effect on the empirical results of adopting the alternative pro-

[27] Actual after-tax reward was $204,000.

[28] As will be seen below, the smoothing inherent in the approach chosen also serves to reduce the over-all tax burden associated with a *before-tax* salary alternative to the option.

cedure depends on subsequent events. In cases where the stock price later recovers, the current equivalent will once again become positive and, in the end, only its pattern and not its aggregate value will have been altered.[29] If, however, the price does not recover sufficiently, the optionee will have been credited with too much salary. His current equivalent, under which payments were awarded for at least a few years, will be more valuable than the option itself, which is either entirely worthless or nearly so. Fortunately, this second situation arises fairly infrequently; even when it does, the spreading out of any initial positive increments will keep the resulting error from being very great.[30] The position may therefore be taken that to rule negative elements out of the current equivalent is not only a sensible concession to practicality but is also unlikely to have much effect on the findings.[31]

The same sort of reasoning applies to situations in which the executive never does exercise his option because the market price of the shares involved falls below and remains below the option price. In principle again, any incremental salary payments credited to him at the time a profit seemed to be in prospect should be recovered via an eventual levy on salary. By convention here, they are not.

The Before-Tax Current Equivalent

Given a definition of the reward provided by an option and a format for determining its after-tax salary counterpart, the final step is to compute a before-tax current equivalent: that series of additions to the executive's actual before-tax salary which will generate the various annual increments implied by the (sum of the) after-tax equivalent(s). A vehicle is thereby obtained which permits the relative importance of stock options and other compensation devices to be measured on a common pre-tax basis and which can be used subsequently to assess the "efficiency" of a particular option by comparing its cost with that

---

[29] For an example, see the illustration in Chapter 6, pp. 97–101.

[30] The extent of the "error" involved and the frequency of its occurrence empirically are discussed below in Chapter 12.

[31] While this is true for the time period covered by this study, it may or may not be so in the future. Stock market conditions will not necessarily continue to be favorable, and the possibility of unprofitable stock option experiences may well increase.

of its current income substitute. Because the underlying after-tax equivalent is constructed in a way that should prevent wide variations in its constituent annual figures, the necessary before-tax increments will also be "smoothed." This will help keep their aggregate amount—and thus their total cost to the firm—as low as possible, since a progressive personal income tax schedule subjects fluctuating incomes to a higher over-all effective rate than stable ones.

Summary

A stock option is a deferred and contingent compensation device whose effectiveness is most appropriately measured *after* the fact. Despite the uncertainties involved, it is possible to design a current income alternative that covers the same span of years as the term of the option, that has the same time-adjusted after-tax value, that could be used as an operational substitute for the option, and that should have the same incentive features. Within such a framework, the rewards provided by stock options—even though unique in their characteristics—can be meaningfully compared with an executive's other earnings.[32]

[32] Once again, the reader is referred to Appendix G, which describes the manner in which the procedures developed above can be modified to fit the changes in the tax treatment of stock options embodied in the Revenue Act of 1964.

5

OTHER COMPENSATION ARRANGEMENTS

While salary and bonus, pensions, deferred compensation, and stock options certainly comprise the bulk of the corporate executive's compensation package, they are not the whole story. Most firms make at least some use of other devices. For our purposes such arrangements may be separated into two groups: those which are very important in a particular firm's reward structure and are well reported on in its proxy statements; and those which are common to almost all firms but of lesser significance and are not spelled out for individual executives in any published source. The first category, which includes such schemes as profit-sharing and stock bonus plans, commands attention because it is occasionally important enough to distort both time series data and comparisons among firms if ignored. For example, one company in the sample uses a profit-sharing plan as a substitute for a pension; it would be inappropriate to group the experience of that firm's executives with the experience of those of other firms which do provide pensions unless their profit-sharing rewards are also evaluated by means of a "current equivalent." The second category, however, consisting of the now-familiar "fringe benefits," such as life insurance, medical insurance, expense account privileges, etc., is almost certainly more uniform in terms of value among different companies and is also likely not to represent a very sizeable proportion of the total pay package for the top executives of the large publicly held firms which comprise the current sample.[1] The complete lack of information about these ar-

[1] Some support for this claim insofar as expense accounts are concerned can be found in Challis A. Hall, Jr., *Effects of Taxation on Executive Compensation and Retirement Plans,* Cambridge, Mass., 1951, where he says (p. 14): "Ac-

rangements in proxy statements would, of course, make it impossible to evaluate them empirically in any event. Nonetheless, because they *could* be handled within the same sort of analytical framework that has been developed above for more visible instruments, if sufficient information were available, they will be discussed briefly here, in the interest of comprehensiveness, before we turn to profit-sharing and stock bonus plans. Even the latter need not be examined in the detail afforded the three major supplements to salary and bonus, since much of the analysis thus far presented is directly applicable to them as well.

Life and Medical Insurance

The group insurance benefits financed by a corporation for its employees may cover a broad range of contingencies. Whatever the combination of provisions in question, their monetary value can readily be appraised by determining whether and to what extent similar arrangements are available to individual employees elsewhere should they seek to obtain equivalent protection on their own. The worth of a firm's insurance program to one of its executives, for instance, can be measured by asking: How much would his salary have to be increased in order that he be as well off via that increase as he is as a participant in the observed plan? The amount of the required increase is the current income equivalent of whatever the arrangement may include. Since individual life and medical insurance policies which duplicate the features of almost any corporate plan are sold by private insuring agencies, the job of finding an appropriate index of value from the executive's standpoint is a simple one. The annual premium which would enable him to purchase an individual insurance policy having the same benefit structure as his firm's plan is precisely the after-tax current equivalent of the latter instrument.[2]

One issue in this connection might be the time period over which

cording to executives interviewed, company-paid-for expenses of the type which really reduce executives' buying costs and represent extra income are of negligible importance in large companies."

[2] As was true before, it may be necessary to define "same" in terms of present value if for some reason the company plan cannot be exactly duplicated on an individual basis. It is also necessary, of course, to deduct the present value of the contributions the executive must make toward the plan, if it is contributory.

such premiums should be thought of as being spread. For medical insurance this is not a problem, since premium rates do not depend on the policyholder's age and are, in fact, quoted on an annual basis subject to change depending on the insurance experience. The only possible figure is the relevant calendar year's current annual rate. In the case of life insurance, however, the time period *is* a decision variable. The position here is that, if the insurance remains in effect only so long as the executive in question is an active employee, the equivalent individual arrangement should be considered to be a *term* life insurance policy covering—and paid for in annual installments over—that same interval.[3] If, instead, the insurance supplied by the corporation becomes paid up and the executive acquires title to it upon retirement, then a standard "x-payment" individual life insurance policy is the appropriate alternative—where x is the number of years from the time the executive first comes under the company's plan through his normal retirement age. In either case, if the amount of the death benefit is raised by the corporation as the man's career progresses, the complete after-tax current equivalent over his working life will consist of several concurrent and overlapping streams of premium payments, each one corresponding to a particular benefit increase.[4]

Both life and health insurance can therefore be analyzed with little difficulty. Very close, or even perfect, substitutes are available to executives individually from insurance companies. The annual premium cost of those substitutes is a convenient and precise statement of the value —in terms of additional current income—of a corporation's group insurance program.

Expense Accounts and Payments in Kind

The compensation represented by the provision of various goods and services to the executive by his employer, either through assuming their

[3] Take, for example, a man who joins a firm at age 25 and is provided with $10,000 worth of life insurance good until his retirement at age 65. The after-tax current equivalent of that benefit is, in the view here, the forty equal annual premiums that would purchase a $10,000, forty-year individual term insurance policy. If term life policies of this duration are not commonly available, the premiums for a *series* of, say, five- or ten-year policies would do as well.

[4] In the same manner in which increases in pension benefits were treated.

cost, as with meal and travel allowances, or by furnishing them directly —company cars and rent-free housing, for example—is still easier to assess, at least in theory. To the extent that expense account payments permit the executive to consume rather than merely meet legitimate business-induced expenses, they should be defined as additions to income. Their after-tax current equivalent in any year would simply be the dollar amount by which such payments exceed actual expenses in that year. The really sticky definitional problems of where and how to draw the line between consumption and "necessary" expenses will be left open, however, since it is not possible to do anything empirically with this component of the pay package for lack of published figures on even *gross* expense account awards to particular individuals. Nonetheless, the principle is clear and the methodology of valuing such devices in a "current equivalent" manner an obvious one. They are, in fact, extra current income and should be so regarded. Employer-provided housing, automobiles, domestic servants, and similar emoluments fall in the same category. These items are worth to their recipient exactly their replacement cost on the open market and may be characterized by an after-tax current equivalent equal to that cost. If the beneficiary of such services is unfortunate enough—or perhaps unskillful enough—already to be taxed on the basis of their market value, then the indicated current equivalent should be smaller by the amount of the tax.

It seems fair to conclude, therefore, that there are no conceptual barriers to measuring the compensation implicit in these schemes. The approach is simply to determine the outlay that would be required of the executive were he to provide the same services or benefits on his own. That figure then provides an index of the value of the compensation arrangement in question which not only enables a comparison with other rewards but does so in what should be the clearest possible manner: as an equivalent salary increase.

Stock Bonuses

The stock bonuses employed by corporations come in several different forms. While in each instance they consist of awards made to the executive in shares of his company's stock, the timing and duration of the payments involved may vary considerably. The variant which is easiest to handle is that in which, like a straight cash bonus, there is but a single payment occurring at the end of the year during which the services that gave rise to the bonus were performed. Such a payment is taxed to the executive as ordinary income and valued for that purpose by the IRS at the market price of the shares on the date they are transferred.[5] This type of bonus may be treated just as a cash award would be. It is worth, in after-tax terms, the gross market value of the stock received minus the applicable tax liability, and its "after-tax current equivalent" is simply that same amount.[6]

A second common arrangement is also very much like a form of cash bonus already discussed. In it, payments are spread over a period of several years immediately following the award year rather than being made in a single lump sum. A series of four or five equal annual installments is the most frequent choice. In this case again, the installments are taxed as ordinary income at their market value when received, and therefore their after-tax current equivalent will be defined as the corresponding series of net additions to salary. The only difference between this scheme and that in which the bonus is in the form of cash is that the final value of the award is not fixed at the time it is made but instead depends in part on stock price developments during the next few years. This means that it is necessary to record the price of the firm's stock on four or five separate dates rather than on just one in order to construct the desired current equivalent. This is a simple task, however, and merely implies that the appropriate alternative to this kind of stock bonus is conceived to be a series of salary increments which themselves are a function of the firm's stock price

---

[5] *Internal Revenue Code,* Section 402.

[6] It should be stressed that it is again irrelevant to the valuation process whether the executive under consideration promptly disposes of the shares he receives or instead retains them in his portfolio. In the latter case he will, upon their eventual sale, be taxed in addition at capital gains rates on any appreciation in their value subsequent to the date they were received (*Internal Revenue Code,* Section 402). On that date, however, he formally acquires a particular valuable asset, is assessed a tax thereon, and is then free to do with it as he pleases. Whatever his decision, the results experienced are not part of the bonus transaction itself and should not be regarded as such. The same argument was made earlier in connection with stock option profits.

over time. There is nothing conceptually incorrect—or even administratively inconvenient—in such an arrangement.

The third, and most interesting, variety of stock bonus is really just another form of deferred compensation. Rather than a given amount of cash being set aside for payment to the executive following his retirement, a given number of shares of stock are so allocated. Thus, the executive may stand to receive a series of stock allotments beginning at age 65, continuing for a specified number of years, and taxable at ordinary income rates. If he should die before attaining retirement age or thereafter before receiving his bonus in full, his estate is entitled to the remaining shares. As is evident, the difference again between such a promise and a cash-payment contract is the dependence of the value of the ultimate receipt on interim stock price movements. However, since the objective is to derive a current income equivalent which applies—as all previous ones have—only to the executive's active working life, it is not possible to wait until the time of each scheduled receipt of stock before fixing the amount of that equivalent.[7] An alternative must be designed which, as in the case of a stock option, anticipates the final outcome. The approach that is suggested here defines the after-tax current equivalent of a deferred stock bonus to be a series of annual salary increments which: (1) begin in the year the bonus is awarded; (2) continue to the executive's normal retirement age; (3) have the same prospective after-tax present value as that estimated for the deferred bonus payments; (4) are revised each year in response to any change in this estimate.

For example, suppose that, in 1950, an executive age 50 is promised a deferred stock bonus of 1,000 shares per year in each of the first five years following his retirement at age 65. At the time of this promise, the market price of his firm's stock is $25 per share. The initial estimate of the ultimate value of his bonus is therefore $25,000 per year, before taxes, for five years. Given the size of the man's salary in 1950, some "outside income" may be projected for him in retirement.[8] With that figure and an estimate of deductions and exemptions, the after-tax value of the five bonus payments can be determined, as in the case of

---

[7] In which case, of course, it would not really be a *current* income substitute for the deferred payments.

[8] See pp. 21–22.

a conventional deferred compensation arrangement. The present value of this expectation as of 1950 is then calculated,[9] and the first stage of the after-tax current equivalent specified to be simply that series of fifteen equal annual additions to after-tax salary which, if received from 1950 through 1964, would have the same present value.[10] The amount of the current equivalent for the year 1950 is, accordingly, the first payment in that series. Suppose further that, in 1951, the stock rises in price to $30 per share. Our estimate of the worth of the deferred bonus is now revised upward by $5,000 per year, the additional after-tax present value implied by that revision computed, and a second stream of *fourteen* payments established having a present value equal to the *increment*. The current equivalent for 1951 is then the sum of this new figure plus the one from the 1950 calculations. The process is repeated every year up to and including age 65, the result being a current equivalent consisting once again of a number of over-lapping "layers" and covering the full time period from the date the bonus arrangement is instituted up to the executive's retirement. By this latter date, the executive will have been credited with extra income over the years equal in value to that dollar amount which, after taxes, his bonus now promises him. He, therefore, will have been made as well off—which is the test here of "equivalence." [11]

The effect, then, is to consider the deferred stock bonus to be simply a deferred compensation contract which happens to require not just one but a series of appraisals in order to be analyzed completely. All the ancillary arguments offered previously in support of the current equivalent designed for such contracts are therefore applicable and will not be

[9] Discounting for both futurity and mortality, using for the latter the 1951 Group Annuity Table referred to earlier. The present value of the death benefits payable under the bonus arrangement is also included in this calculation. They are of the same form as in the case of a regular deferred compensation contract.

[10] Mortality as well as futurity is relevant to *this* computation also. Again, the reasoning has been developed previously in connection with deferred compensation arrangements.

[11] He also, it may be noted, would in practice have been provided during this period with the same incentive to concern himself with the price of his firm's stock as the bonus in question would have engendered, since the size of the current equivalent constructed is tied to *actual* stock price developments over time. See the related discussion in connection with stock options.

reiterated.[12] In the empirical portion of the study, in fact, the two devices are treated as a single category of reward.

Profit-Sharing Plans

If the valuation model just outlined is accepted, there is little that need be added to permit profit-sharing plans to be dealt with. The typical arrangement, including all the ones there will be occasion to examine here, provides that in each year a certain sum related to his firm's profits be set aside in the executive's name and used to purchase shares of its stock for him on the open market.[13] The award, however, is not taxed to the executive when it is made. Instead, the shares purchased are kept in trust by the company until he retires, at which time he takes title to them and is taxed on the full amount of their then-current market value at the capital gains rate.[14] This sort of plan, therefore, differs from a deferred stock bonus in two respects: the award is made initially in terms of a specified dollar figure rather than a given number of shares; and the executive receives all his benefits immediately upon retirement instead of in several installments.[15]

The first of these differences is purely nominal, since the "cash" awarded is immediately transformed into stock. In fact, the number of shares thus acquired is specifically recorded in the firm's proxy statements. The second may appear a more substantive difference, but in fact simply means that the present value of only a single prospective receipt need be considered for plans of this kind. In addition, since the capital gains tax—at the income levels relevant here—is a flat rate, the

[12] One change that should be made is in the discount rate used to arrive at the various present values. In the case of deferred compensation arrangements, 2½ per cent per annum was adopted and rationalized on the basis of the low degree of uncertainty associated with the postretirement benefits anticipated. A deferred stock bonus is more like a stock option in this respect, however, since the eventual outcomes may well vary considerably. Accordingly, the 5 per cent per annum after-tax figure used for stock options is taken to be an appropriate choice for stock bonuses as well.

[13] In some cases, authorized but unissued or treasury shares are "purchased" from the company itself.

[14] *Internal Revenue Code,* Section 402.

[15] As with deferred compensation and stock bonuses, the executive's estate claims his accumulated profit share if he should die *prior* to retirement.

computations are actually a bit easier than in the stock bonus situation. As stock prices vary following an award, the after-tax value of the lump-sum benefit anticipated changes by precisely 75 per cent of that amount.

Given the similarity between such plans and deferred stock bonuses, the conclusion is that their "current equivalents" may be constructed in the same manner. Thus, when stock is allotted in a particular year to an executive's profit-sharing account, its observed market price at that time is used as an initial estimate of the size of the benefit he will eventually receive. A series of equal annual payments beginning then, running through his expected retirement age, and having the same after-tax present value as the estimate thus obtained, constitutes the first component of the current equivalent for that award. Each time stock prices change thereafter up to retirement, an additional—and successively shorter—series of payments is added to this basic stream.[16] The total of all such payments over time represents the complete after-tax current income counterpart of the profit-sharing award. In effect, the valuation procedure established in the last section is adopted virtually without alteration, and its suitability depends on the validity of the arguments made there.[17]

Other Benefit Formats

Every stock bonus and profit-sharing plan does not, of course, look exactly like the arrangements described above as "typical." The precise duration and timing of benefit payments may vary widely from company to company, as may the conditions to be satisfied by the executive in return for those payments. Space limitations and a desire not to become too preoccupied with detail militate against examining here each possible combination of provisions. It should be true, however, that just about any peculiarity that may arise can be taken care of within the framework discussed on the preceding pages, simply by computing

[16] In order to keep the number of computations and the data collection effort required within manageable bounds, the stock price will be examined for change only once a year—on the anniversary of the original award.

[17] Including the appropriateness of a 5 per cent per annum discount rate and the desirability of discounting for mortality as well as futurity in determining the size of the payments in the current equivalent.

the after-tax present values of the relevant benefits and proceeding from there to the same sort of sequentially adjusted current income equivalent suggested. Appendix H contains full statements of the present value and current equivalent formulas for the prototype deferred stock bonus and profit-sharing plans, and may be used as a reference point for the analysis of other devices in these two general categories.

One variant of these basic arrangements which does deserve mention here should serve to illustrate the kind of adaptation to different circumstances that is possible. It sometimes happens that a particular plan will provide for benefits payable partly in cash and partly in shares of stock. If this should occur, the plan may simply be treated as two separate instruments, the cash-benefit portion analyzed as would be a conventional cash bonus or deferred compensation contract and the stock-benefit portion as just indicated. The current equivalents of the two pieces thus determined can then be added together to form the current equivalent of the whole package.

Savings Plans

There is a final class of compensation arrangements which has not yet been considered and which does not quite fit into either of the two groupings that were established at the beginning of this chapter. In recent years there has been a small but growing trend toward adoption by corporations of what are usually referred to as "savings" or "thrift" plans. While it is not difficult in principle to evaluate the compensation these devices provide and to redefine them in equivalent current income terms, the information which appears in published sources is almost invariably insufficient to permit the application of those techniques to the experience of actual executives. On the other hand, it is not possible either to say with the confidence displayed in the case of group insurance benefits that we may safely ignore savings plans and not be concerned about introducing some distortion into an empirical analysis of compensation histories. It is not that such plans are more valuable in the aggregate than company-provided insurance—indeed, they are not—but they are less universally employed and also less uniformly designed. Therefore, for a few of the firms which use them, they can be a reasonably important item of compensation. There is little choice here but to ignore them, however, since the reporting in proxy statements is just not complete enough to allow the necessary story to be told in a systematic fashion. Certainly for the large majority of the companies in the present sample, savings plans were either insignificant or nonexistent as of the end of the time period studied. In no case did a rough estimate of the value of a particular scheme even approach that of any of the major compensation devices employed by the same firm, let alone their combined worth. Of necessity, and with some justification, therefore, savings plans are excluded from the current empirical investigation.

It may be useful, however, to indicate how such arrangements would be analyzed if it were possible to do so. The typical savings plan involves an annual contribution by the executive of a portion of his salary—usually on the order of 2 to 6 per cent—to a fund which is managed for its employees by the corporation. The firm itself also contributes a specified amount to the fund in the man's name, in some cases matching his contribution but more commonly adding, say, 50 per cent as much. The fund is then invested in a specified portfolio of securities and the results thereof distributed to the executive upon his retirement. Contributions to the plan by the executive are not tax-deductible, but neither is he taxed on his employer's contributions until he actually collects his benefit. At that time he pays a capital gains tax on the difference between the payment received and his own total contributions.[18]

Variations in plans among companies arise not only in the size of the executive's contributions [19] and in the degree to which the firm supplements those amounts but also in the composition of the portfolio to which the investment fund is committed. In connection with this last item, three choices predominate: all government bonds, part governments and part common stock of the employer corporation, all common stock of the employer. Seldom are the bonds or the shares of other firms acquired—or even permitted. As it turns out, the reason savings

---

[18] *Internal Revenue Code,* Section 402.

[19] In most instances, the executive is free to choose from among a range of possible contribution rates in deciding upon the extent of his participation in the plan. In one situation observed, for example, he could pick any figure from 2 to 5 per cent of his salary and have the company automatically match that contribution.

plans are difficult to treat empirically is the inadequate reporting of the investment results realized from the plan's portfolio, especially as they relate to an individual executive's account.[20] In the case of a stock bonus or profit-sharing plan, because we are told the number of shares involved to begin with, it is possible to trace changes in their value over time and therefore to construct a current equivalent which reflects those changes. The same kind of information is unavailable for savings plans, however, and there is no indication given of the effect of subsequent transactions by the fund's managers. All one can do is speculate on the status of a particular individual's account at any point in time—and then only in the most general way. Were it necessary for corporations to publish such a statement each year for their senior executives, savings plans could be converted into current income equivalents with little difficulty. Appendix H outlines the suggested approach, which is similar to that developed for profit-sharing arrangements and utilizes the same kind of sequential adjustment process. In fact, a savings plan which specifies that its funds are to be invested entirely in the common stock of the employer corporation is really just a contributory profit-sharing plan.

Summary

The manner in which a group of rewards which are either not commonly used or not thoroughly reported on by corporations may be evaluated by means of "current income equivalents" has been described. Intentionally, the discussion has been less exhaustive than it was for the major compensation devices treated in previous chapters. That it could appropriately be so illustrates what seems an important point: Once an analytical framework and some basic principles of valuation are established, they can be adapted to virtually any compensation arrangement, no matter how peculiar its characteristics.

Company-provided life and medical insurance, expense accounts, payments in kind, and savings plan benefits must be excluded from the empirical investigation that follows because of a lack of published information relating to the experience of individual executives. For all

---

[20] Occasionally, however, even the rate of the executive's contributions and the nature of the portfolio are not clearly stated.

but the last device, this omission is deemed very unlikely to affect the profile of the results. While the same conclusion is perhaps less appropriate for savings plans, the problem is still not a serious one, and its impact is widely scattered in any event. Were sufficient data available, however, all these rewards could easily be converted into current income equivalents and compared with the other components of the pay package.

The reporting of stock bonus and profit-sharing plans permits a more satisfactory solution. There is enough evidence in proxy statements about such plans to allow their role in compensating the executive to be fully assessed. The key to an analysis of both instruments was seen to be a periodic reappraisal of the size of the benefits anticipated thereunder and a corresponding series of adjustments in their current income counterparts. Hopefully, the procedures described have succeeded in capturing the spirit as well as measuring the monetary value of the two devices.

6

THE COMPENSATION PACKAGE

The various elements of the executive's compensation package having been considered separately, it remains then to integrate their analysis. Since the valuation procedures relevant to each reward are largely self-contained, it should not be necessary to devote much additional space to an examination of conceptual matters. This chapter will therefore concentrate on a numerical example, applying the techniques developed earlier to the compensation history of a single executive. The figures presented are entirely fictitious and are designed primarily to illustrate the handling of a wide range of circumstances involving changes in compensation that can and do arise. They are not intended to represent a "typical" executive in the sample analyzed below in any meaningful sense. On the other hand, the experience described is not an unrealistic one, and it may legitimately be used to convey a feeling for at least the orders of magnitude that will be dealt with empirically.

Interdependence Among Rewards

If the federal income tax were proportional rather than progressive, it would be possible to appraise each of the corporate executive's rewards in complete isolation. The size and pattern of his other income would have no effect on the value to him of whatever item of compensation were being considered at the moment. A progressive rate structure, however, creates an interdependence among certain forms of reward which must be taken into account in fitting the pieces of the pay package together.

Stock options, profit-sharing plans, and all other schemes which provide benefits taxable only at capital gains rates present no problem in this connection. The relevant tax *is* a flat percentage—at least for the executives in the sample here—and such devices may therefore be evaluated without reference to their immediate context.

Pensions and deferred compensation arrangements are less conveniently handled. Since the benefits they confer are viewed as ordinary income by the IRS, the taxes due thereon are in part a function of how much other income is being received by the executive concurrently. The tax liabilities applicable to an executive's pension benefits, for example, were seen above to be influenced by the amount of "outside income" that was anticipated for him in retirement.[1] They will also be affected by the presence of any deferred compensation payments. Under a schedule of increasing marginal tax rates, the larger the executive's income, the higher is his tax bill as a per cent of that income—and the less valuable to him is each dollar represented there. Thus, if aggregate tax liabilities are apportioned among several different sources of income in relation to their respective before-tax magnitudes, a given reward will necessarily have associated with it a smaller after-tax counterpart the greater are the amounts of any other benefits received simultaneously.[2] Each time an executive is promised a larger pension by his company, therefore, the after-tax value of his prospective deferred compensation falls. In response, the after-tax current income equivalent contrived for the arrangement must also be reduced. Increases in deferred compensation awards have a symmetrical effect on the worth of a constant pension benefit. Accordingly, this sort of adjustment process will be built into the analysis as an appropriate expression of the interrelated nature of the executive's portfolio of rewards. Its impact will become evident in the calculations that follow.

An Illustrative Case History

Let us then turn to an application of the techniques developed in the preceding chapters. For this purpose, the compensation experience of a

[1] See Chapter 2.

[2] To illustrate: Suppose an individual's annual income is $20,000 and he pays $8,000 in taxes each year. Suppose further that he suddenly enjoys an increase to $30,000 before taxes, due to a new source of income, and that his total tax bill becomes $15,000 as a result of a progressive tax structure. If 20/30 of this new tax is attributed to the original income stream, its after-tax amount drops from $12,000 to $10,000 per annum.

fictitious executive will be offered—one which exemplifies most of the important and interesting combinations of circumstances that are confronted empirically. While it would be possible to illustrate literally all the peculiar situations that can occur, it would not be particularly efficient to attempt to do so. An understanding of the analysis and an adequate appraisal of its validity can be provided with a more modest body of data.

Consider the following case history:

Year	Salary	Noncontributory Pension	Contributory Pension	Deferred Compensation
1945	$ 75,000	—	—	—
1946	75,000	$10,000	—	—
1947	75,000	12,000	—	—
1948	90,000	12,000	—	—
1949	90,000	12,000	$15,000	—
1950	90,000	12,000	15,000	—
1951	90,000	12,000	15,000	$5,000
1952	90,000	15,000	15,000	5,000
1953	90,000	15,000	15,000	6,000
1954	100,000	15,000	15,000	6,000
1955	100,000	15,000	15,000	6,000
1956	100,000	15,000	15,000	6,000
1957	100,000	15,000	15,000	6,000
1958	100,000	15,000	15,000	6,000
1959	100,000	20,000	15,000	6,000
1960	—retired at age 65—			

The column entitled "Salary" refers in this instance only to before-tax salary but should in general be interpreted to include the before-tax amounts of any cash or stock bonus payments as well. Since, as we have seen, all three rewards take the form of current income and are taxed identically, they may be so combined.

The noncontributory pension figures record the amount of the annual retirement benefit promised the executive by his company as of the indicated years. The contributory pension column does the same for the prospective annual benefit under that arrangement. Thus, in 1951, our man, who is then 56 years old, expects to receive $15,000 of contributory and $12,000 of noncontributory pension benefits yearly beginning at age 65. The contributions required of him in return are not tabulated but are, of course, relevant to the analysis. In this connection, it will be assumed that initially the plan calls for an employee to contribute 4 per cent of his gross salary—a figure which is subsequently reduced to 3 per cent as a means of increasing the value of the arrangement (more on this later).

Deferred compensation denotes the annual payment to be made to the executive after his retirement under the terms of a specific deferred-pay contract with him, of the type discussed in Chapter 3. Let us suppose that ten years is the duration of this particular agreement, i.e., he stands to receive the amount indicated each year from age 65 through age 74. Once again, it is irrelevant to the calculations whether such payments are to be in the form of cash in the amounts listed or in shares of the corporation's common stock having the same prospective value. In the latter case it would have been necessary prior to the tabulations to estimate the size of the anticipated payments from the stock's market price and the given number of shares promised in the contract. Whichever way the data were obtained, their magnitude is our only concern here. The tax treatment of both types of payments is identical, and their "current equivalents" are constructed in the same manner.

In addition to the rewards shown, the executive in question will be specified to have been granted two stock options: One in 1952 for 1,000 shares at $95 per share, having a term of seven years; one in 1954 for another 1,000 shares at an option price of $110 and with a five-year term. In both cases the option price is assumed to have been at least 95 per cent of the stock's market price on the date of granting, and both options thus are eligible for capital gains tax treatment of any profits realized therefrom. The end-of-year market prices of the company's stock (adjusted for all stock splits or stock dividends that occurred during the relevant interval) were as follows:

1952	$120
1953	130
1954	110
1955	95
1956	120
1957	150
1958	150
1959	180

Sometime in 1957 the first option was exercised on a day when the stock's market price was $150 per share. In 1958 the second option was exercised under identical conditions. These two instruments and the salary, pension, and deferred compensation payments depicted therefore comprise the executive's complete compensation package over the period of interest.[3]

THE YEAR 1945

The man is 50 years old. His remuneration consists only of payments made in the form of current taxable income in the amount of $75,000. Assuming that he enjoys $11,250 of income from other sources (15 per cent of $75,000) and imputing to him nontaxable deductions and exemptions equal to $8,625 (10 per cent of the total $86,250 current income), we find that his 1945 tax bill, at the rates then in effect, would have been $50,625. If 7,500/8,625 of this tax is attributed to his salary, an after-tax figure of $30,978 is obtained.

THE YEAR 1946

The executive's salary remains at $75,000, but the company he works for adopts a pension plan for the first time. The plan is noncontributory, and according to its provisions he stands to receive $10,000 per year for life upon his retirement at age 65. An "outside" income of $11,250 is projected for him in retirement—the same amount as he currently is estimated to receive—and deductions and exemptions are assumed to continue at 10 per cent. The pension, which is fully taxable except for such deductions, is credited with 1,000/2,125 of the resulting expected after-tax income (computed using 1946 rates). If this annual figure is discounted for its futurity and the man's hypothesized mortality prospects, we find that the after-tax present value of the pension to him as of 1946 is $48,705. It turns out after some testing that an individual annuity policy of the type suggested in Chapter 2, which provided an annual retirement benefit of $6,717, would have the same present value. This figure is substantially less than the original $10,000 pension

---

[3] The fact that he is shown not to come under a pension plan until he is 50 years old should not, parenthetically, seem unusual. Most of the firms in the sample studied—indeed, most American corporations—did not begin to provide pensions for their employees until the 1940's. Consequently, many executives came under such plans relatively late in their careers.

benefit for two reasons. First, an individual annuity is less heavily taxed than a noncontributory pension because its purchaser is allowed to re-coup his premium payments tax-free after retirement by excluding a portion of the benefits he receives from taxable income.[4] Secondly, there are certain preretirement death benefits associated with the annuity, and these also have a significant present value.[5] Thus, the 51-year-old owner of a $6,717-annual-benefit individual retirement annuity was, in 1946, as well off as a 51-year-old executive who was promised a $10,000 noncontributory pension.

It would have required an annual premium of $4,868 beginning in 1946 and continuing through 1959 (the last expected year of the man's employment) to purchase such an annuity from an insurance company under the schedule of premium rates then in effect.[6] The figure $4,868 therefore constitutes the first element in the after-tax current income equivalent of the executive's pension. It defines the expenditure out of each succeeding year's after-tax income that would be necessary on the part of the executive were he to seek to put himself in the same position his pension puts him—and also, in consequence, specifies the amount of additional after-tax current income from his employer that could be sub-stituted for the pension and just maintain the total value of the compen-sation package.

Finally, tax rates in 1946 being somewhat lower than in 1945, the after-tax amount of the man's salary becomes $35,094, using the same rule for apportioning tax liabilities between salary and outside income as before.

THE YEAR 1947

The company's pension plan is liberalized, and, as a result, our execu-tive's promised annual retirement benefit increases to $12,000. His anticipated postretirement income therefore rises to $23,250 since, with salary unchanged, the prediction of $11,250 of outside income still ap-plies. Now 1,200/2,325 of the estimated annual after-tax total is credited to the pension, 1947 tax rates being used in the computations.

---

[4] As indicated in Chapter 2 and in Appendix D.
[5] See again Chapter 2.
[6] The derivation of this schedule from the premiums quoted by two large insurance companies is described in Appendix K.

After discounting, the extra $2,000 benefit is observed to add $8,844 to the after-tax present value of the pension, i.e., $8,844 is the difference between the present value, *as of 1947,* of the new, higher pension benefit and the present value that would have been in prospect had that benefit still been $10,000. As might be expected, given a progressive tax structure, an increase of 20 per cent in pretax annual benefits generates an increase of less than 20 per cent in after-tax present value (8,844/ 48,705). The disparity would be even greater were the executive not one year closer now to retirement.

In this instance an additional individual annuity benefit of $1,141 would raise the total present value of that instrument to the executive by the same amount as his pension increase, taking into consideration the proportionately smaller tax bill for annuities and their attendant death benefit provisions. The purchase of this second annuity contract by our man would, in turn, necessitate annual premiums higher by $1,048 than those indicated in 1946—again with the expectation that they run through 1959. This means that his aggregate pension current equivalent for 1947 becomes $5,916. Annual payments in this amount to an insurance company would permit the acquisition of an individual retirement annuity providing benefits now totaling $7,858. Since tax rates in 1947 were the same as those in 1946, after-tax salary remains $35,094.

The results of the analysis thus far, then, may be summarized in the following manner:

Year	Before-Tax Salary	After-Tax Salary	Pension After-Tax Current Equivalent
1945	$75,000	$30,978	—
1946	75,000	35,094	$4,868
1947	75,000	35,094	5,916

And we begin to see take shape the sort of profile of the executive's compensation package toward which our efforts are directed.

THE YEAR 1948

The one change that occurs is an increase from $75,000 to $90,000 in the man's annual salary. By convention, the estimate of his outside income is therefore raised to $13,500 per annum. When the applicable taxes are recomputed at 1948 rates, which were lower than in 1947, a figure of $52,760 is obtained for his after-tax salary.

This is not quite the whole story, however, because of the impact of a change in *current* income on our prediction of the size of *future* receipts. If the practice of projecting today's "outside income" into retirement is continued, we must also now adjust our assessment of the worth of the executive's pension. We expect him to enjoy a larger total postretirement income than we did last year—$25,500 vs. $23,250—and it follows that the after-tax annual benefit his unchanged before-tax pension promise will provide must decline. The calculations show a resulting loss in present value as of 1948 of $704.[7]

Even as it stands, this loss is not very great (on the order of 1 per cent of the pension's total present value), and its impact on the current equivalent is further diminished by the effect of the additional outside income on the value of the individual annuity offered as an alternative to the pension. Thus, any extra income anticipated in retirement raises the over-all tax bill on the hypothesized annuity benefits as well, since they are expected to occur in the same environment the pension would have. The present value of the individual annuity therefore also falls slightly in response to an increase in current salary. Because it does not fall by as much as that of the pension,[8] the current equivalent must still be adjusted downward in order to restore balance between the two instruments. Calculations—using 1948 tax rates throughout—indicate that the executive would be as well off as he is now with his pension if he had in prospect an annuity benefit smaller by $72 per annum than the one suggested last year. Lowering the benefit by that amount calls, by coincidence, for a reduction also of $72 in the annual premiums payable to the insurance company in 1948 and in each of the next eleven years. The revised pension current income equivalent for 1948 is, accordingly, $5,844.

[7] The present value as of 1948 of the after-tax annual benefit a $12,000 pension would provide if received in concert with $11,250 of outside income is first determined. A second present value, assuming outside income equal instead to $13,500, is then computed. The difference between the two turns out to be $704. At each stage the 1948 income tax schedule is used.

[8] This will always be true, since a portion of the annuity benefits are tax-free and thus unaffected by any changes in "outside income."

THE YEAR 1949

A contributory pension plan is added to the existing noncontributory one. Under it the executive is promised an extra $15,000 annually at retirement and is required to contribute 4 per cent of his before-tax salary toward its financing—a total of $3,600 per annum at present levels. His salary and noncontributory pension rights do not change.

The contributory plan provides benefits in two forms: the $15,000 lifetime annual payment beginning at age 65; and a return of the interest-accumulated value of the executive's contributions if he should die before retiring or before receiving retirement benefits in total equal to that accumulated value.[9] The two can be evaluated separately.

The retirement benefit, which is taxable only to the extent that it is deemed by the IRS to be a product of the company's and not the executive's contributions, may be combined with the noncontributory benefit, and a joint incremental after-tax present value as of 1949 calculated. This figure comes out to $86,944, utilizing $13,500 once again as the estimate of annual postretirement outside income. The net present value of the man's expected contributions through age 64—which are not tax-deductible—and the prospective death benefits they provide is a *negative* $27,436.[10] The result is an over-all increase in the present value of the pension equal to $59,508.

It would take an additional individual retirement annuity of $7,175 payable to the same executive to match this increase. The extra yearly premiums necessary for its purchase, starting in 1949, are $8,040, which pushes the after-tax current equivalent of the combined pensions up to $13,884 per annum. There will be no attempt to separate that figure into amounts attributable to contributory and noncontributory pension benefits, since the procedures involved in doing so are not only tedious but more than a little arbitrary. Apart from this, there seems little real reason to make the distinction. Corporations clearly plan their retire-

[9] See Chapter 2 above and Appendix D.
[10] This also is a predictable outcome. The probability that a man age 54 will live to make all eleven contributions up to his scheduled retirement age is quite large—on the order of 0.85 according to the 1951 Group Annuity Table. Since the complement of this figure is the probability that those same contributions will be recovered by his estate as a death benefit, the odds are heavily weighted toward the negative present value represented by the obligation to make contributions.

ment plans as a package, and it is reasonable to assume that the executive reacts in similar fashion.

THE YEAR 1950

Let us suppose that the corporation decides to liberalize its new contributory pension plan by reducing the employee contribution rate to 3 per cent of salary, while leaving benefits unchanged. Our man now foresees a series of contributions amounting to $2,700 yearly instead of the previous $3,600.

This reduction affects the after-tax present value of his pension not only by making the burden of contributing lighter, but also—in the opposite direction—by increasing slightly the tax bill on the plan's prospective annual retirement benefits. Smaller employee contributions mean that less of each retirement benefit will be considered tax-free as a recovery of those contributions. On balance, certainly, the result will be to raise the present value of the pension. In this case, even though the present value of the retirement benefits declines by $1,664, the lower contribution rate is worth an extra $6,247 to the executive.[11] Over-all, he gains $4,583 in 1950 after-tax present value.

An individual retirement annuity benefit larger by $530 than the current one and costing an additional $664 per year for the next ten years would be as valuable to him. The pension's current equivalent, therefore, rises to a new total of $14,548 per year. Since 1950 tax rates were the same as those of 1948 and 1949, the executive's after-tax salary remains at $52,760.

THE YEAR 1951

The corporation and our executive enter into a deferred compensation agreement whereby he is to receive upon retirement $5,000 a year for ten years. His pension rights, contributions, and salary continue at their 1950 levels.

The executive's total anticipated annual income during the first ten years of his retirement now becomes $45,500: $27,000 in pension, $13,500 of outside income, and the new $5,000 deferred compensation promise. Excluded from taxable income are the deductions and exemp-

---

[11] As before, this latter figure also incorporates the effect of lower death benefits all along the line.

Year	Before-Tax Salary	After-Tax Salary	Pension After-Tax Current Equivalent	Deferred Compensation After-Tax Current Equivalent
1945	$75,000	$30,978	—	—
1946	75,000	35,094	$ 4,868	—
1947	75,000	35,094	5,916	—
1948	90,000	52,760	5,844	—
1949	90,000	52,760	13,884	—
1950	90,000	52,760	14,548	—
1951	90,000	50,884	14,208	$2,697

tions it is assumed he will claim [12] and the portion of the contributory pension which is tax-free as a return of his contributions. The after-tax counterpart of each receipt may then be determined and their present values as of 1951 computed. The result is a reduction of $2,153 in the worth of the pension package due to the higher over-all tax rates brought about by the addition of deferred compensation to the package. The current equivalent of the pension is correspondingly diminished by $340 per annum—the amount by which the annual premiums payable to an insurance company could be cut so as to bring about a reduction in prospective individual annuity benefits also having a present value of $2,153. Equilibrium is therefore restored between the pension and its substitute, at least as both are perceived by the executive.

The after-tax present value of the deferred compensation is calculated at $26,839, which includes the value of the death benefits it provides. Thus, if the executive should die prior to attaining age 65, his estate will receive $50,000 from the corporation. If he dies thereafter but before reaching age 75, his estate gets the difference betwen $50,000 and the payments already made to him. The after-tax current equivalent of this contract is taken to be that series of equal annual payments beginning in 1951 and continuing through 1959 which, if promised the executive by his company, would seem to him to have the same present value. Since those payments are made contingent upon his remaining

[12] Which now are set at 15 per cent of pretax income by convention. This figure applies from 1951 on (see Appendix A).

with the corporation—and living that long—$2,697 per year for nine years, when discounted for mortality and at 2½ per cent per annum, produces the required present value.

Finally, at 1951 tax rates, which are higher than for 1950, and assuming deductions and exemptions of 15 per cent of gross income, the man's after-tax salary comes to $50,884. His story may, therefore, be brought up to date as shown in the tabulation on page 93.

1952–54: STOCK OPTIONS EXCLUDED

Apart from the stock options he is granted, it is not necessary to examine in much detail the changes that occur in the executive's remuneration during the next three years. Similar situations have already been considered here, and the purpose in repeating them is simply to illustrate their impact when they occur in the context of an existing deferred compensation promise as well as a pension plan. The two stock options can be analyzed independently, since there is no link between them and other rewards through the tax structure.

In 1952 the executive's annual retirement benefit under his firm's noncontributory pension plan is raised to $15,000. The result, due to higher postretirement tax liabilities, is a decrease in the value of his deferred compensation as well as a larger aggregate pension current equivalent. Because only the noncontributory portion of the pension is revised, none of the potential death benefits under either the contributory plan or the deferred compensation contract are affected, and their respective present values are unchanged. The over-all gain in the present value of the pension, however, produces a new current equivalent for it $2,597 higher than last year—enough extra annual premium in this case to permit the purchase of an additional $1,605 individual retirement annuity by the executive. A current equivalent just $32 lower per year than in 1951 results for his deferred compensation.

In 1953 the reverse situation occurs. The annual deferred compensation promise goes up by $1,000 while pension benefits remain constant. Thus, the present value of the latter is reduced through the workings of the progressive tax structure. Calculations indicate that the pension's current equivalent should, in consequence, be $113 per annum less than in 1952 and that of the deferred compensation $680 more.

Finally, in 1954 the man's annual salary is increased to $100,000. This raises our estimate of his postretirement outside income to $15,000 yearly and thereby lowers the perceived after-tax present value of *both* his pension and deferred compensation. The pension package is further influenced because the larger salary automatically generates higher annual contributions to the plan as long as the specified contribution rate continues at 3 per cent. The total effect is to reduce the annual after-tax current equivalent of the pension by $462 and the deferred compensation by $21.

A record of the executive's experience over this three-year period therefore reads:

Year	Before-Tax Salary	After-Tax Salary	Pension Current Equivalent	Deferred Compensation Current Equivalent
1952	$ 90,000	$47,553	$16,805	$2,665
1953	90,000	47,553	16,692	3,345
1954	100,000	54,765	16,230	3,324

The increase in his after-tax salary in 1954 was proportionately greater than the concurrent before-tax increase (approximately 15 per cent compared with 10 per cent) because tax rates that year returned to their pre-Korean war levels.

1955 THROUGH 1959

The preceding years offer examples of virtually all the circumstances worth noting from a methodological standpoint. For that reason, the executive's salary, pension, and deferred compensation benefits are, with one exception, assumed to stay the same from 1954 up to his retirement. Since tax rates did not change during these years, the after-tax salary and current equivalents established in 1954 are valid through 1958. In the following year, however, when the executive is 64 years old, the annual retirement benefit promised him under his firm's noncontributory pension plan is raised to $20,000. The motive in hypothesizing this increment is to indicate the very large impact it has on the present value of the pension and thereby on that instrument's current income equivalent.

If an executive happens to be working for a company which revises its pension benefit schedule significantly upward at a time when he is nearing retirement, that revision is an important "windfall" to him. It would require a sizeable premium payment to an insurance company were he to undertake the purchase of as valuable an individual annuity. The present value of the increased pension benefits is high because the man is almost ready to claim them, and the annual cost of the equivalent annuity is considerable because that cost cannot be spread over a very long period of time. Using such an annuity as a standard of comparison and its purchase price as an index of the worth of the pension is still legitimate, however. The volatility of the current equivalent as an executive approaches retirement age is merely an honest reflection of his situation rather than an indictment of the valuation procedures employed.

To return to the case at hand, the $5,000 annual pension benefit increase has an after-tax present value to the executive as of 1959 equal to $33,594. A single-premium payment to an insurance company of $46,558 would suffice to add benefits having the same present value to his existing annuity.[13] The current equivalent of the pension for 1959 is thus defined to be higher by this amount than in 1958. As a side effect, the present value of the man's deferred compensation falls due to the higher tax bill which now applies to it. The result is to lower its current equivalent for the final year by $695.

If we exclude his stock options for the moment, then, a complete analysis of our executive's compensation history would take the following form:

[13] The fact that the present value of the annuity purchased is less than its cost to the executive should not seem surprising. The difference is accounted for by the insurance company's charges for its administrative expenses and sales commissions. This phenomenon is widely recognized as a common one in connection with insurance policies and related instruments and has been rationalized elsewhere in terms of the expected *utility* value of such arrangements. See, for example: Milton Friedman and Leonard J. Savage, "The Utility Analysis of Choices Involving Risk," *Journal of Political Economy,* August 1948, pp. 279–304. In the case of an annuity, the policyholder is, in effect, insuring himself against the "disutility" associated with the adverse economic consequences of living too long—and is willing to pay a price for that protection.

Year	Before-Tax Salary	After-Tax Salary	Pension After-Tax Current Equivalent	Deferred Compensation Current Equivalent	After-Tax Total Compensation
1945	$ 75,000	$30,978	—	—	$ 30,978
1946	75,000	35,094	$ 4,868	—	39,962
1947	75,000	35,094	5,916	—	41,010
1948	90,000	52,760	5,844	—	58,604
1949	90,000	52,760	13,884	—	66,644
1950	90,000	52,760	14,548	—	67,308
1951	90,000	50,884	14,208	$2,697	67,789
1952	90,000	47,553	16,805	2,665	67,023
1953	90,000	47,553	16,692	3,345	67,590
1954	100,000	54,765	16,230	3,324	74,319
1955	100,000	54,765	16,230	3,324	74,319
1956	100,000	54,765	16,230	3,324	74,319
1957	100,000	54,765	16,230	3,324	74,319
1958	100,000	54,765	16,230	3,324	74,319
1959	100,000	54,765	62,788	2,629	120,182

Such figures permit a variety of conclusions. During the fifteen-year period examined, the man's before-tax salary increased by one-third and its after-tax counterpart by 77 per cent. When the value of his pension rights and deferred compensation are recognized, however, we see that his total after-tax remuneration grew by approximately 290 per cent over the same interval—140 per cent even if the sharp jump in 1959 is ignored. In all, pension and deferred compensation were worth fully 36 per cent as much as after-tax salary. While these statements are not only unstructured but obviously peculiar to this executive's contrived case history, they do suggest the kind of information that can be obtained from actual compensation data and which can be drawn on to provide a more comprehensive picture of the corporate pay package than has heretofore been available.

THE STOCK OPTION EXPERIENCE

During 1952 the executive was granted an option to purchase 1,000 shares of his company's stock for $95 per share at any time within the next seven years. If it is assumed that the market price of the stock was no more than $100 on the date of granting, any profits accruing from the subsequent resale of the shares acquired were to be taxed at capital gains rates according to the law then in effect.

On December 31, 1952, we observe that the option has not yet been exercised but that the stock has risen in price to $120. By the procedure described in Chapter 4, our first estimate of the prospective before-tax value of the option is $25,000, the current $25 price spread on 1,000 shares. Its after-tax value would be set at 75 per cent of that figure but for three factors: the additional deductions and exemptions likely to result from the realization of any profits, the deferral of the associated capital gains tax, and the possibility that the optionee may avoid the tax altogether by passing the stock on in his estate. The upshot of an attempt to take these into account was an arbitrary assumption of 15 per cent for the effective tax rate on stock option gains rather than the statutory 25 per cent. Thus, the option's after-tax worth as of the end of 1952 is specified to be $21,250.

When discounted for futurity (at 5 per cent per annum) and for mortality, a series of seven annual after-tax payments of $3,650 each—beginning in 1953 and continuing through 1959—would have a present value equal to $21,250. If the executive were promised those payments, he would, in the view here, be as well off as he is at the moment with his stock option. They, therefore, are the first elements in the after-tax current income equivalent of that option.

Looking at 1953, we find the stock price standing at $130 on December 31 and the option still unexercised. Its prospective value before taxes has thus increased during the year by $10,000—a price rise of $10 on 1,000 shares—and after taxes by $8,500. In response, a second stream of equal annual payments running now from 1954 through 1959 and having a present value of $8,500 is established. These payments come to $1,655 per annum and form the next "layer" of the current equivalent, which now appears as follows:

Year	Stock Option No. 1 Current Equivalent
1953	$3,650
1954	5,305

In effect, then, the developments under the option are assessed at the close of every year and the current equivalent for the coming years is adjusted to reflect whatever change has taken place.

By December, 1954, the market price of the company's stock has fallen to $110. This decline reduces the option's after-tax value by a total of $17,000 and its current equivalent by $3,862 yearly. In the meantime, a second option having a five-year term has been issued at an exercise price of $110. Since this is also the observed year-end closing price of the stock, the current equivalent of the second option is thus far equal to zero.

During 1955 a further stock price decline occurs, and by the end of the year, the market quotation is only $95 per share. Both options are therefore worthless under present conditions. In the case of the second, this merely implies that its current equivalent remains at zero. However, our methodology indicates that the current equivalent of the first option should now be diminished by $3,512 per annum as a consequence of the $12,750 loss in after-tax value over the year. Since a reduction of that magnitude would make the current equivalent negative—and since such "assessments" have been ruled out [14]—it, too, is set equal to zero.[15]

"Normalcy" is restored in 1956 as the stock price rebounds to $120 at year's end. As a result, the first option gains $21,250 in potential value, after taxes. Three after-tax receipts of $7,569 each in 1957, 1958, and 1959 would leave the executive as well off as this increment; they are, therefore, the next segment of the option's current equivalent. They must, however, be superimposed on what would have been a negative stream of payments but for the constraint specified above. The effect is to bring the current equivalent for 1957 through 1959 up only to $5,500 per annum—the algebraic sum of a $7,569 increase and the negative $2,069 that was the theoretically correct value from 1956. Even though the latter assessment was not executed, it must be used as the basis for subsequent computations if we are to continue to deal each year with the *change* from the preceding situation. Thus the only departure from a

[14] See Chapter 4 above.

[15] If the second option did have a positive current equivalent at this point, the negative figure for the first would instead be subtracted from it and a net value obtained for the two combined. In either case, zero is specified to be the effective lower limit of the resulting combination.

strict adherence to the rules of the game turns out to be in the 1956 figure, and that departure is made up for in succeeding years.

The second option has also acquired a positive value, since the market price of the stock now exceeds the option price by $10 per share. The prescribed after-tax current equivalent comes to $3,027 yearly, and the analysis to date therefore reads:

Year	Stock Option No. 1 Current Equivalent	Stock Option No. 2 Current Equivalent
1953	$3,650	—
1954	5,305	—
1955	1,443	$ 0
1956	0	0
1957	5,500	3,027

During 1957 the first option is exercised by the executive at a time when the price of his firm's stock on the market is $150 per share. The actual profit from the option is therefore $55,000 before taxes and $46,750 after taxes. From the latter figure is subtracted the interest-accumulated value of the payments thus far credited to the executive, leaving a net remuneration of $30,550 still to be accounted for.[16] Accordingly, payments of $15,800 each in 1958 and 1959 complete the current equivalent.

The second option remains unexercised despite the upturn in market conditions and, by the end of 1957, has experienced a further $25,500 increase in prospective after-tax value. The required addition to its current income equivalent is $13,190 annually for the next two years, making the total annual figure $16,217.

Finally, in 1958 this option is also exercised on a day when the relevant market price is $150. A $34,000 after-tax reward is thus obtained by the executive. The result is a $15,330 payment in 1959 which makes up the difference between this figure and the cumulative value of the amounts imputed to him in past years—and, therefore, completes the current equivalent.

[16] Both the prior payments and the after-tax option gain are, as was indicated in Chapter 4, cumulated at 5 per cent per annum to the end of 1957 for purposes of this comparison.

Putting the several pieces of the story together, then, we may record the man's stock option experience as follows:

Year	Stock Option No. 1 Current Equivalent	Stock Option No. 2 Current Equivalent
1953	$ 3,650	—
1954	5,305	—
1955	1,443	$ 0
1956	0	0
1957	5,500	3,027
1958	15,800	16,217
1959	15,800	15,330

Had he enjoyed this sequence of after-tax income receipts, he would, in the view here, have been as well off at each point in time as he was in fact as the beneficiary of the two stock option grants described.

The Before-Tax Viewpoint

After-tax current equivalents of the sort developed above provide the basis for our analysis of the compensation package. Another approach to the same objective is to determine the size of the before-tax salary increases that would have been necessary had the corporation in question actually sought to supply the executive with the calculated after-tax increments.

One issue in this connection has to do with the role of what has been termed here "outside income." If we think of raising by a certain amount an executive's current after-tax remuneration, we must decide whether the increase is to be considered marginal to salary alone or to salary and outside income both. Since the personal tax structure is progressive, it makes a difference which view is adopted, i.e., the higher the income base we start with, the larger will be the additional before-tax payment required for a given after-tax increment. It has been argued throughout that the typical executive almost certainly does receive income from sources other than his employment. The various after-tax figures calculated above all reflect an estimate of the size of those earnings. For that reason, it seems inappropriate to ignore such receipts

in the present context. The income base used in arriving at before-tax
current equivalents should therefore include outside income.

A similar question concerns the manner in which the before-tax
counterparts of multiple after-tax current equivalents are to be established. If, say, pensions are viewed as first in line, the progressiveness
of the personal income tax will cause their before-tax current equivalents
to be relatively less per dollar of after-tax value than those of other
rewards. Indeed, the particular sequence in which the calculations are
made for the several items in the package will completely determine the
answers obtained. A way out of this problem which does not prejudice
the results, however, is to first compute the before-tax increment which,
when added to existing salary and outside income, would be sufficient
to raise the executive's after-tax income by the sum of *all* his after-tax
current equivalents. This total before-tax figure can then simply be
divided up according to the proportion each reward's after-tax equivalent represents of the after-tax total. Any need to specify a particular
order for the various rewards is thereby eliminated; it is assumed that
they all contribute equally to the results obtained. Application of this
procedure to our fictitious executive's case history should serve to
illustrate its impact.

BEFORE-TAX ANALYSIS

Since, in 1945, the executive had no remuneration other than salary,
we may skip that year. In 1946 his before-tax salary was $75,000 and
his outside income $11,250. Of this amount only 90 per cent ($77,625)
is considered taxable, and therefore is the actual before-tax income
subject to statutory tax rates that our computations should be based on.
The portion of the man's income which is taken to be tax-free as deductions and exemptions is excluded from consideration because it does not
affect the tax bill on any additions to income that may be proposed.

The after-tax income attributable to *taxable* before-tax income is
$31,734: the indicated figure of $77,625 less $45,891 in taxes at 1946
rates. Adding to this the $4,868 pension after-tax current equivalent,
we obtain a total of $36,602 as the desired after-tax combined income
level. It turns out that the man would require in this particular year an

aggregate (taxable) before-tax income of $103,688 in order to generate that total. The $26,063 difference between this figure and the original $77,625 is thus the before-tax current income equivalent of his pension for 1946. A salary increase of this magnitude would provide him with just enough extra income—after paying the additional taxes due—to permit him to purchase from an insurance company an individual annuity policy as valuable as his pension.

This procedure is repeated in succeeding years, using in each case the tax rates applicable to the year in question. Through 1950 the result is:

Year	Before-Tax Salary	Before-Tax Pension Current Equivalent	Total Required Before-Tax Income from the Corporation
1945	$75,000	—	$ 75,000
1946	75,000	$26,063	101,063
1947	75,000	32,825	107,825
1948	90,000	16,664	106,664
1949	90,000	41,426	131,426
1950	90,000	42,681	132,681

In 1951 we confront for the first time two after-tax current equivalents, one for the pension and one for a deferred compensation contract. Before-tax salary is $90,000 and imputed outside income $13,500. Now that our estimate of deductions and exemptions stands at 15 per cent of gross income, only $87,975 of the total is taxable. After subtracting from this figure its 1951 tax bill, we end up with $42,993 as the man's relevant basic after-tax income. Given two current equivalents which sum to $16,905 (see page 97 above), the required after-tax total becomes $59,898. A taxable gross income of $162,107 would provide this amount, implying that an increase of $74,132 in the executive's before-tax salary for 1951 is called for. Since 83.5 per cent (14,208/16,905) of the combined *after-tax* current equivalent results from the pension, the same proportionate share of the calculated *before-tax* increment will also be attributed to it. We therefore end up with a $62,305 before-tax current equivalent for the pension and one of $11,827 for the deferred compensation.

The remaining years are operated on in the same manner, stock option current equivalents being included where appropriate. The complete analysis takes the following form:

Year	Before-Tax Salary	Before-Tax Pension Current Equivalent	Before-Tax Deferred Compensation Current Equivalent	Before-Tax Stock Option Current Equivalent	Before-Tax Total Required
1945	$ 75,000	—	—	—	$ 75,000
1946	75,000	$ 26,063	—	—	101,063
1947	75,000	32,825	—	—	107,825
1948	90,000	16,664	—	—	106,664
1949	90,000	41,426	—	—	131,426
1950	90,000	42,681	—	—	132,681
1951	90,000	62,305	$11,827	—	164,132
1952	90,000	89,951	14,264	—	194,215
1953	90,000	102,056	20,451	$ 22,316	234,823
1954	100,000	97,792	20,028	31,964	249,784
1955	100,000	88,641	18,154	7,881	214,676
1956	100,000	84,383	17,282	0	201,665
1957	100,000	103,501	21,197	54,378	279,076
1958	100,000	133,380	27,317	263,119	523,816
1959	100,000	599,602	25,105	287,730	1,012,437

These figures permit us to assess the executive's compensation history in a way that points up perhaps even more clearly the value of the supplements to his salary. Had our executive not been the beneficiary of a pension plan, a deferred compensation arrangement, and two stock option grants over this fifteen-year period, it would have taken more than 2½ times as much salary as he actually received to provide him with the same level of reward. His pension, in particular, was extremely valuable when looked at in this manner, especially if the 1959 benefit change is included: [17] A salary increase equal to 111 per cent of actual

---

[17] As it should be, even though its consequences in terms of a "current equivalent" seem severe. It may be emphasized again that situations of this kind, when they occur, are a result of the compensation experience observed— not our model's idiosyncrasies.

before-tax salary from 1945 on would have been necessary had the corporation taken that route instead.[18]

Obviously, these comparisons are sharper than their after-tax counterparts because of the progressive nature of the personal income tax. The amount of any before-tax salary increase must inevitably be larger in relation to existing before-tax income than is the after-tax increment it generates in relation to existing after-tax income. To acknowledge this, however, is not to imply that a before-tax analysis is any less valid or less meaningful—it is merely different. One could, in fact, argue that it bears even more directly on the matter of the tax-ameliorating properties of deferred and contingent compensation arrangements. Were it not possible for a company to postpone and reduce its executives' tax liabilities by providing pension, stock option, and deferred-pay plans of various kinds rather than having to rely exclusively on salary payments, either the levels of remuneration indicated by the after-tax current equivalents computed would be much lower or salaries would be much higher, or both. The extent to which the use of these devices has allowed the heavy tax bite on current income to be side-stepped is brought into clearer focus by the before-tax comparisons. In this sense the notion of a before-tax current equivalent is both interesting and analytically useful.

Some Comments

The career of the executive whose experiences were examined ended with the event which is by far the most common one in practice: retirement at age 65. Had it been otherwise—through death, resignation, or early retirement—the appropriate response here would have been simply to stop the calculations at that point. Because the relevant contingencies are already incorporated in the procedures employed, none of these occurrences require, as has been discussed elsewhere, any adjustment of the figures generated.

[18] It can be seen from the tabulated values that there does exist now a "feedback" between stock options and other rewards. From 1954 to 1958 the before-tax current equivalents of the man's pension and deferred compensation would, like their after-tax predecessors, have been constant were it not for the influence of the stock options' changing after-tax value on the size of the required total before-tax equivalent.

A final comment concerning environmental assumptions is also in order. While the approach taken here requires individual case histories as the basis from which to draw conclusions, it is clearly not possible to "personalize" the computations as much as might be preferred. Common discount rates, outside income imputations, and deduction and exemption percentages are mandatory. Whether standardization of this sort affects the results very greatly is difficult to determine. Certainly, if the parameters chosen are in some sense characteristic of executives as a class, the numbers they produce will not be far wrong and, in fact, may be better suited to the purpose of generalizing about compensation than very individualized ones. It could legitimately be contended that the proper subject for concern in this area ought instead to be the degree to which those numbers are, in the aggregate, sensitive to changes in the values of the several parameters required. For instance, the effect on the current equivalents of setting the outside income estimate at 25 per cent of salary and bonus or of raising the discount rate on stock options to 10 per cent might be examined. In Chapter 12, therefore, the experience of a "typical" executive, as he is described by the sample now to be developed, will be recast with different assumptions about his behavior and market opportunities in an attempt to determine how crucial those assumptions really are.

Summary

The application of the methodology outlined in previous chapters to the compensation history of a single executive has been considered in detail. Both before- and after-tax descriptions of the size and structure of the compensation package were generated and discussed, employing in each case the concept of a "current income equivalent" appropriately defined. The problems encountered in evaluating several rewards simultaneously and in combining their current equivalents were explored and, presumably, solved. We therefore stand ready to operate on the sample data and to arrive at some conclusions about executive compensation in practice.

PART II
EMPIRICAL ANALYSIS

7

THE DATA

The focus of any empirical treatment of the executive compensation package must be the individual executive himself. Pension plans, profit-sharing schemes, deferred compensation arrangements, stock options, and other devices have no real meaning as instruments of remuneration except in their application to specific situations. The one sensible way to look at compensation, therefore, is to look at the people being compensated.

Sources of Data

The proxy statements issued by corporations in connection with their annual shareholders' meetings constitute the only regular and comprehensive source of information about the rewards received by individual executives. The Securities and Exchange Commission requires firms listed on organized stock exchanges [1] to report in their proxy statements the salaries, bonuses, pension expectations, stock options, and other major items of compensation of their top officials.[2] As might be expected, the degree to which different companies respond to the spirit as well as the letter of the law varies greatly, but in most cases the information provided is sufficient to permit all the important rewards that executives receive to be analyzed with considerable precision.[3] Since only a

---

[1] And, recently, some firms traded over the counter as well.

[2] Specifically, the requirement since 1954 has been that the compensation of the three highest-paid officers and of any officer earning more than $30,000 per year in salary who is also a director be reported. Prior to 1954, the threshold was $25,000 and, in the early 1940's the form of the disclosure rule itself was somewhat different.

[3] The chief exceptions, as was noted in Chapter 5, being company-provided life and medical insurance arrangements, expense accounts, and savings plans.

small number of the highest-ranking individuals in each firm are re-ported on, however, the analysis here must be confined to their com-pensation experience. While this is a constraint, it is not necessarily a serious one for several reasons.

First, these are the men who make the major policy decisions for their firms and who thereby play a major role in determining the pattern of economic growth and resource utilization observed in the community. If there is some concern about the performance of our economy over time and about the decisions which spark that performance, it makes sense to concentrate a good deal of attention on the people who formulate the crucial policies. Secondly, the rewards received by these same people establish a foundation for pay scales throughout the corporate organization and thus provide a standard by which men at lower management levels are apt to judge the adequacy of their own compensation and toward which they may look for an incentive to move upward. If, as has been claimed in recent years, the after-tax monetary benefits associated with becoming a top executive are not sufficient in themselves to act as an inducement to younger persons to attempt to at-tain that status, we must rely on other types of motivation to fill the gap or resign ourselves to an inadequate supply of the right kind of talent in this area. Finally, if we are interested in the effects of personal income taxation on the attitudes and actions of individuals, senior corporate executives are a logical group to study. Because of their very high in-comes, progressive taxes have an especially large impact on them and they would, as much as any segment of society, be expected to display some reaction thereto. Accordingly, whether out of concern for be-havior now or in the long run, the remuneration of the few men at the top of the corporate pyramid is of considerable importance and merits our attention.

The Sample

While there are a number of possible bases for choosing the specific group of companies from which to draw such a sample, the decision here was to focus on large manufacturing corporations. In part, the feeling was that the leaders of *large* firms are the pace-setters for the nation's managerial class. They frequently represent it to the public, define for it standards of competent performance, and provide in their rewards a benchmark for the compensation of executives in other, smaller companies. A sample having these characteristics can therefore be viewed as an instrument for obtaining as much mileage as possible from a given amount of data as well as being interesting in its own right.

The choice of manufacturing firms in particular was dictated as much by personal preference as by the thought of any unique advantages to be gained. A sample consisting of utilities, financial institutions, transportation firms, companies engaged in retail trade, etc., would very likely have been a suitable alternative.[4] Concentration on a single category of firms in order to develop as coherent and structured a body of data as possible did appear a desirable objective, however. In that connection, large manufacturing corporations have enough in common to make comparisons among them meaningful and enough diversity to make the same comparisons interesting. Therefore, while they are by no means the only sensible choice, they do have some advantages, are obviously prominent in the economy, and constitute a familiar frame of reference. As such, they should be well suited to the task of providing a solid foundation for an empirical analysis of the compensation package.

Selection of Companies

Two questions remain to be answered: (1) What is a "large" company? and (2) How many of them comprise a sufficient sample from which to draw inferences? Since neither question has a very well-defined theoretical solution in the present context, both must be settled somewhat arbitrarily.

The relevant measure of company size is taken to be annual sales volume. While a strong case could be made for profits, total assets, market value of outstanding securities, and several other criteria, the absence of a clear signal from the nature of the problem suggests that

---

[4] On the other hand, the several dimensions of the executive pay package have been somewhat more fully developed by manufacturing corporations than by other sectors of the business community. For example, financial institutions and public utilities have in general used instruments such as stock options less extensively than have manufacturers.

the decision is essentially a matter of taste and convenience. Given a desire to study executives whose actions have a significant impact on the economy, sales may be marginally preferred as an index of size because they seem to provide the best measure of the sheer weight of economic activity undertaken by a company.[5] They are also a convenient choice: the task of ranking manufacturing firms according to their sales volume is performed annually by *Fortune* magazine in its compilation of the five hundred largest American industrial corporations.[6] This service may therefore be exploited and those tabulations used as the source from which to draw a sample. In any event, if sales are adopted as the yardstick, the group of companies chosen will not be very different from that which would result were any one of several other criteria selected instead. It happens that firms with a high level of sales also have high profits, many assets, and a substantial market value. Indeed, almost any common measure of size will yield a very similar list—similar enough that a long search for the "right" measure here is not worthwhile.[7]

The latter point is reinforced when it is recalled that data on the compensation of a particular executive must extend over a period of time if his experience is to be analyzed properly. This means that both the executive and his company must be in the sample for a number of years if they are to appear at all. Because the firm's dimensions will change over such an interval, whichever one is chosen as most indicative of its relative standing in the business community in a given year will not necessarily provide the same ranking in every other year. There is little to be gained, therefore, from an attempt to establish a rigorous case in principle for a criterion that must immediately be compromised in application.

The conclusion this leads one to is the following: A sample consistent with the objectives established can legitimately be chosen by

[5] Even this assertion, of course, must be highly qualified. One could well argue, for example, that total assets as a measure of resources controlled are better suited to the purpose of indicating "impact" or "importance."

[6] The July issue each year contains this list and a discussion of the attributes of the firms included.

[7] For example, if the 1964 list of firms in *Fortune* was reclassified according to asset size, of the first twenty only four would not be present among the first twenty on the revised list.

taking a list of the nation's largest manufacturing companies ranked in a recent year by any one of several characteristics, starting at the top, and simply working down until the desired number is obtained, eliminating along the way those firms whose executives' compensation cannot be properly analyzed because of insufficiencies in the historical data. This is in fact what was done.

The basic decision was to seek a sample of fifty companies in all—a number judged to be enough to allow statements about average values and trends over time to be made with some confidence. As it later turned out, a sample of this size yielded data on approximately 550 individual executives involving almost 8,000 man-years' worth of compensation experience.

The sample was assembled from the *Fortune* magazine tabulation for 1964.[8] Beginning with General Motors, the back proxy statements of some eighty companies were examined for clarity, consistency, completeness, and availability. This last consideration was obviously a crucial one. There are very few extensive collections of corporate proxy statements in existence and even fewer that contain records for more than a half dozen years or so back in time. One such collection—at the Harvard Business School's Baker Library—was accessible to the author. Because that collection is quite comprehensive, missing data was seldom a stumbling block. Of the some eighty corporations checked, only four had to be ruled out because their proxies were not available.

The next question was whether the manner in which the firm chose to respond to the various SEC reporting requirements over the years provided enough information on its executives to permit an analysis of their rewards. Some companies, for instance, supply in their proxy statements the formal schedule of annual retirement benefits for their pension plans as a function of years of employment and average salary but do not translate that schedule into actual benefit promises for individual executives. In certain cases it was possible to perform this translation from information gathered elsewhere and from various bits of data contained in the proxy statements themselves, but most commonly it was not, and companies in this category usually had to be excluded from the sample.

[8] Which ranks firms according to their fiscal 1963 sales. Volume LXX, No. 1, pp. 179–198.

Another problem situation was the one in which the corporation as it was constituted in 1964 had been put together by a series of mergers. When this had happened, there frequently was not sufficient continuity of personnel or of compensation policy to render an analysis of its history very meaningful. Moreover, to the extent that such an effort was possible, it would deal with men who for much of the relevant time period were employed by companies much smaller than those with which the sample sought to concern itself.

A variety of other difficulties was also encountered. One enterprise classified among the top manufacturers—Western Electric—issues no proxy statements of its own because it is a wholly-owned subsidiary of another company. The shares of some firms—Ford Motor Company being perhaps the most prominent example—were not listed on an organized stock exchange until relatively recently and therefore did not have a long enough proxy statement file to be useful. Still others had only a small number of executives at any one time who were also directors and, in consequence, were required to report the compensation of so few men each year that no adequate history could be assembled for any of them. Ultimately, it was necessary to reach down to the corporation which ranked seventy-eighth in sales volume among manufacturing firms in 1963 in order to round out a list of fifty.

The Companies

These were all minor problems, however, and the resulting sample can, as well as any other, be considered representative of very large American industrial corporations. Most, if not all, the firms included would be termed "blue chips" in the language of the investor. A wide range of both size and type of company appears. The full list is presented in Appendix I.

The fifty firms had, in 1963, a combined sales volume of $93.8 billion, assets of $77.8 billion, a net profit of $6.6 billion, and a total equity market value equal to $113.0 billion. As a group they generated approximately 22 per cent of the total sales of all United States manufacturers in that year.[9] The largest—General Motors—had sales of

[9] United States Department of Commerce. *Survey of Current Business,* May 1955, pp. 3–4. Total sales of all manufacturing firms in 1963 were $417.3 billion.

$16.5 billion and the smallest—Tidewater Oil—sales of $660 million.
A breakdown of the sample by industry would read as follows:

Agricultural machinery	2
Aircraft and aerospace	6
Autos	1
Chemicals	4
Containers	2
Electrical and electronics	4
Food and dairy products	4
Nonferrous metals	2
Office equipment	1
Paper	1
Petroleum	9
Rubber	5
Steel	5
Tobacco	2
Miscellaneous	2

While rankings which go back beyond 1955—the first year for which
Fortune compiled its list—are not readily available, it can be seen from
Appendix A that the large majority of these companies have almost
certainly been among, say, the nation's top one hundred manufacturing
corporations throughout the entire last quarter century. Some, of course,
such as IBM, have experienced a very rapid growth in sales in recent
years and therefore were not major companies by that definition in the
1940's. Situations of this sort are in the minority, however, and, to the
extent a choice was necessary, it seemed most appropriate to include in
the sample companies important now but not twenty-five years ago
rather than the reverse.

Time Period Covered

The objective established at the outset was very simply to develop as
much of a history as the data would permit. Since proxy statements were
the key documents, this meant that the study would go back as far as
they did. The year 1940 turned out to be the practical limit of the
analysis. Proxy statements were first required for listed companies by
the then-newly-formed Securities and Exchange Commission in the
late 1930's, but the disclosure rules applicable to them were apparently

not sufficiently well defined to bring about uniform and comprehensive reporting of remuneration until several years later. The timing involved was fortunate because it effectively coincided with the first serious wave of pension plan adoptions by American corporations. It was therefore possible in almost every instance to obtain the provisions of such plans directly from the proxy statements themselves and to observe their translation into benefit promises for individual executives right from the start. Coupled with the long list of executives whose rewards the reporting requirements of the 1940's made public (the initial confusion having been dispelled by rather severe disclosure rules) this circumstance not only made the data for the early years of the study quite complete but eliminated much of the need to estimate compensation data for various individuals who did not attain high positions within their companies until later on.[10] The analysis begins with 1940, therefore, and continues through 1963.

The Executives

Over this period, data were collected in an attempt to provide an evaluation of the rewards in each year of the *five* highest-paid executives in all fifty companies. Once again, the original goal was to reach as far down in the corporate hierarchy as the available information would allow. After several trial runs, the fifth-ranking man seemed to be the lowest which, considering the entire sample of firms, the proxy data would with any reasonable frequency support.

The degree of success achieved in meeting even this objective, while generally high, varied widely from company to company. For five firms it was possible to fill all five slots in each of the twenty-four years and, in two others, all five in every year but one. The worst company in this regard was by far the worst, supplying enough information to fill only thirty-three of the 120 possible spaces. For no other firm were there less than seventy-four filled. In all, out of the 6,000 man-years' worth of compensation history sought,[11] a total of 5,300 were obtained, involving altogether 558 different executives. A tabular summary of the resulting population by years is presented in Appendix J.

[10] The problem of extrapolating certain data for particular executives is discussed below.

[11] That is, fifty companies over twenty-four years.

It was necessary to assemble more than 5,300 man-years of executive experience, however. In order to determine the value of certain of a man's rewards—his pension and deferred compensation, for example— we must analyze his history starting with the year he is *first* promised benefits under such plans. Data for him for a number of years in advance of the time he becomes one of his company's top five executives are therefore likely to be required. This occurred often enough in practice that a total of 7,802 man-years of compensation experience was eventually collected and processed.

One adjective used very casually in the preceding paragraphs requires a little more elaboration. It is really not possible to establish which individuals in a firm are its five "highest-paid" until *after* the value of each man's rewards has been analyzed and the appropriate current income equivalents constructed. Salary alone is clearly an incomplete ranking criterion. Thus it is not correct to state simply that, for the purposes of the empirical portion of the study, data on the top five men in every company were collected. More precisely, data on enough men were collected so that after an analysis of their remuneration the top five would be sure to emerge. It was frequently necessary, therefore, to examine information on a greater number of executives for each firm in each calendar year. Indeed, one of the comparisons the procedures developed here make possible is between the executive rankings within a company implied by salaries and those which result from considering the full range of rewards.[12]

Demographic Data

In addition to the compensation figures provided by the corporation's proxy statements, the individual executive's age and marital status are important to the analysis. Calculations involving mortality considerations of course depend quite heavily on the former, and tax liabilities are greatly affected by the latter. After-tax present value comparisons, therefore, require that both characteristics be identified.

On occasion it was possible either to obtain or to infer the executive's age directly from the proxy statements. For instance, the number of

[12] See below, Chapters 10 and 11.

years remaining until "normal retirement age," i.e., age 65, might be reported in some connection by a company for each of its officers in a particular year. This sort of thing did not happen very often, however, and other sources had to be relied on in the large majority of cases. *Who's Who in America* and *Who's Who in Commerce and Industry* supplied most of the data. Each presents a short biographical sketch of the individuals it records, and both age and marital status are included. For executives who did not appear in one or the other of these, *Poor's Register of Corporations, Directors, and Executives* was the next line of defense. If that also failed, the assumption was made that the executive in question was indeed age 65 when he was observed to retire and that he was married. For approximately forty out of the 558 men in the sample, no conclusive evidence as to birth date or marital status could be found, and the assumption indicated was necessary.

Estimating Data

In situations where data were required for an individual for a period of years prior to the time he appeared in his firm's proxy statements, it was almost always possible to reconstruct the relevant experience by comparing the man's career with that of another, more visible executive in the same firm, and by making use of various pieces of information contained in the proxy statements after he did appear.

Suppose, for example, that an executive who has been laboring anonymously for a company for a number of years finally attains a position such that his compensation is reported. Suppose further that his salary thereafter is seen to follow consistently one step behind that of a fellow executive for whom a long record of data does exist. If, then, there is some indication from the proxy statements or from information in *Who's Who* that they held the same relative positions in the past as well, it is a fairly easy matter to reconstruct the first man's history—at least when it is not necessary to go back too far in time. We may simply impute to him past salary figures which bear each year the same relationship to the other executive's observable past salary as do his current ones. If the man's age, the date of his employment, and the benefit formulas under the corporation's various supplemental compensation plans are known, the benefits that would have been in prospect for him at all those previous salary levels under such plans can also be computed.

Another situation is that in which an executive who has held the same position in his company for some time suddenly appears in its proxy statements not because of a promotion but by virtue of his election to its Board of Directors. From his current salary and a record of the salary levels over time for the several positions in the company just senior to his, his past experience can be approximated reasonably well. Again, any supplemental compensation promises can be estimated either from the provisions of the plans or by extrapolating the current relationship between those benefits and his salary.

It is frequently possible, therefore, to get a good estimate of that portion of an executive's compensation history which is not directly visible in his firm's proxy statements. The latter aid this effort by reporting—as the SEC requires—the positions a man has held during the five years prior to that in which he is first presented to the shareholders for election to a directorship. His biography in *Who's Who* can be referred to in order to supplement such information when it is necessary to have a longer record. Finally, a clue to the early history of many executives who became important in the 1950's is conveniently provided by corporate proxy statements for the years 1942 through 1946. During that time the SEC specified that the compensation of *all* officers of a company who received a salary of $20,000 or more per year had to be reported whether or not they were also directors or were among the firm's three highest-paid executives. While this requirement was subsequently relaxed,[13] enough men came under it for a year or two to make easier and more precise the task of extrapolating data for those who reappeared later on in high positions.

If, after exploring all these possibilities, it turned out that there was just no way to get a pretty good idea of the profile of a man's compensation experience before his name appeared in his firm's proxy statements, he was simply excluded from the sample. The use of "typical" compensation—i.e., salary—growth rates of the sort suggested by previous

[13] See footnote 2 of this chapter.

studies in order to extrapolate data for a man for a long period of time when it could not be obtained from evidence as to his actual experience was taken to be inappropriate and explicitly ruled out. Indeed, the objective here is to do no less than reject the notion of typical as such studies have defined it and to develop a more comprehensive measure which includes all the executive's rewards.

Of the total 7,802 man-years' worth of compensation experience which was eventually analyzed, 1,561 (or 20 per cent) consisted of estimated rather than directly observed data. Those estimates were confined primarily to years in which the various individuals' remuneration was considerably lower than it was when they finally did appear in proxy statements. For this reason, the effect of errors in any of the projections on the results of the analysis is much less significant than even the proportionate number of years involved would suggest. In order not to leave this a matter of faith, however, the impact of some fairly severe mistakes in estimation for a "typical" executive will be considered later on in conjunction with an examination of changes in discount rates, outside income, and other parameters.[14]

Annuity Premium Rates

An appraisal of the worth of a corporation's pension plan to each of its employees centers on the cost to them of a particular instrument—a "nonparticipating" individual retirement annuity. It was necessary, therefore, to construct a schedule of those costs which could be offered as characteristic of the premium rates actually charged by insurance companies over the time period covered by the study. For this purpose, historical data were obtained from two leading firms who have issued substantial numbers of such policies during the last quarter century: Connecticut General Life Insurance Company and The Travelers Insurance Company, both of Hartford, Connecticut. The average in each year of the two firms' quotations was taken to be a reasonable representation of the prices that would have been confronted by an executive had he sought to provide his own retirement income. Appendix K spells out the details and tabulates the resulting schedule.

[14] See Chapter 12.

Summary

The five highest-paid executives in fifty of the nation's largest manufacturing firms constitute the sample to which the valuation techniques developed in previous chapters will be applied. The experience of such men was chosen for scrutiny out of a desire to deal with individuals whose decisions have a significant impact on the economy and whose rewards are likely to set a standard for the compensation not only of their subordinates but of executives in other firms as well. In compiling the sample, the objective was to include as many men and to go back as far in time as the available information would allow. Since corporate proxy statements are the only comprehensive source of data on the remuneration of particular individuals, the dimensions of the study were largely dictated by their characteristics. As it turned out, the histories of 558 different executives representing approximately 7,800 man-years of compensation experience back to 1940 were collected and analyzed. The results of that effort now follow.

8

THE PATTERN OF COMPENSATION OVER TIME

One approach to an analysis of the compensation of executives is an examination of the changes that have taken place over time in the rewards associated with particular positions within the corporate hierarchy. For example, we might focus on what has happened during the last quarter century to the amount and form of the remuneration of the highest-paid executive in each of the fifty sample companies. It would be relevant to ask such questions as: By how much, on average, have salaries increased since 1940? Has total compensation grown more or less rapidly? Has the growth been steady over this period? Which components of the pay package have been the most valuable and most rapidly growing? These issues will be considered here in terms of the experience of the top executive in each firm in every year and also for the combination of all five positions within those firms for which data were collected. The goal is to determine how well executives have fared since the advent both of high personal income taxes and the post-World War II economic boom and to discover how important rewards other than salary and bonus have come to be for them during this period.

Before-Tax Salaries and Bonuses

We may begin by looking at the most familiar measure of an individual's rewards—his aggregate before-tax current remuneration consisting of salary and bonus payments. Table 1 and Chart 1 summarize the history of these payments from 1940 to 1963 for the two categories of executives. The first column in Table 1 and the upper line in Chart 1 represent the average across all fifty companies of the before-tax salary and bonus

TABLE 1

Average Before-Tax Salaries and
Bonuses, 1940–63
(dollars)

Year	Top Executive	Top Five Executives
1940	137,233	81,353
1941	145,281	85,332
1942	145,473	86,825
1943	144,208	87,554
1944	143,612	86,408
1945	142,892	86,852
1946	143,247	92,262
1947	149,446	94,730
1948	161,959	103,295
1949	169,703	108,421
1950	178,452	116,204
1951	183,235	122,664
1952	185,330	125,822
1953	193,556	133,458
1954	197,726	136,752
1955	205,656	143,633
1956	215,767	150,297
1957	207,586	145,848
1958	207,101	140,594
1959	203,708	144,016
1960	200,788	139,744
1961	198,560	137,491
1962	201,622	141,758
1963	210,164	148,553

received by the highest-paid executive in each firm. The lower line and
the second column record a similar series for the full sample of the top
five executives in every company taken as a group. Thus, in the latter
case, the average current remuneration associated with each of the
highest-paid positions is computed and then the mean of those five
values obtained.

CHART 1

Average Before-Tax Salaries and Bonuses, 1940–63

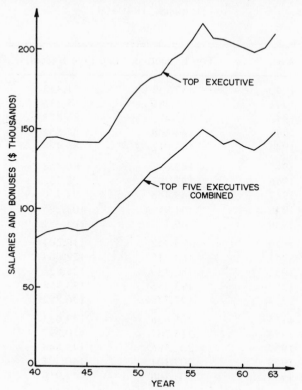

The notion of "highest-paid" refers here only to salary and bonus. As was noted earlier, the executive with the largest amount of such payments may not necessarily be the best-rewarded one when the rest of the pay package is taken into account. For the moment, however, rankings on the basis of current remuneration alone provide the data for the averages compiled.

Those averages are rather surprising in the modest rates of growth they suggest. The before-tax current remuneration of the top executive in each company grew from an average of about $137,000 annually in

1940 to $210,000 by 1963. At the same time, the five highest-paid men together experienced an increase from slightly better than $81,000 on average to approximately $148,500. These changes represent pay raises of 53 and 83 per cent, respectively, over a period of twenty-four years—certainly not very substantial increases by most standards.[1] Between 1940 and 1963 the implied compound annual rates of growth are only about 1.8 and 2.5 per cent for the two groups. The postwar years look somewhat better—the corresponding growth rates from 1945 on being closer to 2.1 and 2.9 per cent per annum—but not significantly so.

Two features of the data are particularly interesting. First, during World War II annual before-tax current remuneration did not increase from its prewar level for either category of executives. A mild advance between 1940 and 1941 is really the only change that is discernible. This result, of course, can be explained by the wage and salary restraint imposed by the federal government during the war.

The postwar pattern, on the other hand, is a much less predictable one: All the growth that took place in the amount of salaries and bonuses received occurred within the ten years from 1945 to 1955; after that point both time series effectively level off. In 1963, average before-tax current remuneration stood at just slightly above its 1955 value in both cases. During the intervening years some fluctuations can be observed. One reason for this is that many of the bonuses involved consisted either of cash payments, which varied in response to the level of a firm's profits, or of shares of stock whose value changed according to stock market conditions. Thus, while salaries were seldom reduced, the bonus component of current remuneration did change from year to year due in part to external circumstances.[2]

Even if we take this into consideration, however, it is clear that the sample executives' direct current rewards did not increase appreciably from 1955 to 1963. Coupled with the enforced stagnation of the early 1940's, the implication is that whatever growth those rewards displayed over the last quarter century was compressed into a single ten-year period.

[1] For some particularly relevant ones, see Chapter 9.

[2] Variations also occur because of normal personnel changes within the sample. Executives are continually retiring and being replaced by younger men whose salaries may not immediately match those of their predecessors.

After-Tax Salaries and Bonuses

A similar but more striking story is revealed in the after-tax current remuneration averages tabulated in Table 2 and pictured in Chart 2. The two executive groups are defined in the same manner as before, and once again each series represents the mean values for all fifty com-

TABLE 2

Average After-Tax Salaries and
Bonuses, 1940–63
(dollars)

Year	Top Executive	Top Five Executives
1940	77,143	51,043
1941	67,202	44,085
1942	52,014	36,571
1943	43,036	31,766
1944	42,959	31,642
1945	42,817	31,767
1946	51,591	38,165
1947	53,050	38,889
1948	77,775	55,742
1949	80,269	57,547
1950	83,007	60,364
1951	79,482	59,490
1952	75,445	56,990
1953	77,716	59,380
1954	83,604	64,213
1955	85,637	66,195
1956	88,177	68,043
1957	86,302	67,101
1958	86,152	65,873
1959	85,767	67,113
1960	84,991	65,866
1961	84,524	65,205
1962	85,274	66,787
1963	87,503	67,947

CHART 2

Average After-Tax Salaries and Bonuses, 1940–63

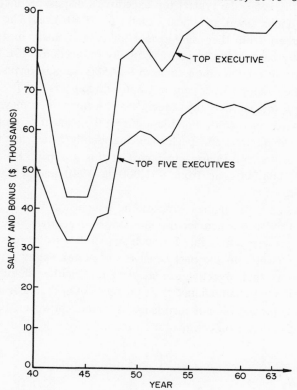

panies. This time, however, the effect of quite modest secular increases in pre-tax compensation and the assessment of personal income taxes at rates much higher than those prior to World War II combine to create a history which suggests that the current earnings of senior executives have improved hardly at all since 1940.

In that year the average after-tax salary and bonus received by the highest-paid executive in each sample company was $77,100. By 1943 this figure had fallen to $43,000 due to heavy wartime taxes and the ceiling on before-tax payments. It remained at that level until 1946, when lower taxes and growing salaries began to have an effect. In 1948 the prewar after-tax figure was reattained and, in 1950, a peak of $83,000 reached. At that point, Korean war tax provisions took hold, and, as late as 1953, the typical top executive's disposable income from salary and bonus stood at almost exactly its 1940 level. The only significant increase from then on—except for a brief flurry in 1956—occurred largely because taxes were eventually reduced. By 1963, average after-tax current remuneration came to $87,500—a gain of just $10,400 since 1940, or about 13 per cent in twenty-three years.

The story for all five top executives together is somewhat more favorable. Their income declined less during the war, grew more sharply immediately thereafter, and performed marginally better in the 1950's. The average after-tax salary and bonus of this group in 1963 was approximately $68,000—up from $51,000 in 1940 and a 33 per cent over-all gain.

As they stand, the figures support the conclusion that is frequently put forward by spokesmen for the interests of executives, i.e., that high taxes have made it impossible for such individuals to be rewarded in a manner comparable to the past because the pretax salary levels necessary to achieve that objective are so great that neither shareholder nor public opinion will countenance their payment.[3] On the basis of the data above, this contention is not surprising. It cannot, however, be accepted until all the evidence on compensation is in.

Total After-Tax Compensation

If, instead of considering only current remuneration, we compute the "after-tax current income equivalents" of the other items in the pay package as well, a rather different history emerges. Table 3 and Chart 3 record the relevant figures for the men who in each year between 1940 and 1963 were their firms' highest-paid employees. In this instance, the term "highest-paid" is an accurate designation. The sample depicted is that in which the executives are ranked within their firms

[3] See, for example, the testimony in 1955 of the then-president of the DuPont Company, Mr. Crawford Greenewalt, in United States Joint Committee on the Economic Report, *Federal Tax Policy for Economic Growth and Stability: Hearings Before the Subcommittee on Tax Policy,* 84th Congress, 1st Session, Washington, D.C., 1955, pp. 137–164.

TABLE 3

Average Total After-Tax Compensation, 1940–63
(dollars)

Year	Top Executive	Top Five Executives
1940	101,979	59,740
1941	91,535	56,885
1942	65,960	44,375
1943	56,467	38,913
1944	63,673	41,873
1945	61,632	41,329
1946	69,043	47,878
1947	78,317	49,989
1948	99,756	67,444
1949	105,311	70,825
1950	122,790	79,011
1951	109,341	77,316
1952	116,657	79,450
1953	131,782	86,181
1954	143,470	93,076
1955	214,430	125,204
1956	235,674	136,960
1957	227,227	133,315
1958	169,436	109,335
1959	211,049	131,247
1960	221,711	133,249
1961	204,274	131,361
1962	224,889	138,754
1963	187,279	121,039
Average: 1955–63	210,663	128,940

CHART 3

Average Total After-Tax Compensation, 1940–63

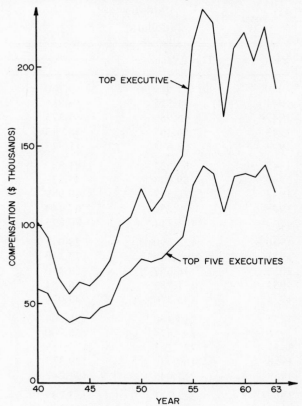

according to their total after-tax income, not just their salaries and bonuses.[4]

Through 1954 the pattern which the data trace out is generally similar to the history of after-tax salaries and bonuses. From its 1940 value, average total compensation fell to a wartime low, rose by about 1948 to its original level, peaked in 1950, and then recovered in 1954 from a brief decline caused by Korean war taxes. In 1955, however, a sub-

[4] See Chapter 10 for a discussion of variations in executive rankings on the basis of total remuneration vs. salary.

stantial jump in total after-tax compensation occurred. The figures there-after, while fluctuating from year to year, suggest that this increase was just maintained. In effect, the same "stagnation" that characterized salary and bonus payments in the late 1950's and early 1960's shows up again, but in the form of income levels significantly higher than those observed prior to 1955. The result is a much less pessimistic view of the compensation experience of executives over time, whether we look only at the top executive in every company or at all five for whom data are available.

The explanation, of course, is one that has been anticipated: a persistent trend toward the use—and liberalization—of forms of reward other than salary and bonus. As will be documented in the following section, all the major supplements to salary have been steadily growing in value. This phenomenon is particularly evident in the mid-1950's and appears most strikingly in the remuneration provided by stock options. Approximately two-thirds of the sharp increase in total after-tax compensation from 1954 to 1955 is accounted for by suddenly higher stock option profits arising from the beginnings of the post-Korean war stock market boom.[5] The volatility of such profits according to market conditions also explains most of the fluctuations in total executive compensation subsequently observed.[6]

Because of those fluctuations, it seems desirable to smooth the stock option data over the interval 1955 through 1963. It was not until then, as we shall see, that options really emerged as a significant item of remuneration. The volatility of the rewards associated with them, however, while an important phenomenon, may tend to obscure some of the longer run trends in *levels* of earnings that are of interest here. The drop in the compensation totals recorded in 1963, for example, is a reflection of the stock market decline of 1962—a decline that was soon reversed.[7] If 1964 figures were calculated, total compensation would again be observed to rise. An "average" stock option current income equivalent for the later years of the study, therefore, should provide a better basis

[5] See below, Table 4 and Chart 5.
[6] Common-stock-based profit-sharing and deferred compensation plans also contribute elements of instability in this connection.
[7] The reduced value of option profits shows up with a lag since the valuation techniques employed adjust the relevant current income equivalents only after "reading" the closing market price of the previous year. See Chapter 4.

CHART 4

Average Total After-Tax Compensation (Stock Option Data Smoothed), 1940–63

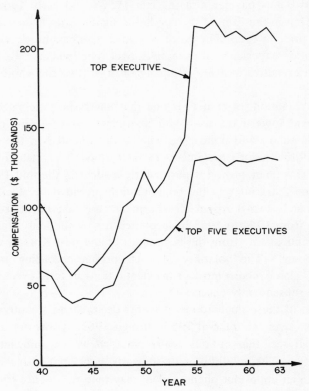

for identifying increases in remuneration over a long period of time than would choosing any single one of those years as a standard. The result of such averaging appears in Chart 4 for both compensation series, the remaining fluctuations being due to the other items in the pay package.[8]

One question which has a bearing on the validity of this procedure is whether the experience of executives with stock options between 1955

[8] Average after-tax stock option profits for the top executives in each firm from 1955 through 1963 were $74,897 per annum. For the top five men, the figure is $34,261.

and 1963 is a fair indication of that which they are likely to confront in the future. If perhaps those years were unusually good ones for realizing stock option profits, it would be misleading to present the compensation levels thus attained as evidence of an established pattern of growth in executive rewards. Two considerations may, in fact, lead us to believe that these profits should be regarded as unusual: The mid- and late 1950's and early 1960's witnessed one of the most vigorous and sustained increases in common stock prices in our history; and the tax law dealing with employee stock options was changed in 1964 in such a manner as to materially reduce their attractiveness.[9] It is by no means assured, therefore, that the happy events of recent years will continue. On the other hand, deferred compensation, profit-sharing, and savings plans are becoming more valuable over time.[10] There is even some evidence (Charts 1 and 2) that salaries and bonuses started moving up again in 1962 and 1963 after a pause of several years. And, of course, the same 1964 tax revision which affected stock options also *reduced* rates on current income receipts. In short, if one were to attempt to predict, on the basis of current trends, the amounts of total after-tax compensation to be enjoyed by top corporate executives over, say, the next five years or so, maintenance of the 1955–63 levels would not be difficult to support even though the composition of those totals might well be expected to change. Accordingly, the aggregate figures obtained by smoothing the observed stock option results should be reasonable ones on which to base some longer-term conclusions.

What, then, may be said about the experience depicted? For one thing, it is clear that all the growth associated with total executive compensation since 1940 took place within the same ten-year interval that generated the entire appreciation in salaries and bonuses—1945 through 1955. Indeed, the situation here is really much stronger. If we "control" for the effect of higher tax rates and eliminate those years in which the pay raises enjoyed by the men in the sample accomplished nothing more than the recovery of after-tax reductions they had experienced in previous periods, the only years in which any substantial increase in remuneration occurred that was subsequently maintained were 1950, 1954, and 1955. When this observation is compared with

[9] See Appendix G.
[10] See below, Charts 6 and 9.

the results summarized in Charts 1 and 2, a further conclusion is indicated (which will be made clearer in the next section by a breakdown of the pay package into its components): The introduction of sizeable supplements to salary, especially stock options, in the postwar period accounted for virtually *all* the increase in the compensation of top executives during the last quarter century. The slowly rising pretax salaries and bonuses seen in Chart 1 just about offset the effect of higher income taxes and would, by themselves, have left executives little better off in terms of after-tax income than they were in 1940.

Because such supplements did appear, however, our assessment of the pattern of executive rewards over time is rather more favorable than that which after-tax current remuneration alone would suggest. The average annual total after-tax compensation enjoyed by the top executive in each firm in the sample during the period 1955 through 1963 comes to $210,663. If that is used as a terminal figure, total remuneration turns out to have grown at an annual rate of approximately 3.2 per cent between 1940 and 1963. Up until 1955, the corresponding rate was 4.8 per cent. If only the interval between the war-induced low of 1945 and the plateau reached in 1955 is considered, an annual rate of fully 12.3 per cent is observed. For all five top executives together, average after-tax remuneration from 1955 to 1963 was $128,940 per annum, and the implied compound annual rates of growth over the three periods indicated were a very similar 3.3, 5.1 and 11.4 per cent, respectively.

A final comment is in order. If we return to the unsmoothed history of Chart 3, it is evident that the aggregate value of the senior corporate executive's compensation package was much more volatile from one year to the next in the later years of the study than it was in the 1940's and early 1950's. It is also true that this volatility is a direct consequence of the manner in which the valuation techniques developed above operate on executives' experiences with stock options and other common stock-oriented rewards. However, the current income equivalents which those techniques generate are regarded here, and were presented earlier, as both accurate and appropriate reflections of the pattern of compensation which is in fact realized by executives. Thus, if the price of a firm's common stock on the market should fall sharply, those individuals holding options to purchase that stock have thereby suffered a diminution of their existing economic positions just as surely as if they already owned the shares involved. It therefore is necessary to recognize this decline as well as any subsequent gains in the current income equivalent of an option.[11] Accordingly, the fluctuations in total compensation depicted are real ones, and they identify a trend which could have important implications.

The issue is frequently raised that corporate executives may not be properly responsive to the welfare of their firms' shareholders now that the era of the owner-manager is past. One answer to such a concern is to point out the sizeable amounts of stock in their companies which, as proxy statements record, almost all senior executives in large firms hold. Even though such holdings seldom approach anything like a majority interest, for many men they are likely to represent a large percentage of their *personal* investment portfolios. Therefore, whatever effect on their behavior an ownership position might be thought of as having, it should be just about as strong under these circumstances as it was in the days before the professional manager appeared. The tendency in recent years to design portions of the compensation package around the firm's common stock—and the results of this policy as evidenced by the increasing variability of rewards—reinforces the tie-in of ownership and management. If a man's remuneration each year is highly sensitive to what happens to the price of his firm's stock, his interest in that price and in the economic well-being of his fellow shareholders cannot help but be intensified. The fact that executive compensation now does in part duplicate the consequences of ownership and the extent to which those consequences are felt by the individuals involved is well illustrated by Chart 3.

Composition of the Package: Top Executive

Separation of total after-tax remuneration into its components highlights and further documents the conclusions offered above. Consider first the experience since 1940 of the highest-paid executive in each

[11] That equivalent stream of payments has, as was noted earlier, some built-in smoothing of widely varying stock prices, which helps modify such situations when they do occur.

firm as it is presented in Table 4 and in Charts 5 through 7.[12] From these data, one development very quickly emerges—the traditional salary and bonus payments no longer constitute the bulk of top executives' compensation. Of the total after-tax rewards received by such men during the ten years from 1940 through 1949, 72 per cent was in the form of salary and bonus. In the nine-year interval beginning in 1955, the corresponding figure was only 38 per cent. In fact, for this sample the absolute level of after-tax direct current remuneration has been very little higher since 1955 than it was in either 1940 or the postwar peak year of 1950. This situation coincides with that depicted previously (Chart 2) for the highest-salaried individuals in the same firms. Clearly, corporations have come to rely much more heavily on noncurrent—and less severely taxed—forms of reward for men who are to be compensated at very high levels. The degree to which the emphasis has shifted since the 1940's is nonetheless rather surprising and strongly indicates the inappropriateness of considering only salary and bonus in any discussion of executive rewards.

A second conclusion which the data suggest is also one which, a priori, might not have been anticipated: pensions have become less important in the pay package over the years. From 1940 through 1949 their current income equivalents amounted to 26 per cent of all compensation, but since 1955 the percentage has dropped to 15. It is not that pensions in themselves are less valuable than they used to be; the average annual current equivalents for the two periods are approximately $20,000 and $31,000, respectively. It is rather that stock options, deferred compensation, and profit-sharing plans have grown in value much more rapidly. In relation to after-tax salary and bonus alone, pensions have been somewhat larger in recent years than they were in the 1940's—39 per cent vs. 36 per cent—but the changes in the other major components of the pay package which have taken place over time have appreciably diminished the role which pensions play in the over-all structure of rewards.

The pattern of the current income equivalents over the relevant interval is worth noting. Several peaks in the figures can be detected:

---

[12] In these tabulations, the current income equivalents of deferred compensation and profit-sharing plans are combined in order to reduce the number of categories of compensation that are recorded and make the various tables and charts easier to read. No important conclusions are obscured by this simplification, and it will therefore be maintained in succeeding sections as well.

TABLE 4

Elements of After-Tax Compensation, Top Executives, 1940–63
(dollars)

Year	Total	Salary and Bonus	Pension	Deferred Compensation and Profit-Sharing	Stock Options
1940	101,979	76,517 (75)	25,299 (25)	163 (0)	— (0)
1941	91,535	65,804 (72)	25,424 (28)	209 (0)	98 (0)
1942	65,960	49,627 (75)	16,061 (25)	272 (0)	— (0)
1943	56,467	42,523 (76)	13,675 (24)	269 (0)	— (0)
1944	63,673	41,795 (66)	21,614 (34)	264 (0)	— (0)
1945	61,632	41,221 (67)	20,112 (33)	299 (0)	— (0)
1946	69,043	48,569 (70)	18,951 (28)	1,523 (2)	— (0)
1947	78,317	51,497 (66)	24,150 (31)	2,670 (3)	— (0)
1948	99,756	75,201 (75)	20,883 (21)	2,829 (3)	843 (1)
1949	105,311	78,767 (75)	18,259 (17)	7,242 (7)	1,043 (1)
1950	122,790	79,852 (65)	30,741 (25)	9,755 (8)	2,442 (2)
1951	109,341	74,623 (68)	24,469 (23)	2,238 (2)	8,011 (7)
1952	116,657	71,927 (62)	22,459 (19)	3,755 (3)	18,516 (16)
1953	131,782	73,100 (56)	25,644 (20)	6,975 (5)	26,063 (20)
1954	143,470	78,353 (54)	26,719 (19)	12,610 (9)	25,788 (18)
1955	214,430	79,478 (37)	46,822 (22)	13,514 (6)	74,616 (35)
1956	235,674	81,347 (35)	38,385 (16)	19,425 (8)	96,517 (41)
1957	227,227	80,736 (36)	39,733 (17)	23,507 (10)	83,251 (37)
1958	169,436	80,985 (48)	31,618 (19)	19,488 (11)	37,345 (22)
1959	211,049	82,167 (39)	31,768 (15)	21,749 (10)	75,365 (36)
1960	221,711	80,299 (36)	28,619 (13)	21,546 (10)	91,247 (41)
1961	204,274	80,297 (39)	19,236 (9)	33,922 (17)	70,819 (35)
1962	224,889	79,112 (35)	26,684 (12)	32,265 (14)	86,828 (39)
1963	187,279	83,073 (44)	18,726 (10)	27,398 (15)	58,082 (31)
Averages:					
1940–49	79,367	57,152 (72)	20,443 (26)	1,574 (2)	198 (0)
1955–63	210,663	80,833 (38)	31,288 (15)	23,645 (11)	74,897 (36)

NOTE: Figures in parentheses denote percentages of total each year.

in 1940 and 1941, in 1944 and 1945, in 1950, and in 1955 through 1957. In each case these peaks coincide with a wave either of pension-plan adoptions by the sample corporations or of liberalizations in the benefit formulas of plans already in effect. Thus, in the early 1940's most firms were introducing pensions for the first time. Late in World War II a second major surge of adoptions occurred. This was followed in many companies by two rounds of benefit increases, some of which took the form of adding a second and separate pension plan to the existing one, in the early and middle 1950's. It should be noted that the 1944

CHART 5

*Average After-Tax Compensation Breakdown,
Top Executive, 1940–63*

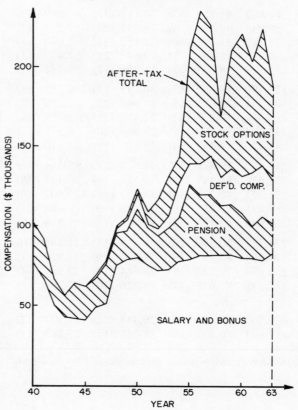

CHART 6

Items of After-Tax Compensation, Top Executive, 1940–63

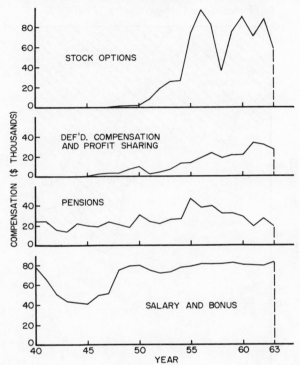

and 1945 pension current equivalent figures appear less significant than they really are in this connection. Just as many of the pensions adopted during those years were reactions to the wartime ceiling on other rewards and to the high tax rates then in effect, so the pensions themselves were less valuable in after-tax terms because of the impact of the same tax rates on the expected postretirement income they would provide.[13] The other concentrations of adoptions and benefit increases took place under less constrained circumstances.

[13] The assumption throughout the computations, it will be recalled, is that the tax rates of the year for which current income equivalents are being determined are expected by the executives under consideration to continue indefinitely. The appropriateness of an assumption of this sort is perhaps most open to question under high wartime tax conditions. The speculations necessary to justify a different set of expectations on the part of the relevant individuals, however, strongly favored maintaining that assumption in every year.

CHART 7

Average After-Tax Compensation Breakdown, Top Executive (Percentage Composition), 1940–63

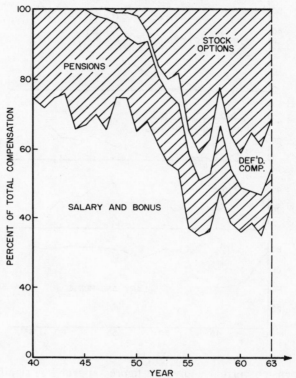

The fact that the resulting pension history is in consequence a series of cycles around a trend rather than a continually rising function is explained by a phenomenon which was pointed out earlier in the numerical example in Chapter 6. If an executive should happen to be awarded a pension for the first time—or should happen to enjoy a substantial increase in the benefits promised him—in a year when he is nearing retirement age, the current income equivalent of that promise is quite large. Therefore, each time we observe a wave of new pension plans or benefit improvements, the older executives in the sample contribute immediately a very sizeable increase to the aggregate pension current equivalent figures. Those executives then retire after several years, and the inclusion of their younger replacements in the sample brings the averages back down again, since the effect of a pension change on the latter's annual current equivalents is not so pronounced.[14] All five top executives taken together present a greater range of ages and circumstances, and the variations over time in the pension figures for that group are somewhat more modest, as we shall see. In any event, while peaks in the pension data are valid symptoms of changes in retirement benefit promises, averages over a span of years are better bases from which to draw conclusions about secular trends.

Table 4 and the accompanying charts make evident the growing significance of deferred compensation, profit-sharing, and stock option plans. For all intents and purposes, none of these devices appeared in the compensation package until after World War II. Even as late as 1951 they accounted for just 9 per cent of the total after-tax annual compensation received by the sample executives. Since 1955, however, they have emerged as major elements in the reward structure, generating fully 47 per cent of the remuneration realized in the final nine years of the study. Stock options alone provided 36 per cent of the total and were, in fact, as important a form of reward as salary and bonus during that period. If we look at Chart 5, it seems fair to conclude that the introduction and expanded utilization of these three instruments were the only real sources of growth in top executive compensation over the last quarter century. Salaries, bonuses, and pension benefits combined just about kept pace with the personal income tax increases experienced since the early 1940's and would alone have done little more than preserve the pre-World War II level of managerial remuneration.

The key attribute of the newer deferred and contingent rewards is, of course, their volatility. This characteristic shows up quite explicitly, especially in Chart 6, when the pay package is dissected, but its implications have already been explored and need not be re-examined. Attention should, however, be called to the fact that we now see that approximately half of the typical top executive's total remuneration in recent years consisted of essentially ownership-oriented rewards. Whatever the behavioral consequences of an ownership attitude may be, they

[14] A similar situation was noted in connection with average salary data.

certainly should be encouraged by a compensation framework weighted this heavily in the direction of such devices. The same weighting also has implications in terms of effective tax progression. Since capital gains rates apply to the income generated by most of these arrangements, it is clear that only a slight majority of the after-tax rewards enjoyed by corporate chief executives nowadays come from sources subject to the high marginal rates of the statutory personal income tax schedule.

Composition of the Package: Top Five Executives

The collective experience of the five highest-paid executives in each firm in the sample is generally similar, as is shown by Table 5 and Charts 8 through 10. Total after-tax compensation grew at about the same rate as in the case of top executives, but current remuneration accounted for a greater share of the growth. This result is consistent with the finding above that the salaries and bonuses of successively lower-ranking individuals increased more rapidly over time (see Charts 1 and 2). Thus, even though the supplements to direct current remuneration introduced in the postwar period have become an important part of every executive's pay package, traditional rewards play a larger role the lower the over-all level of compensation in question.

This pattern is evident in all the computations. The aggregate after-tax remuneration received during the period 1955 through 1963 by the individuals included in Table 5 breaks down as follows:

	Per Cent
Salary and bonus	52
Pension	13
Deferred compensation and profit-sharing	8
Stock options	27

This compares with the corresponding figures for *top* executives:

	Per Cent
Salary and bonus	38
Pension	15
Deferred compensation and profit-sharing	11
Stock options	36

TABLE 5

Elements of After-Tax Compensation, Top Five Executives, 1940–63
(dollars)

Year	Total	Salary and Bonus		Pension		Deferred Compensation and Profit-Sharing		Stock Options	
1940	59,740	51,044	(85)	8,627	(15)	32	(0)	37	(0)
1941	56,885	44,039	(78)	12,732	(22)	41	(0)	73	(0)
1942	44,375	36,390	(82)	7,923	(18)	54	(0)	8	(0)
1943	38,913	31,550	(81)	7,309	(19)	54	(0)	—	(0)
1944	41,873	31,389	(75)	10,432	(25)	52	(0)	—	(0)
1945	41,329	31,580	(77)	9,667	(23)	82	(0)	—	(0)
1946	47,878	38,055	(80)	9,141	(19)	682	(1)	—	(0)
1947	49,989	38,851	(78)	10,455	(21)	680	(1)	3	(0)
1948	67,444	55,636	(83)	10,677	(16)	916	(1)	215	(0)
1949	70,825	57,433	(81)	10,667	(15)	2,476	(4)	249	(0)
1950	79,011	60,266	(76)	14,970	(19)	3,073	(4)	702	(1)
1951	77,316	59,104	(76)	13,943	(18)	1,406	(2)	2,863	(4)
1952	79,450	56,783	(72)	12,826	(16)	2,459	(3)	7,382	(9)
1953	86,181	59,214	(69)	13,993	(16)	3,131	(4)	9,843	(11)
1954	93,076	64,135	(69)	13,519	(15)	5,929	(6)	9,493	(10)
1955	125,204	66,058	(53)	23,274	(18)	5,028	(4)	30,844	(25)
1956	136,960	68,009	(50)	19,045	(14)	8,215	(6)	41,691	(30)
1957	133,315	67,430	(51)	19,807	(15)	9,954	(7)	36,124	(27)
1958	109,335	65,778	(60)	16,964	(15)	8,461	(8)	18,132	(17)
1959	131,247	66,924	(51)	16,583	(13)	11,494	(9)	36,246	(27)
1960	133,249	65,971	(49)	15,447	(12)	11,899	(9)	39,932	(30)
1961	131,361	65,295	(50)	12,944	(10)	16,640	(13)	36,482	(28)
1962	138,754	67,052	(48)	16,112	(12)	12,828	(9)	42,762	(31)
1963	121,039	68,883	(57)	13,922	(11)	12,099	(10)	26,135	(22)
Averages:									
1940–49	51,925	41,597	(80)	9,763	(19)	507	(1)	58	(0)
1955–63	128,940	66,822	(52)	17,122	(13)	10,735	(8)	34,261	(27)

NOTE: Figures in parentheses denote percentages of total each year.

CHART 8

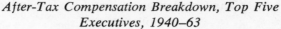

After-Tax Compensation Breakdown, Top Five
Executives, 1940–63

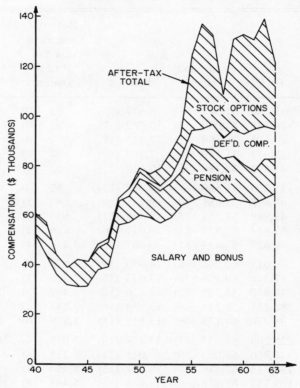

More interesting at the moment, however, is the fact that the same pronounced shift toward ownership-oriented rewards—and away from salary and bonus—has taken place for these men as well. From 1940 to 1949, stock options, deferred compensation, and profit-sharing plans together provided only about 1 per cent of all their after-tax compensation. Pensions supplied 19 per cent, and the remainder was due to salary and bonus.[15] Regardless of which group we choose to consider,

[15] Once again, pensions turn out to have diminished in relative importance over the years, not because of a reduction in their absolute value but because of the more rapid growth of other rewards.

CHART 9

Items of After-Tax Compensation, Top Five Executives, 1940–63

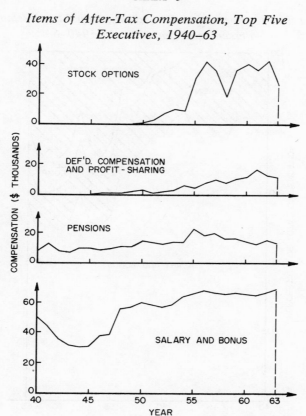

therefore, the historical patterns tell a consistent story. The composition of the pay package has changed significantly over time; it has become more volatile in the process; and its growth in after-tax value is, by and large, a result of innovations in reward.

Before-Tax Current Equivalents

Examination of the before-tax current income equivalents of the various supplements to salary and bonus sharpens these assertions and shows very clearly the impact on executive remuneration of both high ordinary-

CHART 10

After-Tax Compensation Breakdown, Top Five Executives (Percentage Composition), 1940–63

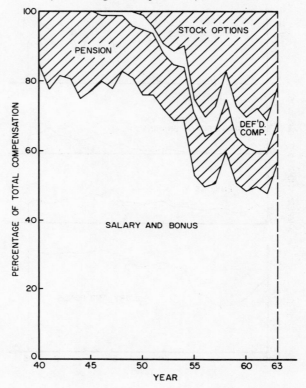

income tax rates and the tax-ameliorating capacity of deferred and contingent arrangements. A computation was made of the amount of before-tax salary and/or bonus that would have been necessary in each year to provide an individual with the level of *total* after-tax income indicated by the averages obtained above for the five executive positions studied. Time series like those constructed for after-tax remuneration were then derived and are presented in Tables 6 and 7 and in Charts 11 through 14.

For example, the question was asked: How much in the way of

TABLE 6

Before-Tax Current Income Equivalents, Top Executives, 1940–63
(dollars)

Year	Salary and Bonus	Pensions	Deferred Compensation and Profit-Sharing	Stock Options	Before-Tax Total
1940	131,364 (65)	69,852 (35)	450 (0)	— (0)	201,666
1941	138,711 (62)	85,518 (38)	703 (0)	330 (0)	225,262
1942	132,679 (53)	113,320 (46)	1,919 (1)	— (0)	247,919
1943	137,631 (38)	217,240 (61)	4,194 (1)	— (0)	359,065
1944	133,399 (27)	348,033 (72)	4,170 (1)	— (0)	485,603
1945	130,063 (28)	321,898 (71)	4,786 (1)	— (0)	456,746
1946	128,263 (47)	134,431 (49)	10,804 (4)	— (0)	273,497
1947	140,486 (42)	174,928 (52)	19,340 (6)	— (0)	334,754
1948	147,436 (58)	91,298 (36)	12,368 (5)	3,681 (1)	254,783
1949	157,589 (56)	82,817 (30)	32,847 (12)	4,731 (2)	277,984
1950	145,900 (43)	139,897 (41)	44,393 (13)	11,113 (3)	341,304
1951	158,164 (33)	226,915 (47)	20,754 (4)	74,281 (16)	480,115
1952	164,667 (25)	248,516 (38)	41,550 (6)	204,885 (31)	659,618
1953	168,893 (20)	294,087 (35)	80,001 (9)	298,892 (36)	841,874
1954	170,712 (20)	275,356 (33)	129,954 (15)	265,761 (32)	841,784
1955	174,647 (11)	503,084 (31)	145,192 (9)	801,719 (49)	1,624,642
1956	181,182 (10)	415,434 (22)	210,233 (11)	1,044,585 (57)	1,851,434
1957	179,045 (10)	428,970 (24)	253,800 (15)	898,814 (51)	1,760,629
1958	179,916 (16)	335,063 (30)	206,519 (18)	395,764 (36)	1,117,262
1959	184,053 (12)	342,546 (22)	234,514 (15)	812,640 (51)	1,573,752
1960	177,517 (10)	308,421 (18)	232,197 (14)	983,349 (58)	1,701,484
1961	177,510 (12)	206,397 (14)	363,963 (24)	759,868 (50)	1,507,738
1962	173,367 (10)	287,262 (16)	348,162 (20)	934,732 (54)	1,743,523
1963	187,517 (14)	200,740 (15)	293,713 (23)	622,630 (48)	1,304,599
Average: 1955–63	179,417 (12)	336,435 (21)	254,255 (16)	806,011 (51)	1,576,118

NOTE: Figures in parentheses denote percentages of total each year.

before-tax salary and bonus would have been required in 1963 to generate for an individual the $187,279 in aggregate after-tax compensation that was, on average, enjoyed by the highest-paid executive in each sample company? The difference between that figure and the actual (average) before-tax salary and bonus received by such executives

TABLE 7

Before-Tax Current Income Equivalents, Top Five Executives,
1940–63
(dollars)

Year	Salary and Bonus	Pensions	Deferred Compensation and Profit-Sharing	Stock Options	Before-Tax Total
1940	77,072 (78)	21,832 (22)	90 (0)	78 (0)	99,072
1941	82,750 (67)	40,550 (33)	140 (0)	223 (0)	123,664
1942	81,923 (63)	47,537 (37)	383 (0)	34 (0)	129,879
1943	81,066 (48)	86,916 (52)	838 (0)	0 (0)	168,821
1944	80,111 (37)	134,976 (63)	834 (0)	0 (0)	215,922
1945	80,630 (39)	123,361 (60)	1,182 (1)	0 (0)	205,174
1946	87,143 (58)	57,366 (39)	4,465 (3)	0 (0)	148,974
1947	90,160 (55)	67,824 (42)	4,719 (3)	17 (0)	162,722
1948	98,016 (70)	37,079 (27)	3,530 (2)	864 (1)	139,491
1949	102,569 (68)	37,507 (25)	9,893 (6)	1,065 (1)	151,035
1950	101,070 (59)	54,211 (32)	12,384 (7)	2,839 (2)	170,505
1951	113,088 (48)	92,702 (39)	9,600 (4)	21,436 (9)	236,828
1952	117,224 (38)	103,749 (34)	21,176 (7)	65,353 (21)	307,503
1953	124,485 (33)	122,756 (33)	29,577 (8)	95,522 (26)	372,340
1954	127,149 (34)	108,787 (29)	49,687 (14)	83,348 (23)	368,972
1955	132,775 (19)	217,905 (31)	49,699 (7)	297,243 (43)	697,624
1956	138,621 (17)	184,300 (23)	82,651 (10)	409,258 (50)	814,831
1957	136,818 (18)	189,802 (24)	98,946 (13)	353,423 (45)	778,991
1958	132,146 (25)	151,226 (29)	79,590 (15)	162,638 (31)	525,601
1959	135,540 (18)	157,437 (21)	112,345 (15)	353,982 (46)	759,305
1960	132,894 (17)	145,169 (19)	112,644 (14)	392,779 (50)	783,488
1961	130,692 (17)	120,426 (16)	162,271 (21)	349,496 (46)	762,885
1962	135,751 (16)	151,964 (18)	127,237 (15)	426,156 (51)	841,109
1963	141,779 (22)	125,696 (20)	116,719 (18)	257,667 (40)	641,863
Average: 1955–63	135,224 (18)	160,436 (22)	104,678 (14)	333,627 (46)	733,966

NOTE: Figures in parentheses denote percentages of total each year.

represents the combined before-tax current income equivalent of their
deferred and contingent rewards, and can be apportioned among pensions, stock options, and deferred compensation according to the procedure outlined in Chapter 6. These calculations were made for each

year and for all five top executive positions. As before, the stock option
data are smoothed over the period 1955–63 in the charts in order to
aid the identification of trends.

We see from Chart 11 that the time pattern of the before-tax current
equivalents resembles that of total after-tax compensation (Chart 4)
but that each change in the figures is accentuated because of the impact
of progressive tax rates. In 1940 the typical top executive's entire compensation package was worth to him, in terms of pretax salary, $201,-
700. For the top five as a group, the figure was $99,000. By 1955, and
continuing thereafter through 1963, these values had increased to ap-

CHART 11

*Average Total Before-Tax Compensation (Stock Option Data
Smoothed), 1940–63*

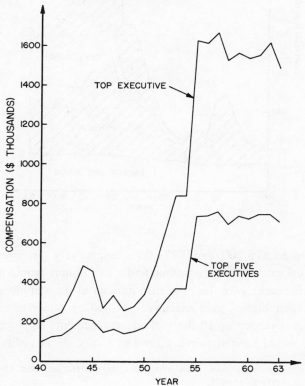

CHART 12

Average Before-Tax Compensation Breakdown, Top Executive, 1940–63

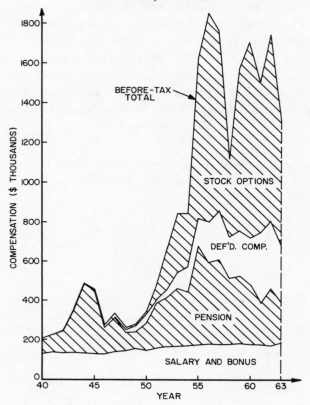

proximately $1,576,000 and $734,000, respectively. In effect, a per capita annual salary of over a million and a half dollars would have been necessary in recent years had the corporations in the sample attempted to reward their highest-paid executives as well by salary alone as they were in fact rewarded by all the various arrangements employed.[16] This alternative would have required a level of salary about eight times the

---

[16] Stock options themselves were worth the equivalent of over $800,000 per year in pretax salary payments.

CHART 13

Average Before-Tax Compensation Breakdown, Top Five Executives, 1940–63

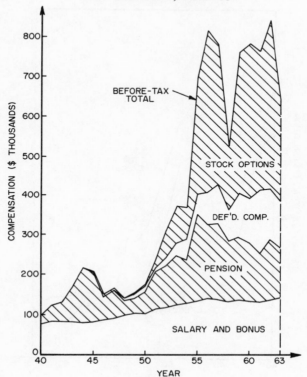

amount actually paid. In the case of the five highest-paid men together, the figure is approximately five times actual salary.[17]

The greater significance of deferred and contingent rewards for top executives as compared with the average for the top five shows up again in these before-tax computations. Actual salary and bonus constitute only about 12 per cent of the before-tax total calculated for the

---

[17] It should be pointed out that if the lower personal tax rate schedule adopted by Congress in 1964 were the applicable one, somewhat smaller total before-tax payments would generate the same levels of after-tax reward. As an offset, of course, the after-tax figures themselves would be higher to begin with for the same reason.

CHART 14

Average Before-Tax Compensation Breakdown: Salary and
Bonus as a Percentage of all Compensation, 1940–63

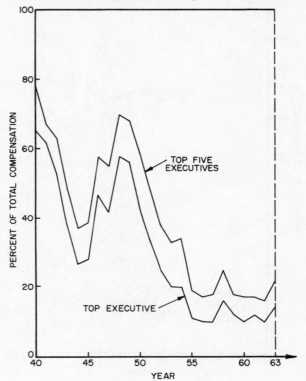

years 1955 through 1963 for the highest-paid man in each firm, but
come to 18 per cent for all five combined.

In certain respects other than in their volatility, however, the behavior of the before-tax current equivalents over time does differ from
that of their after-tax counterparts. The large jump in compensation in
1955 and the maintenance of the new level are again observed, but the
World War II and Korean war years do not follow the previous pattern. The before-tax current equivalent of the total pay package in
both periods rises—and, as it turns out, for the same reason that the
after-tax figures fell. Even though after-tax compensation declined under

the press of higher tax rates, those tax rates also created a situation in which the amount of salary that would have been necessary to substitute for the relevant noncurrent rewards went up even more. In 1944 and 1945, for example, the wave of pension plan adoptions mentioned above did not generate as much in the way of equivalent after-tax earnings as it would have in the presence of lower taxes, but the results *were* sufficient to cause the before-tax equivalents of all pensions to triple within the space of two years, thereby raising significantly the before-tax current income value of the whole package. The same phenomenon recurs during the Korean war, the impetus in that instance coming primarily from increases in stock option, deferred compensation, and profit-sharing benefits.

These computations point up very dramatically the extent to which the introduction of new types of compensation subject to less severe tax treatment has allowed the heavy burden on direct current payments to be circumvented by corporations. Clearly, had such arrangements not been available, the extremely high salary levels required to duplicate the remuneration thereby provided would not have been forthcoming. Executives, in consequence, would not have been anywhere near as well rewarded as they actually were. If we want to speak of the "impact" of taxes on the compensation of top corporate executives, then, the before-tax current equivalent time series derived here permit two significant— and hitherto undocumented—conclusions: (1) had they been applied to all forms of reward, the steeply progressive personal tax rates of the post-World War II period would almost certainly have prevented any substantial growth in after-tax executive remuneration since 1940; and (2) the tax "loopholes" which pensions, stock options, and other deferred and contingent rewards represent have made possible levels of compensation that in recent years were equivalent in value to salary and bonus payments five to eight times as large as those actually paid.

Summary and Comments

The average annual before-tax salaries and bonuses associated with the five highest-paid executive positions in the nation's largest manufacturing corporations have increased by 83 per cent over the last quarter century. For the top executive in each firm alone, the increase amounted to 53 per cent. Because of a rise in personal tax rates during the same interval, however, the corresponding after-tax increments come to only 33 and 13 per cent, respectively. As might be anticipated, a more favorable historical pattern emerges when the values of the major supplements to direct current remuneration are included in the comparisons. The *total* after-tax compensation of the executives in the sample has approximately doubled since 1940, implying a compound rate of growth of slightly in excess of 3 per cent per annum. The latter figure, while a substantial improvement on the 1 per cent or so suggested by after-tax salaries and bonuses, is still quite modest.

The growth in compensation levels which did occur was confined entirely to the ten years immediately following World War II. From 1940 to 1945 total after-tax top executive pay declined steadily, and since 1955 has exhibited no appeciable upward trend. Significantly, virtually all the observed increase in earnings is attributable to the introduction of new forms of reward rather than to an expanded utilization of traditional ones. Stock options in particular have been a key item, providing between 25 and 40 per cent of observed aggregate after-tax remuneration over the last decade. The importance of developing techniques for evaluating all the components of the pay package is underscored by these findings. Salary and bonus alone are no longer sufficient guides to executives' compensation circumstances. In fact, in terms of before-tax current income equivalents, other devices have been worth from four to seven times as much as actual salary and bonus in recent years.

A concomitant of this shift in emphasis away from direct current remuneration has been an increase in the year-to-year variability of the value of the compensation package. Since many of the newer rewards utilize shares of the employer corporation's common stock as the compensation medium, changes in market prices have come to exert a strong influence on top executives' earnings. It is not unlikely, therefore, that a greater degree of managerial identification with shareholder interests has been encouraged by these arrangements—a result which prevailing sentiment would applaud.

The substantial increase in personal income tax rates experienced since 1940 has not only contributed to the slow rate of growth of top executives' after-tax rewards but has obviously provided much of the impetus for the wider use of the other compensation instruments described. Stock options, profit-sharing plans, pensions, and deferred-pay contracts have all been accorded differentially better tax treatment than salary and bonus, and the discovery that they have relegated the latter to a less important compensatory role than in the past is not surprising. What is surprising, however, is the degree to which this has occurred. Nowadays, salary and bonus are not merely less important rewards than before, they are actually minority components of the total pay package for most top executives. It seems fair to conclude that part of this change must have resulted from the favorable stock market conditions of the 1950's and early 1960's rather than from tax considerations alone. Deferred and contingent compensation arrangements would have been much less attractive, and almost certainly have been relied on much less heavily, had they not held out the possibility of very large profits as well as very low taxes. This suggests that if the stock market experience of the last ten or fifteen years is considered unlikely to continue, some revival of direct cash payments can be expected in the near future. A similar line of reasoning also suggests that the same stock market conditions may be at least partially responsible for the lack of growth in salaries and bonuses observed since 1955. The large profits realized by executives from options and other stock-based instruments could well have made increases in direct payments unnecessary in many firms because the levels of reward desired for top management were being attained without those increases.

A second possible explanation for the recent popularity of supplements to current remuneration is their comparative obscurity. While salary and bonus awards to executives are easily understood and can readily be appraised by shareholders when reported on in a firm's proxy statements, the same is not true of other compensation arrangements. By their nature they require for understanding both an informed and a persistent analysis from year to year. Few shareholders are equipped for such an effort, and even fewer are likely to be inclined to pursue it. Thus, a firm that wanted to reward its top executives handsomely but preferred not to advertise the fact might well seek to do so in large part by means other than salary and bonus. The extent to which a desire for concealment is a factor in corporate compensation policy is, of course, pure speculation here. Nonetheless, since the opportunity to conceal does exist, it would be surprising if it were not taken advantage of somewhere along the line.[18]

Finally, a careful approach to financial planning would, in many cases, logically result in a decision to utilize certain deferred and contingent rewards more extensively. For a given level of executive remuneration, it may simply be cheaper from the corporation's standpoint to grant a stock option, for example, than a salary increase. Or, because group annuity contract premium rates are lower than those on individual policies, a company can probably provide retirement income for its employees at a lower cost than that involved in raising their wages and salaries enough to let them make equivalent arrangements on their own. Liquidity constraints could be persuasive in leading certain firms to prefer the postponement of payments permitted by a deferred compensation plan to the immediate cash drain of a salary increase.[19] In short, for any one of several good reasons, it may be more efficient for a firm to utilize forms of reward other than salary and bonus rather extensively. The availability of a wide range of alternative instruments in the postwar period and the concurrent development of improved techniques of financial management could very well have encouraged the sort of restructuring of the executive pay package observed above.[20]

The evidence presented here, then, provides a comprehensive historical profile of the size and composition of the remuneration accruing to top executives in large manufacturing firms. It is hoped that the data generated are not only valuable in themselves but will contribute to further research in this area by casting up the compensation transaction in a way that allows more meaningful statements about its development and characteristics than have previously been possible.

[18] On the other hand, it must be pointed out that it is also possible that subterfuge of the kind darkly—and perhaps unfairly—hinted at here may be discouraged in some cases by its very effectiveness. If the executives who are to be the beneficiaries of such a policy do not themselves fully understand or appreciate the value of the various supplements to salary they are to be awarded, there is little to be gained by the employer corporation in attempting to trade off such rewards against salary in the compensation package.

[19] Of course, the executives involved—particularly younger ones—may have liquidity constraints of their own which create counterpressures in this respect. For the individuals in the current sample, however, this is not apt to be a problem.

[20] In connection with this possibility, the costs of various deferred and contingent compensation arrangements are compared with the costs of their current income equivalents in some detail in Appendix M.

9

HISTORICAL COMPARISONS

A fuller appreciation of the data described in Chapter 8 can be obtained by comparing those time series with the changes that have taken place during the same interval in the surrounding economy. Three standards of comparison in particular appear relevant: increases in the earnings of certain other occupational groups; changes in the prices of the goods and services which executives as consumers confront; and the growth of the corporations which employ the executives.

The Employer Companies

While it may, in general, seem reasonable to believe that the remuneration associated with a given position in a firm should be expected to increase as the firm grows in size and profitability, the rationale for postulating such a relationship depends on some very specific assumptions about the nature of the organization in question. A corporation should be willing to increase the compensation of one of its employees only if his value to the firm—his "marginal revenue product"—rises over time.[1] Were it possible to measure the actual contributions to output of the executives who comprise the sample studied here, a comparison of the resulting rates of growth with the secular increases in earnings outlined above would tell us very quickly whether those earnings have kept pace since the early 1940's. Because the desired figures cannot be obtained directly, however, it is necessary to attempt to estimate the pattern of changes in them from some more visible index of the rate

[1] That is, if the addition of one extra unit of labor input to the firm's production process results in an increase in output, in physical terms, equal to Δx units, which can then be sold at a price (P_x) per unit, the owners of the firm can afford to pay up to the amount $P_x \Delta x$ (its marginal revenue product) for that input.

of growth of the corporations examined: the growth in their sales, assets, or profits, for example. This, of course, is an appropriate alternative only if a case can be made for the proposition that an expansion in the scale of a firm's activities implies a roughly proportionate increase in the productive contributions of each of its senior officers. On that basis, a historical comparison of top executive pay and employer-company size would be meaningful.[2]

As it happens, two considerations offer at least some support for the validity of such an assumption. One is the nature of the services rendered by the individuals whose compensation is at issue. Since it is possible as a firm grows larger for it to add correspondingly to its labor force, it would obviously be improper to contend that the scope—and the impact on profits—of the tasks performed by most of its employees will also increase in proportion. The firm can simply hire more workers for many of its various job categories, and a particular individual's responsibilities may undergo very little change. Top executive functions, on the other hand, are rather less easily shared. A corporation can have only one chief executive, one chief financial officer, one general counsel, regardless of its size. Their distinctive policy-making and over-all administrative responsibilities cannot really be delegated, even though certain details of their day-to-day activities may be.[3] As a company expands, therefore, it is not unlikely that the marginal revenue products of individuals at the level with which the empirical analysis here is concerned may increase at approximately the same rate.

A second factor is the role that inflation has played in generating the historical patterns we observe. To the extent that firms appear to grow larger over time merely because the price level in the community rises, the current-dollar value of the productive contributions of their employees should grow in proportion. If, for example, nothing about a corporation's selling or production activities changes during a particular interval except that the product and factor prices associated therewith increase by a given percentage, the marginal revenue products attrib-

[2] Only in terms of *rates* of growth, however. It is clearly not possible to compare absolute magnitudes.

[3] Indeed, the inability to delegate the key top executive functions is one of the explanations frequently given by economists for asserting that the long-run cost curves of a firm should be expected to rise eventually as it increases in size.

utable to each input employed will increase by that same percentage when measured—as they are here—in current dollars. Insofar as a broad rise in prices has been an element in the apparent expansion of the firms in the sample, then, it is appropriate to use the indicated company rates of growth as estimates of the rates of growth in the value of their top executives' services.

Neither of these arguments, of course, is conclusive, and the link between the historical trends which is hypothesized cannot be more than speculation at this point for lack of an adequate empirical test. In fact, the further issue as to *which* measure of the secular increase in employer-company size is the most suitable proxy for marginal revenue product growth rates remains open, i.e., should a senior officer's value to his firm be expected to grow in proportion to its assets, its sales, its profits, or yet another characteristic of its circumstances? Fortunately, it is not necessary in the present context to attempt to settle the issue. The compensation of the executives in the sample studied has grown substantially less rapidly during the last quarter century than *any* of the observable attributes of the companies they worked for. Whatever our choice of criteria, therefore, the answer we get is unambiguous.

Table 8 lists, for each year from 1940 through 1963, the aggregate figures for the fifty employer companies in six categories of data: total assets, net worth, sales, profits before taxes, profits after taxes, and the total market value of their common stock.[4] When the implied compound annual rates of growth in each of these items are compared with the rates of growth suggested by the compensation time series derived in Chapter 8, the outcome is as shown in the tabulation on page 160. A significant "lag" in remuneration is clearly evident, even when the value of the major supplements to salary and bonus is taken into account.

To the extent, then, that executive marginal revenue product growth rates are similar to those of the various corporate characteristics tabulated, our conclusion must be that compensation has been falling behind since the early 1940's. The explanation may lie simply in higher

[4] The figures were obtained from *Moody's Industrials* and incorporate the results of all mergers and acquisitions during the period.

Total market value was defined for the individual firm as the mean of the high and low prices observed in each year for its stock multiplied by the mean number of shares it had outstanding in that year.

	Annual Growth Rate 1940–1963 (per cent)
Company parameters:	
Assets	7.0
Net worth	6.8
Sales	9.1
Profits before taxes	9.1
Profits after taxes	8.1
Equity market value	10.2
Top executive rewards:	
Before-tax salary and bonus	1.8
After-tax salary and bonus	0.5
Total after-tax compensation	3.2 [a]
Top five executives' rewards:	
Before-tax salary and bonus	2.5
After-tax salary and bonus	1.3
Total after-tax compensation	3.3 [a]

[a] Computed using average compensation for the years 1955 through 1963 as the 1963 figure. See Chapter 8 for the rationale.

personal tax rates, which have not been entirely undone by the use of deferred and contingent rewards,[5] or it may in part be traceable to imperfections in the market for managerial services. Certainly it would not be difficult to identify some possible sources of imperfection. The compensation bargains struck between a large corporation and its top executives may well be subject to so many external pressures (like those generated by the necessity to report the dimensions of the bargain in proxy statements, for instance), may be influenced so much by internal organizational considerations, and may suffer so heavily from a lack of accurate information as to the actual value of the services being purchased that what we might like to think of as the more objective underlying market forces suggested by the theory of the firm in its

[5] It is worth noting that if, despite tax increases, the aggregate after-tax remuneration of top executives *had* grown as rapidly as our best estimate of their marginal revenue products, we might conclude that corporations had been able to "shift" the burden of those taxes to others in the community—either by passing on the cost of higher compensation outlays directly through product price increases or lower profits or by adopting forms of reward which are available only to executives and which enjoy favorable tax treatment, thereby indirectly redistributing the community's total tax bill.

TABLE 8

Characteristics of the Sample Corporations, 1940–63
(million dollars)

Year	Assets	Net Worth	Sales	Before-Tax Profits	After-Tax Profits	Market Value of Equity
1940	16,261	13,283	12,567	1,607	1,085	12,030
1941	18,215	13,786	17,313	2,738	1,251	11,391
1942	19,650	14,315	21,411	2,672	1,020	10,251
1943	20,841	14,830	27,891	3,148	1,063	12,850
1944	21,235	15,057	30,220	3,013	1,143	13,978
1945	20,007	15,522	26,371	2,063	1,159	16,343
1946	20,966	16,692	20,894	1,666	1,267	17,881
1947	24,444	18,935	29,848	3,280	2,031	16,978
1948	27,900	21,598	35,589	4,489	2,780	16,913
1949	28,156	22,891	35,610	4,436	2,794	19,215
1950	31,200	24,393	41,786	6,817	3,557	23,634
1951	35,655	26,897	48,884	7,596	3,088	31,025
1952	38,688	30,061	51,810	6,584	3,013	31,002
1953	41,596	32,065	59,850	7,656	3,417	32,618
1954	43,480	34,768	57,551	7,161	3,888	43,765
1955	48,171	38,609	65,850	9,519	5,009	63,203
1956	53,060	42,629	69,218	8,778	4,816	71,940
1957	57,443	46,298	74,667	9,150	5,091	70,917
1958	60,184	49,650	70,373	7,549	4,344	77,889
1959	63,601	51,420	76,442	8,879	4,909	97,839
1960	66,644	54,212	79,733	9,196	5,058	94,148
1961	71,022	57,694	79,717	9,047	5,116	108,689
1962	74,001	60,003	87,896	10,579	5,908	98,810
1963	77,758	62,545	93,759	11,923	6,552	112,951

traditional form are seldom reflected in the figures we observe. In fact, the situation in question may be close enough to that of bilateral monopoly that we should not expect even in theory a result approaching the purely competitive solution to emerge.[6]

An equally plausible interpretation of the data, however, would be

[6] Especially since the individuals involved are often on *both* sides of the bargaining table.

that employer-company and executive marginal-product rates of growth are quite unconnected and that the comparison with compensation presented is merely a curiosity devoid of analytical content. Given this possibility, it does not appear very fruitful to speculate further here on the probable causes of what may be a completely irrelevant phenomenon. Nonetheless, because there is at least some chance that a valid relationship does exist, and because the lag in earnings growth that this would imply is so pronounced, the comparison seems worth calling attention to.[7]

Professional Incomes

Increases in the earnings of other important occupational groups over the last quarter century provide a second set of standards by which to appraise the observed rates of growth in compensation. Have executives done as well in their chosen field as they might have had they decided instead to channel their energies in other directions? The most logical approach to that question would seem to be by posing as the relevant vocational alternatives lines of endeavor which require a generally similar level of education and professional skill and which might reasonably have been thought of as attractive possibilities by individuals who in fact became executives. By that test, secular changes in the earnings of physicians, lawyers, and dentists appear to be appropriate criteria.

It should be emphasized, however, that if executive incomes turn out to have grown less rapidly than those in the indicated occupations— as we shall see *is,* in fact, the case—our interpretation of such a development must be carefully phrased. The argument which is usually presented by persons concerned with the possibility that managerial rewards are not all they might be runs as follows: [8] The proper administration of the resources which executives in their capacity as stewards of shareholder interests control depends on a continuing supply of talented and energetic individuals to the ranks of management. If the

---

[7] It should also be pointed out that the indicated lag, if real, might be eminently desirable in terms of resource allocation. It is possible that executives were earning *too much* in 1940, and we may simply have witnessed the restoration of more sensible levels of remuneration in recent years.

[8] U.S. Joint Committee on the Economic Report, *Federal Tax Policy for Economic Growth,* pp. 137–164.

rewards such individuals can expect are no longer sufficient to induce them to become executives, the performance of our economy will eventually suffer.

Arguments of this sort are valid, of course, only if it is also established that one or the other of the markets which determine the compensation received in different occupations is functioning improperly and therefore causing any redirection of talent to be a misallocation. There would be nothing wrong, for example, with more bright young men deciding to become doctors instead of businessmen because of a change in relative earnings possibilities, if that change were the result of a market mechanism which efficiently matched compensation with productive contribution in each activity. Indeed, if the market's decisions are to be respected, there *should* be an increasing supply of doctors under those circumstances, and the economy would not suffer in any meaningful sense.

While the discussion in the preceding section raised the possibility that the compensation of top executives may not have increased as rapidly since 1940 as their marginal revenue products—and that there is likely to be considerable friction in the market for managerial services—the same may be true of other professions. There is also reason to suspect that, even if all the relevant markets were operating smoothly, the results generated would not necessarily fully reflect the value of the several occupations being compared. The benefits to society of having an adequate number of doctors, lawyers, and dentists may not be accurately measured solely by the incomes those individuals stand to receive from the pursuit of their professions. A similar argument could be made for executives who, by their decisions, create employment for others and promote economic growth. Left to its own devices, therefore, the private market's perceptions of value might not be a reliable guide to the appropriateness of earnings in various occupations, and the community as a whole might logically decide to subsidize one or the other as a matter of policy in order to bring about a result in which its *collective* preferences were given expression. Judgments about the possible undesirability of historical trends in income must therefore confront this issue as well as that of market imperfections.

The only conclusion, then, that can legitimately be drawn here from such trends is that if, for whatever reason, the compensation of top executives has grown less rapidly over the years than have earnings in other leading professions, the relative attractiveness of those professions will have increased and there should be a movement toward them and away from management by men who are now starting their careers. While there are obviously a wide range of nonpecuniary considerations on which job choices are based, this movement should occur if those considerations have remained fairly stable over time and if income opportunities are taken into account at all in career decisions. The latter assumption at least seems a reasonable one.

Despite its limitations, the information which is available about the incomes of physicians, lawyers, and dentists strongly suggests that all three groups have indeed experienced a more substantial increase in pay since the early 1940's than have senior corporate executives. Physicians and dentists, in particular, have done very well by comparison. The data are summarized in Table 9.

The first, fifth, and eight columns present the results of a series of surveys of the incomes of selected professional occupations conducted by the Department of Commerce and reported on in its *Survey of Current Business*.[9] The figures denote the mean income of nonsalaried lawyers, physicians, and dentists (net of all business expenses but prior to personal income tax payments) as determined from a sample selected by the National Income Division of the Office of Business Economics. Because the last such survey was conducted in 1956, the data in the case of lawyers end in 1954 and for physicians and dentists in 1951.

The figures in the second, sixth, and ninth columns of Table 9 were obtained from reports of the Bureau of the Census.[10] They represent the median income in 1949 and 1959, respectively, of those individuals in the "experienced civilian labor force" who were classified as (1) physicians and surgeons, (2) lawyers and judges, and (3) dentists. Corresponding figures for prior years are not available, since the 1940

9 In August 1949, pp. 18–24; January 1950, pp. 8–16; July 1950, p. 4; July 1951, pp. 9–26; July 1952, pp. 5–7; and December 1956, pp. 26–35.

10 U.S. Bureau of the Census, *U.S. Census of Population: 1950, Volume IV, Special Reports,* Part I, Chapter B, "Occupational Characteristics," Table 19, Washington, 1956, and *U.S. Census of Population: 1960, Subject Reports,* "Occupational Characteristics," Final Report PC(2)-7A, Table 25, Washington, 1963.

TABLE 9

Average Incomes of Physicians, Lawyers, and Dentists, 1940–62

(dollars)

Year	Physicians				Lawyers			Dentists		
	SCB	Census	Med. Econ.	IRS	SCB	Census	IRS	SCB	Census	IRS
1940	4,441	—	—	—	4,507	—	—	3,314	—	—
1941	5,047	—	—	—	4,794	—	—	3,782	—	—
1942	6,735	—	—	—	5,527	—	—	4,625	—	—
1943	8,370	—	9,186	—	5,945	—	—	5,715	—	—
1944	9,802	—	—	—	6,504	—	—	6,649	—	—
1945	10,975	—	—	—	6,861	—	—	6,922	—	—
1946	10,202	—	—	—	6,951	—	—	6,381	—	—
1947	10,726	—	11,300	—	7,437	—	—	6,610	—	—
1948	11,327	—	—	—	8,003	—	—	7,039	—	—
1949	11,744	8,302	—	—	7,971	6,284	—	7,146	6,448	—
1950	12,324	—	—	—	8,349	—	—	7,436	—	—
1951	13,432	—	15,262	—	8,855	—	—	7,820	—	—
1952	—	—	—	—	9,021	—	—	—	—	—
1953	—	—	—	—	9,392	—	—	—	—	—
1954	—	—	18,122	—	10,258	—	—	—	—	—
1955	—	—	—	—	—	—	—	—	—	—
1959	—	15,013	23,888	19,099	—	11,261	11,246	—	12,392	11,385
1960	—	—	—	19,522	—	—	11,373	—	—	11,873
1961	—	—	—	20,222	—	—	12,513	—	—	12,594
1962	—	—	—	21,354	—	—	12,689	—	—	13,710

NOTE: SCB denotes *Survey of Current Business* data; Med. Econ. denotes *Medical Economics* data; IRS denotes Internal Revenue Service data. All figures are mean values except the Census data, which are medians.

and earlier Census data do not provide the same sort of breakdown of income by occupations.

The third column tabulates the findings of a continuing survey by the journal *Medical Economics* as reported in the *Industrial and Labor Relations Review*.[11] The figures once again refer to the mean income of a sample of nonsalaried physicians, but only individuals under sixty-five years of age are included therein.

Finally, the fourth, seventh, and tenth columns are derived from data which have recently begun to be published by the Internal Revenue Service in its *Statistics of Income* series. A breakdown of proprietorship and partnership income receipts by occupational categories, among them physicians and surgeons, dentists, and lawyers, is now available.[12] From these figures it is possible to compute the average earnings of all individuals engaged in private practice in the three professions in each year.[13] This, on a much larger scale, is the same sort of "nonsalaried" group to which the *Survey of Current Business* samples apply. Because the IRS figures allow proprietorships and partnerships reporting net profits to be separated from those having net losses, the former are singled out here as best suited to comparisons with executives, and the averages presented refer only to such individuals.

The difficulty with all these data is, of course, the fact that no one set of figures covers the full range of years in which we are interested. A variety of other sources periodically provides similar information, but each draws on its own particular sample and each presents the same problem. It is necessary, therefore, to superimpose several of the tabulations in order to complete a story which can be compared with the compensation experience of executives.

This will be a legitimate procedure if we can assume that the distribu-

[11] Elton Rayack, "The Supply of Physicians' Services," *ILRR*, January 1964, pp. 221–237.

[12] U.S. Treasury Department, Internal Revenue Service, *Statistics of Income, Business Tax Returns*.

[13] Data which permit accurate computations exist only from 1959 on, however, and the 1963 figures were not yet available at the time of this writing. A useful supplement to the IRS tabulations is research note #13-1965 of the U.S. Department of Health, Education, and Welfare, Social Security Administration, Division of Research and Statistics, entitled *Incomes of Physicians and Dentists from Private Self-Employment Practice: 1960–1962*, Washington, 1965.

tion of incomes within the three professional groups indicated has not changed significantly over the last quarter century. Should that be the case, virtually any sample from among each group which is chosen on a consistent basis from one year to the next will produce a time series for earnings that will closely approximate the rate of growth of the average—whether mean or median—for the whole profession. In consequence, the stringing together of *successive* time series segments, derived from different samples in different periods, will be appropriate to construct a longer historical record, since it is only growth rates and not absolute levels of earnings that are our concern. Strong support for such a solution can be found in the *Survey of Current Business* studies just cited. The relative income distributions (the so-called "Lorenz curves") for all three professions at issue were found to have changed very little over the period for which data were collected by the Department of Commerce.[14] On that evidence, and for lack of an alternative, a sequential approach to estimating earnings increases *will* be undertaken.

The procedure is as follows: The *Survey of Current Business* figures are chosen as the basis for the historical record beginning in 1940. Because these compilations end in the early 1950's, the rate of growth in average professional incomes between 1949 and 1959 will be approximated from the change in the numbers reported by the Bureau of the Census in those two years. For example, the *SCB* survey indicates that the average income of physicians in 1949 was $11,744. According to Census data, the 1959 figure for such individuals was 1.808 times its 1949 value.[15] At that rate of increase, the *SCB* average would have risen to $21,237 by 1959. Similar projections can be made for dentists and lawyers, and the patterns of growth from 1959 on can be derived from the secular changes in the *Statistics of Income* figures. The result (see Table 10) is three time series which—albeit with a few gaps— in effect predict what would have been the outcome of the *SCB* survey had it been conducted in every year from 1940 through 1962. Given

[14] *Survey of Current Business,* January 1950, p. 10; July 1951, p. 12; and December 1956, p. 27.
[15] That is, an increase from a median income of $8,302 to one of $15,013 (see Table 9).

no substantial change in intraprofessional income distributions over time,[16] these series should constitute fairly accurate indexes of the "true" rates of growth in the before-tax earnings of the several professions. Even if they are only rough approximations, the evidence that executives have lost ground relative to the income from these occupations turns out to be sufficiently compelling that considerable errors in the estimates can be tolerated without endangering that conclusion.

The corresponding—and, for comparisons, more relevant—after-tax figures present an additional problem. They depend not simply on the rate of increase but on the magnitude of before-tax earnings. In that connection, it does not seem reasonable to offer the averages compiled in Table 10 as meaningful benchmarks for an appraisal of the time pattern of senior executives' rewards. The same talents and energies which enabled these individuals to reach the top of their chosen field would very likely have produced a similar result in other vocations. Accordingly, the earnings of, say, the top 1 per cent or so of the nation's physicians, lawyers, and dentists might be more appropriate criteria in the present context. As long as the Lorenz curves for the various professions retain their shapes over time, the rates of growth of before-tax earnings for such men will match those of the averages for their contemporaries, but the same will not be true after taxes. In particular, the graduated personal income tax will cause the observed after-tax increases to be less the higher the level of pretax income in question. It would be misleading, therefore, to compute tax liabilities on the basis of the data in Table 10, since this would tend to overstate after-tax growth rates vis-à-vis top executives.

Unfortunately, information of the sort which would permit us to identify the earnings of the most successful individuals in each activity is not available, and it is necessary to attempt to remove the indicated bias in some indirect manner. One possible approach would be to "factor up" the figures derived above by assuming that the average before-tax

---

[16] An assumption which is reinforced when the *Medical Economics* figures listed in the third column of Table 9 are used as a check on the indicated estimate of the 1959 average income of physicians. The values for 1951 and 1959 from that source were $15,262 and $23,888, respectively—a gain of 56.5 per cent in eight years. If the 1951 *SCB* figure of $13,432 is projected to 1959 on that basis, an average income of $21,020 in the latter year is obtained. This figure is within about 1 per cent of the $21,237 estimate derived from the growth in the Census averages.

TABLE 10

Derived Average Before-Tax Earnings of Physicians,
Lawyers, and Dentists, 1940–62
(dollars)

	Physicians		Lawyers		Dentists	
Year	Average Earnings	Index (1962 = 1.000)	Average Earnings	Index (1962 = 1.000)	Average Earnings	Index (1962 = 1.000)
1940	4,441	.187	4,507	.280	3,314	.200
1941	5,047	.213	4,794	.297	3,782	.229
1942	6,735	.284	5,527	.343	4,625	.280
1943	8,370	.353	5,945	.369	5,715	.346
1944	9,802	.413	6,504	.404	6,649	.402
1945	10,975	.462	6,861	.426	6,922	.419
1946	10,202	.430	6,951	.431	6,381	.386
1947	10,726	.452	7,437	.461	6,610	.400
1948	11,327	.477	8,003	.497	7,039	.426
1949	11,744	.495	7,971	.495	7,146	.432
1950	12,324	.519	8,349	.518	7,436	.450
1951	13,432	.566	8,855	.549	7,820	.473
1952	–	–	9,021	.560	–	–
1953	–	–	9,392	.583	–	–
1954	–	–	10,258	.636	–	–
1959	21,237	.894	14,284	.886	13,733	.830
1960	21,707	.914	14,445	.896	14,322	.866
1961	22,485	.947	15,893	.986	15,192	.919
1962	23,744	1.000	16,117	1.000	16,538	1.000

income of the top professional men in the country in recent years has been equal to the average before-tax salary and bonus received by the executives in our sample. The historical record for such men could then be reconstructed simply by hypothesizing a pattern of pretax earnings increases like that suggested by Table 10 but which ends up instead at the higher level specified. In this way, something very much like the impact of heavier progressive taxes on executives' rewards over time would be attributed to the professions as well.

To illustrate: The before-tax direct current remuneration of senior corporate executives was discovered to reach a plateau in 1955 and remain at just about the same level through 1963.[17] Over that period the five highest-salaried men in each of fifty companies studied here enjoyed, on average, an annual before-tax salary and bonus of $143,548. If we assume that the individuals at the upper end of the income distribution within the medical profession, which is apparently the most affluent nowadays of the three examined, had average earnings in 1962 equal to that figure, their prior experience can be estimated by making use of the index numbers recorded in Table 10. Thus, for 1961, a value of $135,938 ($143,548 × 0.947) is obtained; for 1960, one of $131,234 ($143,548 × 0.914); and so on, back to 1940. If it is further assumed that the most successful lawyers and dentists had incomes in 1962 which stood in the same relationship to those of top physicians as the over-all averages for that year for the three professions would suggest, their earnings histories can be developed along similar lines. On this basis, the 1962 figure for lawyers will be 16,117/23,744, and for dentists 16,538/23,744, of that for physicians—which values come to $97,439 and $99,984, respectively. Corresponding figures for earlier years can then be generated from the observed rates of growth of incomes in the legal and dental professions. In effect, the convention is that for lack of more concrete evidence, the same degree of progressivity in tax rates which has recently been associated with top executive salaries and bonuses should also be applied to professional incomes. While the procedure adopted to accomplish this is certainly an arbitrary one, and is by no means the only possible solution, it at least operates in the right direction to remove the bias that clearly would be present were the figures in Table 10 used as they stand. The resulting before- and after-tax time series are recorded in Table 11. The after-tax figures were obtained by assuming the same percentage of deductions and exemptions,[18] and of "outside income," [19] as in the case of executives.

A comparison, therefore, of these data with the compensation history of the executive sample documents the differences in the several rates of growth. In Table 12 and Chart 15, the after-tax incomes of the three professional groups and the total after-tax compensation of senior executives are collected. For convenience and ease of interpretation, the

[17] See Table 1 and Chart 1.
[18] That is, 10 per cent of total income up to 1950; 15 per cent thereafter.
[19] 15 per cent of earnings from professional employment.

TABLE 11

Adjusted Average Incomes of Physicians, Lawyers, and Dentists,
1940–62
(dollars)

	Physicians		Lawyers		Dentists	
Year	Before-Tax	After-Tax	Before-Tax	After-Tax	Before-Tax	After-Tax
1940	26,849	22,425	27,248	22,701	20,035	17,525
1941	30,513	20,983	28,983	20,150	22,865	16,778
1942	40,718	23,187	33,415	20,079	27,961	17,583
1943	50,603	24,366	35,942	19,458	34,551	18,919
1944	59,260	26,911	39,321	20,676	40,198	20,984
1945	66,352	28,834	41,480	21,436	41,848	21,565
1946	61,678	30,849	42,024	23,723	38,578	22,309
1947	64,846	31,904	44,962	24,865	39,962	22,876
1948	68,480	42,962	48,384	32,852	42,556	29,746
1949	71,001	44,185	48,190	32,748	43,203	30,091
1950	74,507	45,852	50,476	33,960	44,956	31,025
1951	81,206	47,248	53,535	34,839	47,277	31,567
1952	–	–	54,538	32,912	–	–
1953	–	–	56,781	33,877	–	–
1954	–	–	62,017	38,690	–	–
1959	128,393	64,973	86,357	49,378	83,026	48,001
1960	131,234	65,929	87,330	49,780	86,587	49,473
1961	135,938	67,515	96,084	53,246	91,846	51,601
1962	143,548	70,071	97,439	53,771	99,984	54,759

patterns over time are recast in the form of index numbers, 1940 being
the base year for all series.[20] Since, in that respect, the record of after-
tax remuneration received by both the top executive in each of the fifty
companies studied and by the top five together is almost identical, only
the experience of the latter is depicted in Chart 15.[21]

It can be seen from these tabulations that executives *have* trailed
other professions over the last quarter century in the rate of growth of

[20] The figures for executives are those compiled in Table 3. As has been
done on several previous occasions, the rewards generated by stock options
during the period 1955 through 1963 have been averaged over that period.

[21] Also in that chart, the pattern of growth in professional earnings in years
for which data are unavailable is approximated by a straight line.

TABLE 12

Comparative Growth in After-Tax Incomes: Executives vs. the Professions, 1940–63
(1940 = 1.000)

Year	Physicians	Lawyers	Dentists	Top Executives	Top Five Executives
1940	1.000	1.000	1.000	1.000	1.000
1941	0.936	0.888	0.957	0.898	0.952
1942	1.034	0.884	1.003	0.647	0.742
1943	1.087	0.857	1.080	0.554	0.651
1944	1.200	0.911	1.197	0.624	0.701
1945	1.286	0.944	1.231	0.604	0.692
1946	1.376	1.045	1.273	0.677	0.801
1947	1.423	1.095	1.305	0.768	0.837
1948	1.916	1.447	1.697	0.978	1.129
1949	1.970	1.443	1.717	1.033	1.186
1950	2.045	1.496	1.770	1.204	1.322
1951	2.107	1.535	1.801	1.072	1.294
1952	–	1.450	–	1.144	1.330
1953	–	1.492	–	1.292	1.442
1954	–	1.704	–	1.407	1.558
1955	–	–	–	2.105	2.153
1956	–	–	–	2.099	2.168
1957	–	–	–	2.146	2.200
1958	–	–	–	2.030	2.100
1959	2.897	2.175	2.739	2.065	2.164
1960	2.940	2.193	2.823	2.014	2.136
1961	3.010	2.346	2.944	2.043	2.162
1962	3.125	2.369	3.125	2.088	2.180
1963	–	–	–	2.001	2.162

after-tax incomes—even when the value to them of the major supplements to their salaries and bonuses is recognized.[22] Physicians and den-

[22] The question as to whether these relationships may be affected by items of income which could not be included therein is a difficult one to answer. Self-employed professional men such as physicians, lawyers, and dentists almost certainly have a greater opportunity that do executives to mix elements of personal consumption with their actual business expenses in reporting the net

CHART 15

Growth in After-Tax Earnings of Executives and Other Professional Groups, 1940–63

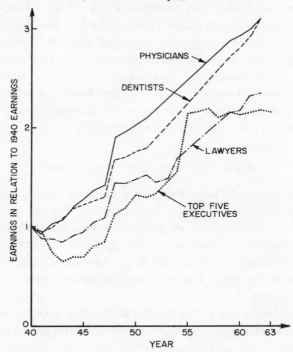

income figures recorded above. While to that extent their earnings are really higher than the figures suggest, this does not present a problem here unless the *degree* of underreporting has changed significantly over the years. Thus, as long as growth rates and not absolute levels are at issue, only changes in the relative importance of any missing data are of concern. Even though increases in personal tax rates over the period studied may have encouraged the self-employed to rely more heavily on "hidden" consumption expenditures and caused the rate of growth of their incomes to be somewhat greater than it appears from the available data to have been, it should be remembered that there may be a similar bias contained in the executive compensation time series. Because of the limitations of the information available in corporate proxy statements, certain rewards enjoyed by executives—e.g., company-provided life and health insurance benefits—could not be appraised empirically. Since the value of those rewards is also likely to have been increasing over time, the historical trend in total executive pay may be mildly understated as it stands, and this understatement should offset, at least in part, any which is associated with the earnings of the professions.

tists did substantially better, enjoying between 1940 and 1962 a compound annual rate of earnings growth equal to approximately 5.2 per cent as compared with 3.3 per cent for executives. While lawyers in general did less well,[23] they still managed a 3.9 per cent rate of growth. These comparisons are, of course, strengthened by the fact that average annual professional earnings have been and apparently continue to be steadily rising over time, whereas the compensation of corporate executives seems at the moment to have reached a plateau.[24] Moreover, the indicated gap between executives and the professions is sufficiently wide that any errors in estimating the relevant data would have to be fairly large in order to undo the conclusions offered.[25]

Other Corporate Employee Groups

Another occupational "category" whose earnings—or, at least, secular changes therein—are of interest in connection with the experience of top executives is the group of individuals who labor at lower levels within the corporate organization. The question is whether the compensation differentials between the senior officers of large manufacturing firms and the rest of their firms' employees have narrowed or widened over time.

One very simple way to attempt to answer this question would be to examine the circumstances of those individuals who are in effect at the opposite end of the corporate hierarchy: the wage-earning production labor force and firms' newly-hired management trainees. The latter are by no means likely to be the lowest-paid employees in a company, but they do occupy the bottom rung on the *management* ladder and are relevant for that reason. While it would also be desirable to examine

[23] In fact, in 1940 lawyers earned more on average than either physicians or dentists but by 1962 were the lowest-paid of the three professions (see Table 10).

[24] And, as noted earlier, the maintenance of even that "plateau" depends either on a continuing opportunity for executives to realize stock option profits comparable to those of the late 1950's and early 1960's, or an offsetting rise in the value of their other rewards.

[25] Appendix L discusses some alternative assumptions about the tax rates on professional incomes. Under any reasonable set of possible conditions, executives consistently appear to have fallen behind. Because the rate of growth of their rewards has been so uneven over the interval studied, however, there are subperiods in which they have done better than the professions—1945 to 1950 and 1952 to 1955, for example (see Chart 15).

the rewards of middle-management personnel, information that would permit us to do so is not available in any published source. Data relating to the other two groups of employees do exist, however, and should serve to indicate whether senior executives are losing ground within their own companies as well as within the professional community.

According to the Bureau of Labor Statistics, the average gross weekly wages of manufacturing production workers rose from $24.96 in 1940 to $99.63 in 1963, an increase of some 300 per cent.[26] While these figures incorporate the effect not only of higher hourly wage rates but also of changes in the length of the average work week, they are not affected significantly by the second factor. The number of hours worked per week per employee in manufacturing was only slightly greater in 1963 than in 1940—40.5 and 38.1 hours, respectively.[27] The story would therefore not be much different if it were cast in terms of hourly wage rates instead.[28] Because the weekly figures seem a better measure of changes in actual gross earnings, they will be adopted for the comparisons here.

An important class of rewards which is not included in these figures, however, is the so-called "fringe benefit" package. Production workers clearly enjoy more in the way of such items as pensions, life and health insurance, vacations and holidays, and sick leave, nowadays than they did in the early 1940's. The Chamber of Commerce estimates that the additional cost of such arrangements to a typical employer company currently comes to approximately one-fourth of the basic wage bill itself.[29] Wage data alone will, as a result, understate the true rate of growth of workers' total compensation, especially when compared with the earnings of top executives for whom supplements to salary and bonus have been very carefully taken into account. The problem which is confronted in performing a similar analysis for production workers is that the data which are available relate to the *cost* of fringe benefits, not to their *value* from the employees' standpoint. The total compensa-

[26] *Employment and Earnings Statistics for the United States, 1909–64,* Bulletin No. 1312-2, Washington, 1964, Table 3, p. xvi.

[27] *Ibid.,* p. xvi.

[28] The relevant values are: $0.655 per hour in 1940 and $2.46 in 1963, a gain of 276 per cent on that basis. *Ibid.,* p. xvi.

[29] Including payments required under Social Security, workmen's compensation, and unemployment compensation legislation. Chamber of Commerce of the United States, *Fringe Benefits: 1963,* Washington, 1964, p. 9.

tion time series derived above for executives consist of estimates as to how much various deferred and contingent forms of reward are worth as judged by their recipients' alternative market opportunities to secure equivalent arrangements on an individual basis. An effort of that sort is impossible for a large and anonymous body of wage-earners. Fortunately, it also turns out that it is not really necessary for purposes of the present discussion. Manufacturing production workers' wages alone grew at a sufficiently rapid pace since 1940 to permit us to conclude that the rate of growth of their aggregate remuneration—whatever that figure might be—comfortably exceeded the corresponding rate for top executives.

Table 13 presents, for every year from 1940 through 1963, the BLS calculations of average gross weekly earnings in manufacturing and, more importantly, average "spendable" weekly earnings.[30] The latter is estimated by the BLS by deducting the federal income and Social Security tax liability that would be applicable to a married worker with two children employed all year long and receiving the indicated gross before-tax income each week.[31] The third column in the table is the spendable income series in index number form, with 1940 chosen as the base year. The fourth column reproduces, again with 1940 as the base, the total after-tax compensation history of the top five senior executive sample recorded previously in Table 12. A comparison of these last two series reveals very clearly the higher rate of growth in earnings realized by production workers, even in the absence of any allowance for the value of their wage supplements.

A similar story emerges if we examine the secular increase in the starting salaries of management trainees—which in the view here means the starting salaries of MBA graduates. While again it is impossible to say much about such individuals' fringe benefits, there is an additional problem in developing a meaningful time series. Most of the schools of business which are now regarded as among the nation's best did not really attain that status until midway through the time period under consideration. The historical record of growth in the starting salaries of their graduates will therefore reflect not only the general economic forces

[30] *Employment and Earnings Statistics,* p. 646.

[31] The fact that Social Security taxes are deducted in these computations but were not in determining the amount of executives' after-tax income means that a slight additional bias in favor of executives is built into the comparisons.

TABLE 13

Comparison of Manufacturing Production Workers' and
Top Executives' Earnings, 1940–63

Year	Workers' Gross Weekly Earnings (dollars)	Workers' Spendable Weekly Earnings (dollars)	Workers' Spendable Earnings Index (1940 = 1.000)	Executive Compensation Index (1940 = 1.000)
1940	24.96	24.71	1.000	1.000
1941	29.48	29.19	1.181	0.952
1942	36.68	36.31	1.469	0.742
1943	43.07	41.33	1.673	0.651
1944	45.70	43.76	1.771	0.701
1945	44.20	42.59	1.724	0.692
1946	43.32	42.79	1.732	0.801
1947	49.17	47.58	1.926	0.837
1948	53.12	52.31	2.117	1.129
1949	53.88	52.95	2.143	1.186
1950	58.32	56.36	2.281	1.322
1951	63.34	60.18	2.435	1.294
1952	67.16	62.98	2.549	1.330
1953	70.47	65.60	2.655	1.442
1954	70.49	65.65	2.657	1.558
1955	75.70	69.79	2.824	2.153
1956	78.78	72.25	2.924	2.168
1957	81.59	74.31	3.007	2.200
1958	82.71	75.23	3.045	2.100
1959	88.26	79.40	3.213	2.164
1960	89.72	80.11	3.242	2.136
1961	92.34	82.18	3.326	2.162
1962	96.56	85.53	3.461	2.180
1963	99.63	87.78	3.552	2.162

which impinge upon the segment of the labor market in which we are
interested, but will have built into it the effect of substantial changes in
the quality of the various schools as well. The result is almost certain
to be an upward bias in the data over time which would distort any

comparisons with increases in top executive remuneration. Given also that the experience of the graduates of *leading* institutions would seem to be the most desirable basis of comparison, the solution is simply to concentrate on a school or schools in that category whose relative standing in the academic community —or, perhaps more to the point, whose relative reputation among prospective employers—has not changed significantly since the early 1940's. There is at least one institution, the Harvard Business School, about which most observers would probably agree in this connection, and the growth in the starting salaries of its graduates over the last twenty-five years should provide an appropriate and convenient historical standard for our purposes here.[32]

The relevant data are presented in Table 14.[33] The first column records the mean before-tax starting salaries of Harvard MBA graduates from 1940 to 1963, and the second the after-tax counterpart of those figures. The latter were computed in the same manner as were executives' after-tax rewards and the after-tax earnings of the professional groups discussed in the preceding section, i.e., by assuming in determining tax liabilities the same percentages of deductions and exemptions and of outside income in relation to salary. The third column restates the second as an index based again on 1940 and the fourth is a duplicate of the after-tax series for the executive sample contained in Tables 12 and 13. Chart 16 summarizes the pertinent comparisons by combining these data with those developed for manufacturing production workers.[34]

There is evidence, then, that the compensation "spread" between the highest and lowest employee levels in large manufacturing corporations has narrowed—in relative terms, at least—during the last quarter century. Top executives' earnings have grown considerably more slowly

[32] If the same is true of several other schools, the experience of their graduates should be quite similar, and little will be lost by not considering them explicitly.

[33] The author is indebted to the Director of Placement at the Harvard University Graduate School of Business Administration, Mr. John Steele, for supplying the information for these time series.

[34] It should be noted that the use of starting salaries for an entire MBA class in such comparisons implicitly assumes that the pay of those graduates who actually join *manufacturing* firms—and who therefore comprise the particular group whose rewards are really of interest—has grown at the same rate as that of their contemporaries who chose to accept jobs in other sectors of business. There seems to be no real reason to question this assumption, but attention should be called to the fact that it is inherent in the comparisons presented.

TABLE 14

Comparison of MBA Starting Salaries and Top Executives'
Earnings, 1940–63

Year	Before-Tax MBA Starting Salary (dollars)	After-Tax MBA Starting Salary (dollars)	MBA After-Tax Salary Index (1940 = 1.000)	Executive Compensation Index (1940 = 1.000)
1940	1,550	1,489	1.000	1.000
1941	1,800	1,638	1.100	0.952
1942	2,100	1,730	1.162	0.742
1943	2,490	1,964	1.319	0.651
1944	n.a.	n.a.	n.a.	0.701
1945	n.a.	n.a.	n.a.	0.692
1946	3,136 [a]	2,579 [a]	1.732	0.801
1947	3,396	2,790	1.874	0.837
1948	3,685	3,134	2.105	1.129
1949	3,602	3,063	2.057	1.186
1950	3,683	3,132	2.103	1.322
1951	4,200	3,484	2.340	1.294
1952	4,571	3,698	2.484	1.330
1953	4,894	3,954	2.655	1.442
1954	4,943	4,088	2.745	1.558
1955	5,882	4,851	3.258	2.153
1956	6,021	4,964	3.334	2.168
1957	6,483	5,340	3.586	2.200
1958	6,475	5,334	3.582	2.100
1959	6,909	5,686	3.819	2.164
1960	7,330	6,028	4.048	2.136
1961	7,666	6,302	4.232	2.162
1962	8,291	6,806	4.571	2.180
1963	8,982	7,345	4.933	2.162

[a] For September graduates; all other figures refer to June graduates.
n.a. = not available

CHART 16

After-Tax Earnings of Executives, Production Workers,
and Recent MBA Graduates, 1940–63

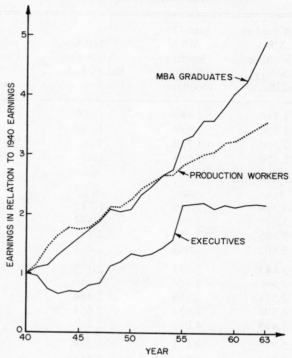

than those of either their firms' production workers or new management trainees. Apparently, the role which unions have played in the labor market since the early 1940's and the increasing intensity of the competition for promising young managerial recruits have exceeded any similar pressures on senior executives' rewards. Whatever the explanation, the differences in the rates of growth of earnings are unmistakable and appear, if anything, to be widening in recent years.

Real Income

A final standard by which to judge the historical performance of top executive compensation is the behavior of the prices which executives, in their role as consumers of goods and services, must confront. If, for example, we take the Bureau of Labor Statistics' familiar Consumer Price Index series as a reasonable approximation of secular changes in purchasing power, we may use that series to determine how well the men in the sample have fared over the years in terms of "real" income.[35] Table 15 and Chart 17 restate in this manner the total after-tax compensation experience of the highest-paid executive in each sample company and of the five highest-paid as a group. The year 1940 is chosen as the base for the price index, which is recorded in Table 16, and all income figures are therefore in 1940 dollars. Once again, executive stock option profits were averaged over the period 1955 to 1963 in order to highlight longer-term trends.[36]

Comparison with the undeflated experience depicted in Charts 15 and 16 reveals that the historical pattern of aggregate remuneration is transformed from one of modest, albeit uneven, growth to one of stagnation. The wartime drop in after-tax compensation appears sharper, the postwar recovery not as substantial, and the experience of the 1950's and early 1960's less impressive than the current-dollar time series indicated. A downward trend in total compensation, in constant dollars, following the peak year of 1955 is now evident.

Upon adjusting for price changes, therefore, we find that the several deferred and contingent compensation devices incorporated into the pay package since World War II and used extensively since the mid-1950's have resulted not in amounts of top executive remuneration higher than ever before but instead have simply enabled real incomes to be restored to approximately their 1940 levels. Put another way, the men in the sample would be just about *half* as well off now as they

---

[35] Ideally, a price index based on the "market basket" of goods and services purchased by high-income families should be employed. Since no such index exists, the CPI is the only possible choice. If there is any bias introduced thereby, it seems likely to be in the direction of *understating* the actual price increases faced by executives. Thus, services almost certainly represent a larger proportion of total consumption for high-income families than for those units whose expenditures are examined in compiling the CPI. Given that the prices of services have, in general, been increasing more rapidly over time than those of goods, a high-income consumer price index would be expected to indicate a sharper decline in purchasing power since 1940 than the CPI itself. If so, the consequence here will be too optimistic a picture of top executives' real income histories.

[36] That is, they were averaged in absolute dollar terms prior to being adjusted for price changes.

TABLE 15

Executives' Real Total After-Tax Compensation, 1940–63
(figures in 1940 dollars)

Year	Top Executive	Top Five Executives
1940	101,979	59,740
1941	87,093	54,125
1942	56,667	38,122
1943	45,750	31,483
1944	50,695	33,338
1945	47,962	32,163
1946	49,564	34,370
1947	49,132	31,361
1948	58,099	39,280
1949	61,911	41,637
1950	71,514	46,017
1951	58,944	41,680
1952	61,560	41,926
1953	68,996	45,121
1954	74,802	48,528
1955	112,297	67,270
1956	110,380	66,734
1957	109,000	65,464
1958	100,284	60,787
1959	101,241	62,145
1960	97,189	60,377
1961	97,589	60,487
1962	98,592	60,302
1963	93,364	59,087
Average: 1955–63	102,204	62,517

TABLE 16

Consumer Price Index,
1940–63
(1940 = 1.000)

Year	Index Value
1940	1.000
1941	1.051
1942	1.164
1943	1.236
1944	1.256
1945	1.285
1946	1.393
1947	1.594
1948	1.717
1949	1.701
1950	1.717
1951	1.855
1952	1.895
1953	1.910
1954	1.918
1955	1.912
1956	1.941
1957	2.008
1958	2.064
1959	2.080
1960	2.113
1961	2.135
1962	2.160
1963	2.186

SOURCE: U.S. Department of Commerce, Bureau of the Census, *Statistical Abstract of the United States: 1965,* Washington, D.C., 1965, p. 361.

CHART 17

"Real" After-Tax Total Compensation, 1940–63

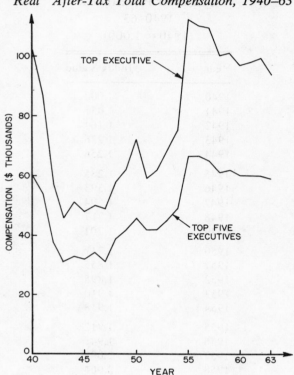

were before World War II had the salaries and bonuses they received been their only rewards.[37]

While a price index of the type employed in arriving at these conclusions may not tell the whole story with regard to changes in the amount and, especially, the quality of consumer-good purchasing power per dollar of expenditure, it would certainly require a major modification of that index to make the record of the executives considered look very favorable. Moreover, in its present terms their real income during

[37] Since, as was observed previously, these payments generated roughly half the aggregate after-tax compensation they enjoyed from 1955 through 1963. See Tables 4 and 5.

the later years of the study is, if anything, overstated. The current income equivalents of the various supplements to salary and bonus each year have been combined with the same year's actual receipts from the latter in deriving the time series depicted. Thus, items that permit current consumption and those that represent the possibility of future consumption have been added together without adjustment. In order to do so legitimately, it is necessary to assume that prices will not change in the interim—or, more appropriately, that the executives involved believe each year they will not. Given that the concern here is with measuring the impact of just such changes, this assumption is obviously incorrect. If prices are likely to rise over time, as they seem to, the effect is to impute too high a real income value to the current equivalent of every deferred reward. Since those rewards have provided effectively all the observed secular increase in top executives' (undeflated) after-tax compensation, the consequence is an overstatement of the growth—or an understatement of the decline—in their aggregate real income over time.[38] The task of prescribing a different set of price expectations for each of the twenty-four years of the study was sufficiently unattractive, however, that accepting and acknowledging the probable bias appeared the better alternative.

Summary

By any one of several criteria, the compensation of top executives in large manufacturing firms has not increased very rapidly during the last quarter century. The corporations whose affairs they administer—and therefore, under certain not unreasonable assumptions, the productive contributions of the executives themselves—grew considerably faster in every important respect. The after-tax incomes enjoyed by other leading professional groups in the community, among them physicians, lawyers, and dentists, now stand at anywhere from two and one-half to three times their 1940 levels, while executives' earnings have just about doubled. At the opposite end of the corporate employee hierarchy, manufacturing production workers have been awarded substantially larger pay increases, and the starting salaries paid by firms to their man-

[38] Added to which, of course, is the suspicion expressed above that the CPI is too mild a deflator of high-income families' purchasing power.

agement trainees rose by some 400 per cent over the period studied. Perhaps as importantly from the executives' standpoint, if secular increases in the prices of consumer goods and services are taken into account, the men in the sample turn out to have experienced no increase in their "real" income since 1940.

10

CROSS-SECTIONAL PATTERNS

Another perspective on the compensation package can be obtained by looking beyond the collective experience outlined above and focusing on the relationships *among* the executives who comprise the sample. Have the salary differentials between the top five executive positions narrowed or widened over the years? What about total compensation differentials? Do deferred and contingent rewards become more or less important the farther down in the corporate hierarchy we go? Is the pay package more volatile at higher levels? The answers to these and other questions require a cross-sectional analysis which the preceding chapters do not provide. While such an analysis must still be confined to the small group of senior officers for whom proxy statement compensation information is available, certain trends observed within that group can perhaps be extrapolated to lower management levels as well.

Before-Tax Salaries and Bonuses

Separate before-tax salary and bonus time series for the individuals who received the five largest amounts of such payments in each firm in each year from 1940 to 1963 are recorded in Table 17 and Chart 18. The numbers contained therein represent averages across the sample companies throughout. Table 18 and Chart 19 restate the series in ratio form, using the highest current remuneration payment in every year as a base. Thus, in 1940, the executives with the second largest amounts of salary and bonus in each company received, on average, 61 per cent as much as did the top executives in the same firms in that year. The third-highest-salaried men received 51 per cent as much, and so on down the line.

Two conclusions are immediately suggested by the data. First, the

TABLE 17

Average Before-Tax Salaries and Bonuses, 1940–63
(dollars)

Year	Executive Ranking				
	First	Second	Third	Fourth	Fifth
1940	137,233	83,366	69,603	60,822	54,742
1941	145,281	89,678	71,570	64,059	56,073
1942	145,473	91,243	73,944	66,958	56,508
1943	144,208	93,952	75,929	66,613	57,073
1944	143,612	92,495	72,860	65,696	57,377
1945	142,892	91,580	74,200	65,365	60,226
1946	143,247	99,537	81,691	70,857	65,979
1947	149,446	101,976	82,401	73,845	65,986
1948	161,959	110,567	88,182	79,719	76,049
1949	169,703	116,943	91,554	84,828	79,079
1950	178,452	127,835	100,472	90,560	83,702
1951	183,235	135,817	106,432	98,044	89,792
1952	185,330	137,619	113,319	100,805	92,041
1953	193,556	145,816	119,312	107,386	101,223
1954	197,726	149,805	123,476	109,588	103,170
1955	205,656	157,171	130,730	117,067	107,543
1956	215,767	162,774	136,632	120,898	115,417
1957	207,586	159,765	132,415	117,402	112,075
1958	207,101	151,223	126,566	112,099	105,983
1959	203,708	155,487	133,003	117,075	110,807
1960	200,788	151,390	130,029	114,097	102,421
1961	198,560	145,128	126,970	112,484	104,315
1962	201,622	152,526	134,502	115,635	104,507
1963	210,164	160,684	139,812	122,217	109,890

salary and bonus differentials between the several executive positions become successively greater the higher the level of compensation considered. This relationship holds in virtually every year studied, the only exceptions being the war years 1942, 1943, and 1944, when the gap between the fourth- and fifth-ranking executives was, on average, slightly greater than that between the third and fourth. By far the most striking salary increment in every instance is that between the top executive and the second-ranking man. In fact, this increment alone is larger in all cases than the total salary differential separating the other four men in the sample.

The second phenomenon which appears, however, is a steady narrowing of this gap over time, at least in percentage terms. In the early 1940's the annual salary and bonus awards associated with the first two executive positions in each firm differed by a little more than $50,000 on average—or by between 35 and 40 per cent of the top executive's pay. During the last nine years of the study, when a plateau of sorts was reached, the $50,000 differential was still pretty much intact, but it

CHART 18

Average Before-Tax Salaries and Bonuses Profile, 1940–63

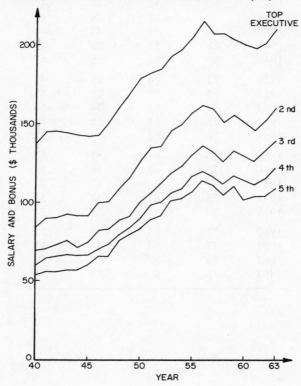

TABLE 18

Before-Tax Salaries and Bonuses in Relation to Top Executive's Salary and Bonus, 1940–63
(per cent)

Year	Executive Ranking			
	Second	Third	Fourth	Fifth
1940	61	51	44	40
1941	62	49	44	39
1942	63	51	46	39
1943	65	53	46	40
1944	64	51	46	40
1945	64	52	46	42
1946	69	57	49	46
1947	68	55	49	44
1948	68	54	49	47
1949	69	54	50	47
1950	72	56	51	47
1951	74	58	54	49
1952	74	61	54	50
1953	75	62	55	52
1954	76	62	55	52
1955	76	64	57	52
1956	75	63	56	53
1957	77	64	57	54
1958	73	61	54	51
1959	76	65	57	54
1960	75	65	57	51
1961	73	64	57	53
1962	76	67	57	52
1963	76	67	58	52

CHART 19

Before-Tax Salaries and Bonuses in Relation to Top Executive's, 1940–63

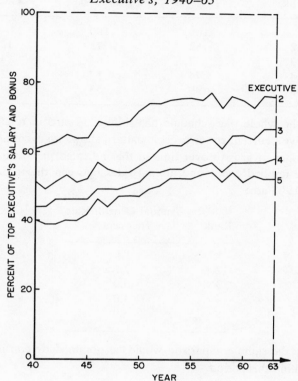

constituted then only a 25 per cent increment in total current remuneration between the two positions. Thus, the men at both levels have enjoyed just about the same absolute dollar increase in annual salary and bonus since the early 1940's.

A similar development is reflected in the other three time series. Each of the lower-ranking executive positions gained relative to the highest-paid one. Moreover, they did so in such a manner as to maintain almost exactly the percentage differences among themselves. When the experience of the prewar years 1940 and 1941 is compared with that of the period 1955 through 1963, the average annual salary-plus-bonus of

the top five executive positions in each company expressed as a per
cent of the remuneration of the highest-paid officer appear as follows:

Rank	1940–41	1955–63	Gain
1	100	100	—
2	62	75	13
3	50	64	14
4	44	57	13
5	39	53	14

In effect, the whole pay schedule has shifted upward in relation to the
top executive's current rewards. This pattern shows up even more clearly
when the rates of growth over time in the indicated payments are computed. The implied compound annual rates between the terminal years
1940 and 1963 are:

Rank	Annual Growth Rate (per cent)
1	1.8
2	2.8
3	3.0
4	3.0
5	3.0

Essentially the same comparison would be obtained by considering any
interval within this period.

After-Tax Salaries and Bonuses

As would be expected, the after-tax current remuneration time series
tell a similar and somewhat stronger story, since the influence of a
progressive personal income tax schedule is added to narrowing before-
tax differentials. Tables 19 and 20 and Charts 20 and 21 present the
after-tax data in both absolute and percentage terms, using the same
format as above.

Again, the largest increment in average salary and bonus payments
occurs between the first two executive rankings. In this case, however,
that increment is considerably smaller than its before-tax counterpart.

TABLE 19

Average After-Tax Salaries and Bonuses, 1940–63
(dollars)

	Executive Ranking				
Year	First	Second	Third	Fourth	Fifth
1940	77,143	53,521	45,766	41,159	37,627
1941	67,202	46,395	38,924	35,735	32,173
1942	52,014	38,431	33,423	31,178	27,811
1943	43,036	33,698	29,766	27,452	24,878
1944	42,959	33,465	29,190	27,388	25,210
1945	42,817	33,222	29,418	27,339	26,044
1946	51,591	40,539	35,557	32,312	30,828
1947	53,050	41,255	35,865	33,389	30,886
1948	77,775	59,448	50,191	46,489	44,804
1949	80,269	61,643	51,535	48,505	45,785
1950	83,007	65,356	55,072	50,717	47,674
1951	79,482	64,296	54,611	51,214	47,850
1952	75,445	61,167	53,499	49,090	45,752
1953	77,716	63,772	55,572	51,205	48,640
1954	83,604	69,175	60,557	55,162	52,569
1955	85,637	71,338	62,707	57,560	53,737
1956	88,177	73,094	64,277	58,583	56,089
1957	86,302	72,346	63,009	57,392	56,454
1958	86,152	69,967	61,680	56,591	54,976
1959	85,767	71,653	64,188	58,564	55,394
1960	84,991	70,685	63,003	57,806	52,846
1961	84,524	68,613	62,231	56,862	53,798
1962	85,274	70,896	65,123	58,327	54,320
1963	87,503	73,419	66,643	57,122	55,046

TABLE 20

After-Tax Salaries and Bonuses in
Relation to Top Executive's Salary
and Bonus, 1940–63
(per cent)

| Year | Executive Ranking | | | |
	Second	Third	Fourth	Fifth
1940	69	59	53	49
1941	69	58	53	48
1942	74	64	60	53
1943	78	69	64	58
1944	78	68	64	59
1945	78	69	64	61
1946	79	69	63	60
1947	78	68	63	58
1948	76	65	60	58
1949	77	64	60	57
1950	79	66	61	57
1951	81	69	64	60
1952	81	71	65	61
1953	82	72	66	63
1954	83	72	66	63
1955	83	73	67	63
1956	83	73	66	64
1957	84	73	67	65
1958	81	72	66	64
1959	84	75	68	65
1960	83	74	68	62
1961	81	74	67	64
1962	83	76	68	64
1963	84	76	65	63

CHART 20

Average After-Tax Salaries and Bonuses Profile, 1940–63

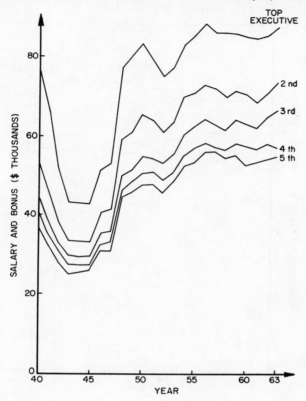

In relation to the top executive's rewards, the differential came to 31 per cent in the early 1940's and about 17 per cent from 1955 on. If we compare on that basis the changes over time on the after-tax salary and bonus profile across all five positions, the result (in per cent) is:

Rank	1940–41	1955–63	Gain
1	100	100	—
2	69	83	14
3	59	74	15
4	53	67	14
5	48	64	16

CHART 21

*After-Tax Salaries and Bonuses in Relation to Top
Executive's, 1940–63*

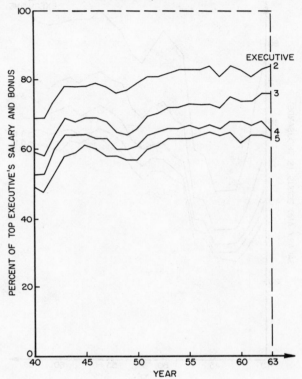

Thus, on average, the four men immediately below the top executive in
each company experienced substantially more rapid increases in take-
home pay than he did. In fact, the absolute as well as the percentage
differences declined in every instance (see Table 19). While all these
gains were larger than in the before-tax case, the four men still just about
maintained their positions relative to each other. The after-tax annual
rates of salary and bonus growth from 1940 to 1963 are:

Rank	Annual Growth Rate (per cent)
1	0.5
2	1.4
3	1.6
4	1.6
5	1.7

None of these, of course, is very great, confirming the judgments made in the last chapter.

Both the before- and after-tax current remuneration data therefore lead to essentially the same conclusions: (1) Salary and bonus differentials increase steadily and sharply as we examine successively higher executive levels within the corporate hierarchy. (2) There is an especially large differential between the first two positions. (3) The latter gap has narrowed significantly in percentage terms over the last quarter century. (4) The annual salaries and bonuses of the four men just below the top executive have not changed appreciably in relation to one another in that time.

Predictably, the second of these conclusions is somewhat weaker on an after-tax basis and the third somewhat stronger—a consequence in both cases of progressive personal income taxes.

The fact that the direct current remuneration of the top executive in each firm has not risen as rapidly over time as that of his immediate subordinates, of course, does not necessarily imply that by a more comprehensive index of performance he has also lost ground to them. It may well be that he has regularly enjoyed more in the way of other rewards than they have and that a different story will emerge when the rest of the compensation package is made a part of the historical comparisons.

Total After-Tax Compensation

Tables 21 and 22 and Charts 22 and 23 present time series from 1940 to 1963 for those executives who received, according to the valuation procedures employed here, the five largest amounts of *total* after-tax

TABLE 21

Average Total After-Tax Compensation, 1940–63
(dollars)

| Year | Executive Ranking | | | | |
	First	Second	Third	Fourth	Fifth
1940	101,979	60,355	50,080	45,262	41,023
1941	91,535	64,014	51,669	40,964	36,245
1942	65,960	47,778	40,460	36,278	31,400
1943	56,467	41,394	35,809	31,930	28,964
1944	63,673	45,991	37,392	32,689	29,622
1945	61,632	44,624	37,001	32,942	30,446
1946	69,043	52,210	42,818	39,201	36,120
1947	78,317	52,072	44,136	39,500	35,919
1948	99,756	72,274	60,239	53,740	51,210
1949	105,311	77,738	62,293	56,901	51,881
1950	122,790	84,192	69,584	61,925	56,565
1951	109,341	83,806	72,920	64,304	56,209
1952	116,657	85,777	73,412	64,281	57,122
1953	131,782	93,651	78,843	66,983	59,644
1954	143,470	101,337	83,193	72,480	64,901
1955	214,711	142,318	114,199	93,925	77,955
1956	214,054	143,996	114,157	94,262	81,181
1957	218,872	143,992	118,499	93,073	82,821
1958	206,987	141,588	113,916	87,065	77,762
1959	210,581	138,979	124,813	92,399	79,539
1960	205,361	141,439	116,882	92,892	81,311
1961	208,352	149,837	112,862	91,533	83,115
1962	212,958	137,538	120,568	98,234	81,964
1963	204,094	139,243	124,547	100,965	76,973
Average: 1955–63	210,663	142,103	117,827	93,816	80,291

NOTE: Stock option profits averaged, 1955–63.

TABLE 22

Total After-Tax Compensation in Relation to Top Executive's Compensation, 1940–63
(per cent)

| | Executive Ranking | | | |
Year	Second	Third	Fourth	Fifth
1940	59	49	44	40
1941	70	56	45	40
1942	72	61	55	48
1943	73	63	57	51
1944	72	59	51	47
1945	72	60	53	49
1946	76	62	57	52
1947	67	56	50	46
1948	73	60	54	51
1949	74	59	54	49
1950	69	57	50	46
1951	77	67	59	51
1952	74	63	55	49
1953	71	60	51	45
1954	71	58	51	45
1955	66	53	44	36
1956	67	53	44	38
1957	66	54	43	38
1958	68	55	42	38
1959	66	59	44	38
1960	69	57	45	40
1961	72	54	44	40
1962	65	57	46	39
1963	68	61	50	38
Average: 1955–63	67	56	45	38

NOTE: Stock option profits averaged, 1955–63.

CHART 22

Total After-Tax Compensation Profile (Stock Option Data Smoothed), 1940–63

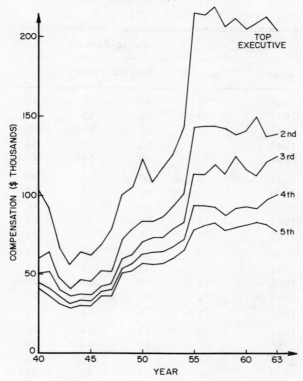

compensation in each of the sample companies in each year. The current income equivalents of the various supplements to salary and bonus are included in these figures, and the numbers recorded represent mean values for the entire sample. Stock option profits realized during the period 1955 through 1963 are spread evenly over that period both in the tables and in the charts in order to facilitate interpretation of the results.

The issue raised in the preceding section can therefore be resolved: when the whole pay package is taken into account, the highest-paid executive *does* turn out to have done just about as well in terms of rates of compensation growth as his colleagues. A comparison between the experience of the last two pre-World War II years and the plateau in total remuneration observed from 1955 on shows the following:

Executive Rank	Average After-Tax Compensation 1940–41	Average After-Tax Compensation 1955–63	Implied Annual Growth Rate (per cent) [a]	Compensation as a Per Cent of Top Executive's	
				1940–41	1955–63
1	$96,757	$210,663	3.4	100	100
2	62,185	142,103	3.6	64	67
3	50,875	117,827	3.6	53	56
4	43,113	93,816	3.4	45	45
5	38,634	80,291	3.2	40	38

[a] Based on a twenty-four-year interval, i.e., as if the two averages calculated applied to the terminal years 1940 and 1963.

As was suggested earlier, and as will be confirmed by the compensation breakdown presented below, this result is not difficult to explain. Deferred and contingent rewards have been employed more extensively at higher executive levels. In fact, the extent to which such arrangements appear to have evened out the disparities in compensation growth rates implied by the salary and bonus time series argues strongly for two propositions: first, that corporations make a conscious effort to consider the value of the entire pay package in planning their executives' remuneration; and second, that as part of this effort, they recognize the effect of personal income taxes very explicitly, since the total compensation data tabulated are in after-tax terms throughout. While neither of these is a terribly surprising conclusion, both now have a documentation that has heretofore been lacking.

It should be stressed, however, that it is necessary in this connection to accept the techniques used here to construct "current income equivalents" for supplements to salary and bonus as appropriate—and also to suppose that the corporations in the sample perceive the value of those supplements in much the same way. The former is perhaps easier to justify than the latter. On the other hand, the individuals who in practice make the relevant appraisals are both intelligent and economically sophisticated, and the comparisons at issue have all been cast in

CHART 23

*Total After-Tax Compensation in Relation to Top
Executive's, 1940–63*

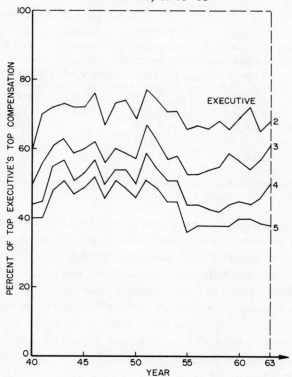

terms of averages across fifty firms and over a period of years. It is not
unreasonable, therefore, to expect that the informal, implicit—or even
temporarily erroneous—compensation valuation procedures actually employed by these firms will operate to produce a consensus which ap-
proximates the "correct" one. The historical evidence certainly points
in that direction—and it offers clear support for the hypothesis that the
top executive compensation package is comprehensively planned to
achieve a specified level of after-tax reward.

The other phenomenon which emerges from the figures concerns the
compensation differentials between the five executive positions. The

pattern which the salary and bonus data exhibited again appears: each successive step upward on the corporate ladder carries with it a progressively greater increment in total after-tax remuneration. The increment between the top two positions continues to be by far the most substantial, exceeding the next three combined. In this case, however, the close similarity of the growth rates in the five compensation time series implies that the *absolute* differentials are steadily widening over time:

Increment in Rank	Increment in After-Tax Compensation 1940–41	Increment in After-Tax Compensation 1955–63	Increment as Per Cent of Top Executive's Compensation	
			1940–41	1955–63
1–2	$34,572	$68,560	36	33
2–3	11,310	24,276	12	12
3–4	7,762	24,011	8	11
4–5	4,479	13,525	5	6

Therefore, if only at the senior executive level, the total compensation profile in large manufacturing firms is, except for a scale factor, just about the same now as it was prior to World War II.[1]

Composition of the Package

Separation of the pay package into its components further amplifies these conclusions. Tables 23 through 27 depict the make-up over time of the total remuneration associated with the five positions. Chart 24 summarizes that information in its most pertinent form: after-tax salary and bonus as a per cent of all after-tax compensation. The secular trend noted in Chapter 8 toward a diminishing role for direct current remuneration is, of course, still quite apparent. The more interesting feature of the data at the moment, however, is the consistently increasing importance of pensions, deferred pay, profit-sharing plans, and stock options at successively higher compensation levels. That pattern is followed in virtually every year studied and is especially marked from 1955 on.

If we compare the decade of the 1940's with the last nine years

[1] The differentials between positions 2 and 3 and between 3 and 4 have, however, tended to become more alike over the years.

TABLE 23

Elements of After-Tax Compensation, Top Executive, 1940–63
(dollars)

Year	Salary and Bonus	Pension	Deferred Compensation and Profit-Sharing	Stock Options	Total
1940	76,517 (75)	25,299 (25)	163 (0)	— (0)	101,979
1941	65,804 (72)	25,424 (28)	209 (0)	98 (0)	91,535
1942	49,627 (75)	16,061 (25)	272 (0)	— (0)	65,960
1943	42,523 (76)	13,675 (24)	269 (0)	— (0)	56,467
1944	41,795 (66)	21,614 (34)	264 (0)	— (0)	63,673
1945	41,221 (67)	20,112 (33)	299 (0)	— (0)	61,632
1946	48,569 (70)	18,951 (28)	1,523 (2)	— (0)	69,043
1947	51,497 (66)	24,150 (31)	2,670 (3)	— (0)	78,317
1948	75,201 (75)	20,883 (21)	2,829 (3)	842 (1)	99,756
1949	78,767 (75)	18,259 (17)	7,242 (7)	1,043 (1)	105,311
1950	79,852 (65)	30,741 (25)	9,755 (8)	2,442 (2)	122,790
1951	74,623 (68)	24,469 (23)	2,238 (2)	8,010 (7)	109,341
1952	71,927 (62)	22,459 (19)	3,755 (3)	18,516 (16)	116,657
1953	73,100 (56)	25,644 (19)	6,976 (5)	26,063 (20)	131,782
1954	78,353 (54)	26,719 (19)	12,610 (9)	25,788 (18)	143,470
1955	79,478 (37)	46,822 (22)	13,513 (6)	74,616 (35)	214,430
1956	81,347 (35)	38,385 (16)	19,425 (8)	96,517 (41)	235,674
1957	80,736 (36)	39,733 (17)	23,508 (10)	83,252 (37)	227,227
1958	80,985 (48)	31,618 (19)	19,488 (11)	37,346 (22)	169,436
1959	82,167 (39)	31,768 (15)	21,749 (10)	75,365 (36)	211,049
1960	80,299 (36)	28,619 (13)	21,546 (10)	91,247 (41)	221,711
1961	80,297 (39)	19,236 (9)	33,921 (17)	70,819 (35)	204,274
1962	79,113 (35)	26,684 (13)	32,365 (14)	86,828 (39)	224,889
1963	83,073 (44)	18,726 (10)	27,399 (15)	58,082 (31)	187,279
Averages:					
1940–49	57,152 (72)	20,443 (26)	1,574 (2)	198 (0)	79,367
1955–63	80,833 (38)	31,288 (15)	23,645 (11)	74,897 (36)	210,663

NOTE: Figures in parentheses denote percentages of total each year.

TABLE 24

Elements of After-Tax Compensation, Second-Ranking Executive,
1940–63
(dollars)

Year	Salary and Bonus	Pension	Deferred Compensation and Profit-Sharing	Stock Options	Total
1940	52,715 (87)	7,611 (13)	— (0)	29 (0)	60,355
1941	46,069 (72)	17,895 (28)	— (0)	50 (0)	64,014
1942	39,191 (82)	8,587 (18)	— (0)	— (0)	47,778
1943	32,473 (78)	8,921 (22)	— (0)	— (0)	41,394
1944	32,601 (71)	13,390 (29)	— (0)	— (0)	45,991
1945	33,341 (75)	11,247 (25)	36 (0)	— (0)	44,624
1946	41,213 (79)	9,724 (19)	1,273 (2)	— (0)	52,210
1947	40,958 (79)	10,999 (21)	115 (0)	— (0)	52,072
1948	58,556 (81)	12,553 (17)	1,146 (2)	19 (0)	72,274
1949	60,998 (79)	12,680 (16)	4,009 (5)	52 (0)	77,738
1950	65,179 (78)	15,369 (18)	3,408 (4)	237 (0)	84,192
1951	64,968 (78)	14,523 (17)	2,242 (3)	2,074 (2)	83,806
1952	59,270 (69)	13,636 (16)	5,938 (7)	6,933 (8)	85,777
1953	63,403 (68)	14,982 (16)	4,442 (5)	10,824 (11)	93,651
1954	69,261 (68)	14,964 (15)	7,106 (7)	10,007 (10)	101,337
1955	71,704 (53)	25,320 (19)	5,753 (4)	32,993 (24)	135,770
1956	72,788 (50)	20,158 (14)	11,509 (8)	41,144 (28)	145,599
1957	71,808 (50)	20,663 (15)	11,981 (8)	38,800 (27)	143,251
1958	69,919 (59)	20,558 (17)	11,570 (10)	16,832 (14)	118,879
1959	67,813 (48)	17,554 (12)	14,071 (10)	43,491 (30)	142,929
1960	71,572 (48)	16,003 (11)	14,323 (9)	48,683 (32)	150,581
1961	68,363 (45)	16,383 (11)	25,550 (17)	40,157 (27)	150,453
1962	72,604 (46)	17,252 (11)	8,140 (5)	59,112 (38)	157,109
1963	72,509 (54)	17,049 (13)	10,144 (7)	34,656 (26)	134,358
Averages:					
1940–49	43,811 (79)	11,361 (20)	658 (1)	15 (0)	55,845
1955–63	71,009 (50)	18,993 (13)	12,560 (9)	39,541 (28)	142,103

NOTE: Figures in parentheses denote percentages of total each year.

TABLE 25

Elements of After-Tax Compensation, Third-Ranking Executive,
1940–63
(dollars)

Year	Salary and Bonus	Pension	Deferred Compensation and Profit-Sharing	Stock Options		Total
1940	46,295 (92)	3,715 (8)	— (0)	70	(0)	50,080
1941	38,935 (75)	12,635 (25)	— (0)	98	(0)	51,669
1942	33,601 (83)	6,859 (17)	— (0)	—	(0)	40,460
1943	30,062 (84)	5,747 (16)	— (0)	—	(0)	35,809
1944	29,505 (79)	7,887 (21)	— (0)	—	(0)	37,392
1945	29,229 (79)	7,738 (21)	33 (0)	—	(0)	37,001
1946	36,245 (85)	6,486 (15)	87 (0)	—	(0)	42,818
1947	35,874 (81)	7,822 (18)	432 (1)	8	(0)	44,136
1948	51,561 (86)	8,336 (14)	253 (0)	89	(0)	60,239
1949	51,869 (83)	9,801 (16)	572 (1)	52	(0)	62,293
1950	56,004 (80)	12,219 (18)	1,041 (2)	321	(0)	69,584
1951	54,580 (75)	14,941 (21)	1,604 (2)	1,795	(2)	72,920
1952	54,270 (74)	12,788 (17)	1,091 (2)	5,263	(7)	73,412
1953	55,664 (71)	14,378 (18)	2,127 (3)	6,675	(8)	78,843
1954	61,179 (73)	10,615 (13)	5,464 (7)	5,934	(7)	83,193
1955	63,116 (58)	19,516 (18)	3,163 (3)	23,193	(21)	108,988
1956	65,479 (56)	14,746 (13)	5,528 (5)	30,981	(26)	116,734
1957	64,798 (55)	16,740 (14)	8,558 (7)	28,267	(24)	118,362
1958	64,678 (64)	14,209 (14)	6,624 (7)	15,683	(15)	101,195
1959	68,140 (53)	14,697 (11)	13,572 (11)	32,850	(25)	129,259
1960	66,987 (57)	12,483 (10)	9,008 (8)	29,676	(25)	118,154
1961	65,864 (57)	9,648 (8)	8,946 (8)	31,928	(27)	116,386
1962	68,273 (52)	11,989 (9)	11,903 (9)	38,330	(30)	130,494
1963	70,468 (58)	13,476 (11)	12,200 (10)	24,731	(21)	120,874
Averages:						
1940–49	38,318 (83)	7,703 (17)	138 (0)	32	(0)	46,191
1955–63	66,432 (56)	14,167 (12)	8,834 (8)	28,404	(24)	117,827

NOTE: Figures in parentheses denote percentages of total each year.

TABLE 26

Elements of After-Tax Compensation, Fourth-Ranking Executive,
1940–63
(dollars)

Year	Salary and Bonus	Pension	Deferred Compensation and Profit-Sharing	Stock Options	Total
1940	41,713 (92)	3,465 (8)	— (0)	84 (0)	45,262
1941	36,692 (90)	4,174 (10)	— (0)	98 (0)	40,964
1942	31,620 (87)	4,619 (13)	— (0)	39 (0)	36,278
1943	27,583 (86)	4,347 (14)	— (0)	— (0)	31,930
1944	27,502 (84)	5,187 (16)	— (0)	— (0)	32,689
1945	27,699 (84)	5,203 (16)	40 (0)	— (0)	32,942
1946	32,562 (83)	6,123 (16)	516 (1)	— (0)	39,201
1947	33,653 (85)	5,673 (14)	174 (1)	— (0)	39,500
1948	47,334 (88)	6,009 (11)	290 (1)	107 (0)	53,740
1949	49,422 (87)	7,024 (12)	401 (1)	54 (0)	56,901
1950	50,704 (82)	10,179 (17)	786 (1)	256 (0)	61,925
1951	53,097 (83)	9,140 (14)	490 (1)	1,577 (2)	64,304
1952	51,117 (80)	8,458 (13)	1,310 (2)	3,396 (5)	64,281
1953	52,808 (79)	8,123 (12)	1,798 (3)	4,253 (6)	66,983
1954	57,400 (79)	8,333 (12)	3,889 (5)	2,858 (4)	72,480
1955	60,512 (67)	14,892 (17)	1,891 (2)	13,005 (14)	90,301
1956	61,902 (63)	12,525 (13)	3,204 (3)	20,858 (21)	98,491
1957	59,733 (64)	13,090 (14)	3,622 (4)	16,400 (18)	92,844
1958	58,281 (69)	9,886 (11)	2,268 (3)	14,304 (17)	84,740
1959	61,469 (65)	9,488 (10)	4,813 (5)	18,890 (20)	94,660
1960	57,939 (62)	10,596 (11)	7,728 (8)	17,794 (19)	94,057
1961	56,786 (58)	10,203 (11)	7,915 (8)	22,491 (23)	97,395
1962	58,544 (58)	14,419 (14)	8,642 (9)	18,497 (19)	100,102
1963	65,768 (72)	11,254 (12)	7,313 (8)	7,422 (8)	91,758
Averages:					
1940–49	35,578 (87)	5,182 (13)	142 (0)	38 (0)	40,942
1955–63	60,104 (64)	11,817 (12)	5,266 (6)	16,629 (18)	93,816

NOTE: Figures in parentheses denote percentages of total each year.

TABLE 27

Elements of After-Tax Compensation, Fifth-Ranking Executive, 1940–63
(dollars)

Year	Salary and Bonus	Pension	Deferred Compensation and Profit-Sharing	Stock Options	Total
1940	37,978 (93)	3,045 (7)	— (0)	— (0)	41,023
1941	32,694 (90)	3,530 (10)	— (0)	20 (0)	36,245
1942	27,912 (89)	3,488 (11)	— (0)	— (0)	31,400
1943	25,109 (87)	3,855 (13)	— (0)	— (0)	28,964
1944	25,541 (86)	4,081 (14)	— (0)	— (0)	29,622
1945	26,412 (87)	4,034 (13)	— (0)	— (0)	30,446
1946	31,688 (88)	4,423 (12)	10 (0)	— (0)	36,120
1947	32,272 (90)	3,630 (10)	8 (0)	9 (0)	35,919
1948	45,529 (89)	5,605 (11)	58 (0)	17 (0)	51,210
1949	46,108 (89)	5,570 (11)	156 (0)	46 (0)	51,881
1950	49,589 (88)	6,343 (11)	379 (1)	254 (0)	56,565
1951	48,262 (86)	6,646 (12)	439 (1)	862 (1)	56,209
1952	47,330 (83)	6,789 (12)	202 (0)	2,802 (5)	57,122
1953	51,096 (86)	6,831 (11)	323 (1)	1,394 (2)	59,644
1954	54,476 (84)	6,964 (11)	582 (1)	2,879 (4)	64,901
1955	55,481 (72)	9,822 (13)	816 (1)	10,411 (14)	76,531
1956	58,528 (66)	9,409 (11)	1,409 (2)	18,954 (21)	88,300
1957	60,075 (71)	8,810 (10)	2,102 (3)	13,903 (16)	84,889
1958	55,025 (76)	8,547 (12)	2,355 (3)	6,496 (9)	72,423
1959	55,032 (70)	9,408 (12)	3,264 (4)	10,633 (14)	78,337
1960	53,061 (65)	9,543 (12)	6,872 (8)	12,267 (15)	81,743
1961	55,163 (62)	9,250 (11)	6,867 (8)	17,018 (19)	88,298
1962	56,725 (70)	10,218 (12)	3,185 (4)	11,045 (14)	81,174
1963	52,599 (74)	9,103 (13)	3,436 (5)	5,786 (8)	70,924
Averages:					
1940–49	33,124 (89)	4,126 (11)	23 (0)	9 (0)	37,282
1955–63	55,743 (69)	9,346 (12)	3,367 (4)	11,835 (15)	80,291

NOTE: Figures in parentheses denote percentages of total each year.

CHART 24

After-Tax Salary and Bonus as a Percentage of
Total After-Tax Compensation, 1940–63

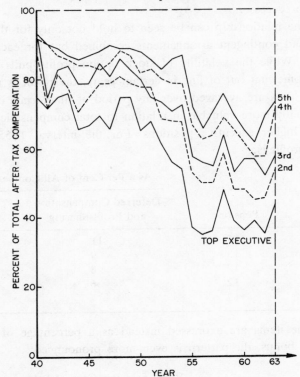

recorded, the breakdown of the total after-tax remuneration received in
each of those periods is as follows:

Executive Rank	Salary and Bonus as Per Cent of All Compensation	
	1940–49	1955–63
1	72	38
2	79	50
3	83	56
4	87	64
5	89	69

Supplements to salary and bonus therefore turn out to be twice as important in recent years for the top executive in each company as for the fifth-ranking man, and more than twice as important as for his own pre-1950 predecessors.

The same relationship can be seen to hold not only for the several deferred and contingent arrangements combined but for each one individually. While the volatility of stock option profits pulls the comparisons somewhat out of line in certain years, the result is unmistakable if the data are averaged over any period of time: *each* device becomes steadily more valuable in relation to total compensation at progressively higher executive positions. For the interval 1955 through 1963 the profile is: [2]

| | | As a Per Cent of All Compensation: | |
Executive Rank	Pensions	Deferred Compensation and Profit-Sharing	Stock Options
1	15	11	36
2	13	9	28
3	12	8	24
4	12	6	18
5	12	4	15

If the same items are expressed instead as a percentage of after-tax salary and bonus, the pattern is even more pronounced:

| | | Value as a Per Cent of Salary and Bonus: | |
Executive Rank	Pensions	Deferred Compensation and Profit-Sharing	Stock Options
1	39	29	93
2	27	18	56
3	21	13	43
4	20	9	28
5	17	6	21

[2] Similar comparisons for other periods would not be meaningful, since it was not until the mid-1950's that many of these arrangements began to be widely used.

The increasing emphasis on stock options in particular has a very powerful effect on the over-all results, since they were by far the most sizeable adjunct to current remuneration during this period. Indeed, they were so profitable that "adjunct" is really too mild a description.

It is also worth noting that the value of an individual's prospective pension benefits increases in importance as compared with his salary and bonus at successively higher levels just as do the other arrangements indicated. This is somewhat unexpected, because in most instances the promised benefits are specified to be a direct function of salary by the provisions of the corporation's retirement plan. The fact that the comparisons here are on an after-tax basis accounts for part of the observed progression (i.e., if pension benefits are proportional to before-tax salary, they will rise steadily in relation to after-tax salary) but certainly not all of it. The rest is apparently a "real" phenomenon resulting from differences in ages, years of employment, career salary patterns, and other factors.

The most likely explanation for such a consistent and unequivocal trend in the composition of the pay package is, of course, a reaction by firms to the heavy personal income tax burden on very large salary and bonus payments. The availability of deferred and contingent compensation devices provides them with an obvious alternative whose attractiveness increases steadily the greater the aggregate remuneration to be generated. The responses which the cross-section data identify are therefore appropriate and predictable ones.

There may, however, be another consideration which has contributed to the popularity of these devices, especially in the case of the top executives of business firms such as those examined here—and it is in connection with the *top* executive that we observe most clearly the role of various supplements in making up for a lag in the rate of growth of direct cash payments. Given the SEC's proxy statement disclosure rules, a large corporation may find it more prudent from the standpoint of shareholder or labor relations to reward its highest-paid employee by relying heavily on deferred and contingent arrangements. Even though the salaries and bonuses of the firm's other senior officials are also published each year, the largest figure reported is likely to command the most public attention and be the focal point of any criticism. Thus the historical patterns recorded above may in part be a reflection of a concern by corporations with the appearance as well as the substance of the compensation bargain.[3]

Variability of Compensation

A final aspect of the pay package which the time series above highlight is the variability of aggregate after-tax rewards from year to year. The fact that an increasing reliance on common stock-based compensation instruments has in recent years caused the value of an executive's remuneration to become more sensitive to market conditions and thereby more volatile has been pointed out on several occasions. Given now a total compensation profile across all five top executive positions, it is possible to examine the relationships among those positions in this dimension as well.

For that purpose, the period from 1955 to 1963 again seems the most appropriate on which to focus. The patterns observed in earlier years reflect the influence both of growth trends in before-tax compensation and of several changes in tax rates. The resulting variability of after-tax rewards at different executive levels in those years is, accordingly, only in small part a function of conscious compensation policy differences. After 1955, however, personal tax rates did not vary, and aggregate executive remuneration effectively reached a plateau. At the same time, those rewards which give rise to most of the volatility in which we are interested finally came into their own. The last nine years of the study therefore provide as "controlled" an environment as we are likely to find for any cross-sectional analysis.

The pattern that emerges from the data for those years is summarized in the tabulation on the following page. It turns out that, in general, the higher an executive's total compensation, the more volatile it is, both in absolute terms and in relation to average pay. This pattern is followed quite consistently as far down as the fourth-ranking executive position in each company, but seems to falter thereafter. A more extensive sample covering a greater range of management levels would

[3] A similar point was made in Chapter 8.

| Executive Rank | Total After-Tax Compensation: 1955–63 (dollars) | | | Variability Indexes | |
	Mean(μ)	Range(R)	Standard Deviation(σ) [a]	R/μ	σ/μ
1	210,663	66,238	19,793	0.314	0.094
2	142,103	38,230	10,648	0.270	0.075
3	117,827	29,299	8,556	0.249	0.073
4	93,816	15,362	4,408	0.164	0.047
5	80,291	17,376	5,961	0.216	0.074

[a] Computed in each instance on the basis of the nine observed deviations from the 1955–63 mean.

therefore be especially useful in this case. Because the importance of ownership-oriented rewards increases steadily at higher ranks, the volatility of aggregate remuneration would normally be expected to display the same tendency. As things stand, however, it is impossible to tell whether the apparent departure from that expectation in the fifth-ranking position is due to some special set of circumstances related to the particular group of executives studied or is characteristic of an actual levelling-off of the degree of compensation variability at the point indicated.

The extent as well as the pattern of such variability is worth emphasizing. Even during a period when over-all compensation rates reached a plateau, the same executive position within the typical large manufacturing corporation was subject to anywhere from a 16 to a 32 per cent variation in total after-tax remuneration from one year to the next, depending on how well that corporation's performance was received by the investing public. This finding suggests a degree of stock market involvement by the executives affected which should go a long way toward encouraging an entrepreneurial attitude on their part. It is also clear that the much-maligned [4] stock option is primarily responsible for this development. A comparison of the fluctuations in the annual stock option "current income equivalents" observed since 1955 with the measures of variability tabulated above for the whole compensation package illustrates the latter point.

[4] By groups other than executives, that is. See, for example: *The Stock Option Scandal*, Industrial Union Department, AFL-CIO, Washington, D.C., 1959; Erwin N. Griswold, "Are Stock Options Getting Out of Hand?," *Harvard Business Review*, November–December 1960, pp. 49–55.

Executive Rank	Total Compensation		Stock Options		Relative Variability	
	R_t	σ_t	R_s	σ_s [a]	R_s/R_t	σ_s/σ_t
1	$66,238	$19,793	$59,171	$17,181	0.893	0.868
2	38,230	10,648	42,280	10,894	1.106	1.023
3	29,299	8,556	22,647	6,159	0.773	0.720
4	15,362	4,408	15,069	4,289	0.981	0.973
5	17,376	5,961	13,168	4,099	0.758	0.688

[a] Determined according to the nine deviations from the 1955–63 mean stock option current equivalent.

Stock options clearly exerted the major influence during this interval. In fact, the total after-tax compensation of the second-ranking executives would have been even more volatile had other rewards not operated to dampen the fluctuations that resulted from changing option profits.

Executive Ages

While the concern thus far has been with the size and form of the income enjoyed by executives, there are several other characteristics of their employment circumstances which necessarily become apparent in the course of generating data on compensation. Two of these are so easily identified and tabulated, and are sufficiently interesting, that a short digression seems in order.

Table 28 and Chart 25 indicate, for every year from 1940 to 1963, the average (mean) age of the individuals who occupied the five highest-paid executive positions in the companies studied. The figures in parentheses in Table 28 denote the number of men actually represented in the sample in each year at each of those five positions (see Appendix J).

The most striking feature of the resulting history is the fact that top executives in the late 1950's and early 1960's turn out, on average, to be about four or five years older than their predecessors of the early 1940's. The forty-seven men who were the highest-paid individuals in their respective firms in 1963 had an average age of fifty-nine years. In 1940 the comparable figure for the forty-nine men who held similar positions at that time was only fifty-five years. This pattern holds throughout. The executives occupying each of the next three lower

TABLE 28

Average Age of Executives, 1940–63

Year	Executive Ranking				
	First	Second	Third	Fourth	Fifth
1940	56 (49)	53 (48)	54 (44)	53 (45)	51 (44)
1941	56 (49)	55 (48)	54 (47)	55 (46)	52 (45)
1942	56 (49)	55 (49)	56 (47)	55 (45)	54 (46)
1943	57 (49)	55 (49)	56 (47)	54 (47)	55 (45)
1944	58 (50)	58 (50)	56 (48)	55 (47)	52 (46)
1945	59 (50)	56 (50)	56 (48)	55 (46)	54 (45)
1946	59 (50)	57 (49)	56 (49)	56 (47)	55 (44)
1947	59 (50)	57 (49)	57 (49)	53 (47)	54 (46)
1948	59 (50)	57 (50)	56 (50)	55 (48)	55 (43)
1949	59 (50)	57 (50)	56 (50)	55 (48)	56 (43)
1950	60 (50)	58 (50)	56 (49)	57 (49)	56 (46)
1951	59 (50)	59 (50)	57 (49)	56 (46)	54 (47)
1952	60 (50)	58 (50)	56 (47)	57 (47)	56 (46)
1953	60 (50)	60 (50)	56 (46)	55 (47)	55 (40)
1954	61 (50)	59 (50)	56 (47)	57 (45)	56 (41)
1955	62 (50)	59 (50)	58 (46)	56 (43)	56 (38)
1956	61 (50)	61 (48)	59 (46)	56 (42)	55 (31)
1957	61 (50)	60 (48)	57 (45)	57 (40)	55 (29)
1958	61 (50)	58 (49)	59 (40)	56 (38)	56 (29)
1959	61 (50)	58 (48)	59 (38)	56 (32)	55 (29)
1960	60 (50)	59 (46)	57 (33)	57 (32)	55 (24)
1961	59 (49)	60 (44)	58 (32)	56 (27)	57 (23)
1962	60 (48)	59 (40)	59 (30)	57 (24)	58 (19)
1963	60 (47)	59 (37)	58 (30)	58 (21)	60 (13)

NOTE: Figures in parentheses denote the number of executives in the sample at each position in each year.

positions in 1963 appear to be approximately five years older than their pre-World War II counterparts, and the typical fifth-ranking executive fully eight years older.

A careful interpretation of these figures is called for before the trend which they signal can be accepted as conclusive, however. By the nature

CHART 25

Average Executive Ages, by Rank, 1940–63

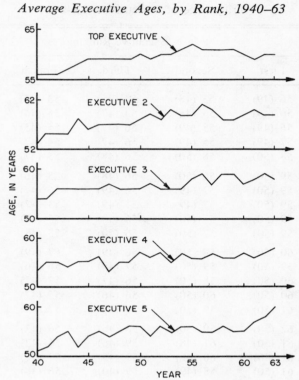

of the process involved in collecting the sample described, the tendency toward an increasing average age in each executive rank over time will almost certainly be somewhat overstated as it stands. The more frequent gaps in the data in the later years of the study result from an inability to reconstruct the early compensation experience of individuals who did not become top executives until very recently. Since such individuals were participants in pension, deferred compensation, and profit-sharing plans for a number of years prior to their appearance in their firm's proxy statements, they had a substantial history of benefit promises which was relevant to an evaluation of their present rewards but was impossible to compile—and which eliminated them from consideration here.[5] When eventually they did attain important executive positions, they were in most cases, certainly, younger than their immediate predecessors. Therefore, the sample depicted above may consist, in years when it drops significantly below a total of fifty men in a particular rank, of a disproportionate number of older executives. If so, the average ages calculated for those years will be higher than the true averages for a full sample of fifty. Because this situation occurs primarily in the more recent years indicated, an upward bias over time is likely to result.

Perhaps the least ambiguous way to handle this bias is simply to accept as valid only those figures which are generated by a set of observations sufficiently close to a complete sample that there can be little doubt as to their accuracy, or at least sufficiently close that some limits can be placed on the probable extent of their inaccuracy. A rule of thumb that might be appropriate for this purpose is the following: Let us suppose that the executives *missing* from the sample in recent years are five years younger on average than the ones *included*—an assumption which seems a fairly strong one. On that basis, the calculated average age of a sample of size forty will at most be one full year greater than the "real" average age of the whole group of fifty it purports to represent.[6] If then the figures tabulated for each executive rank are disregarded past the point where there are no longer forty or more individuals contributing data thereto, it should be possible to make statements about developments to that point at least with considerable confidence.[7]

[5] This problem was discussed previously in Chapter 7.

[6] Thus, if the average age of a group of forty men is x, the average age of a group of fifty—the last ten of which are aged $x - 5$—is:

$$x' = \frac{40x + 10(x - 5)}{50} = x - 1.$$

[7] Problems of this sort should show up only in connection with average age calculations. There is no reason to suspect that the compensation figures derived above might also be distorted to any significant extent. While the current income equivalents of such items as pensions and deferred compensation may be slightly overstated for a sample consisting of a greater percentage of older individuals than the "true" population, salary and bonus levels should be peculiar to the *position* rather than the individual. Further, stock options may well be used less extensively for executives nearing retirement age and, in the aggregate, might be slightly understated here, balancing in the total package any upward bias in the pension and deferred compensation figures. In no case, however, should there be any serious distortions, particularly since there are not many years in which the question arises at all. This contention is supported

The result is a slightly attenuated historical record, but a set of conclusions which are hardly less emphatic than those suggested by the raw
data. They may be summarized as follows:

Executive Rank	Last Year with Forty Observations	Calculated Average Age in That Year	Average Age in 1940	Age Increase [a]
1	1963	60	56	4
2	1962	59	53	5–6
3	1958	59	54	4–5
4	1957	57	53	3–4
5	1954	56	51	4–5

[a] The larger figure is the indicated difference from these tabulations and the
lower one that difference reduced by the one-year "maximum" bias likely to
result from a sample of only forty executives.

This indicates a mean increase of five years if the reported figures are
accepted and four years if the smaller "adjusted" ones are preferred. It
seems reasonable to believe, therefore, that the top executives in all
five positions in recent years *were* noticeably older than their pre-World
War II predecessors.

The other characteristic of the data which is noteworthy is the steady
increase in average executive age within each year at successively higher
positions. Up to the point where the averages begin to become suspect
due to the probable sampling bias discussed, there is a quite consistent
four- to five-year age differential between the fifth-ranking executive and
the highest-paid man. Such an observation, of course, fits the notion of
some sort of normal progression by an individual to higher positions in
his firm with increasing age and experience.

If this phenomenon is predictable, however, the general trend toward
a higher average age in *all* positions is not. Given that retirement at 65
has become a more common and more formal commitment in recent

by the marked regularity of the pattern of the compensation data among the
five executive positions examined. If a bias were present, it should be expected
to manifest itself in a more noticeable fashion than any of the computations thus
far suggest. In the case of the fifth-ranking executive, for example, the indicated
average age rose quite sharply from 1960 to 1963 as the size of the sample
simultaneously declined. Nowhere in the compensation time series is there a
counterpart of such a phenomenon. When any sudden increases or decreases in
remuneration occur, they invariably appear in all five positions—not in just
one—and they are of the same order of magnitude throughout.

years, the expectation might well be that senior executives would on average be younger now than they were prior to World War II. One conjures up visions of venerable and misanthropic robber barons still clutching the reins of industrial power in those earlier years but being steadily replaced over time by a youthful and energetic meritocracy of professional managers. Nonetheless, the results do not seem to support that particular view of life—indeed, they seem to contradict it.

Of the many possible explanations that might be offered, the one that has the most appeal here because it retains the general outlines of the plot suggested is the following: It could be that although executives frequently remained in active employment beyond age 65 in days gone by, they also assumed their respective positions at an earlier stage in their careers. Suppose that twenty-five years ago the top executive in most firms did not retire until he was age 68, but that he likewise became the top executive when he was only age 50. Under stable conditions a cross section of such individuals would show them to be on average 59 years old. Suppose further that nowadays every top executive retires at age 65 but that he usually does not attain that rank until he is fully 61 years old. The average age of this sort of a group would therefore be 63 years. In short, if the *frequency* of job changes among senior corporate executives has increased over time—more men now being given a chance at the top positions—the results tabulated can be rationalized despite a trend toward earlier retirement.

Job Tenure

Evidence on job tenure that would permit a test of this hypothesis is available within the current sample. The average length of time the individuals who are the five highest-paid executives in each firm typically hold their respective positions can be calculated, and any trends over time in that regard identified. A move toward significantly shorter terms of office since the early 1940's would be expected to emerge if the explanation suggested above is valid.

Table 29 presents the results of such an analysis for six different benchmark years covering the period studied. Thus, in 1950, the men who were the highest-paid executives in the sample companies had, on average, enjoyed that status for 5.1 years previously and would continue

TABLE 29

Executive Job Tenure, by Position, 1940–63

Executive Ranking	1940	1945	1950	1955	1960	1963
Average Number of Years in Position Prior to Date						
1	—	3.5	5.1	6.0	4.6	4.9
2	—	2.2	3.2	2.8	3.2	3.4
3	—	1.9	2.1	2.8	2.0	3.0
4	—	2.0	1.6	2.6	2.5	2.5
5	—	1.8	1.9	2.1	2.6	3.0
Average Number of Years in Position After Date						
1	8.2	5.2	4.6	2.7	1.7	—
2	4.8	3.5	3.0	1.7	1.3	—
3	3.4	2.6	2.2	1.3	1.0	—
4	3.3	2.2	1.9	1.6	0.9	—
5	2.5	2.4	1.6	1.5	1.0	—
Total Number of Years Position Occupied						
1	n.a.	9.7	10.7	9.7	7.3	n.a.
2	n.a.	6.7	7.2	5.5	5.5	n.a.
3	n.a.	5.5	5.2	5.1	4.0	n.a.
4	n.a.	5.2	5.5	5.2	4.4	n.a.
5	n.a.	5.2	5.5	4.6	4.6	n.a.

to do so for 4.6 more—a total of 10.7 years counting 1950 itself.[8] Since the data do not begin until 1940, of course, there is no record of the number of years served in the various positions prior to that time—and, similarly, no record of tenure past 1963. The 1945 "before" and the 1960 "after" computations are likely to be biased to a certain extent for the same reason.

The total job tenure figures listed at the bottom of the table are the pertinent ones. As it turns out, they do display some tendency to decrease over time, particularly if the 1945 figure is adjusted upward to

[8] A similar analysis was performed on the basis of executive rankings by salary and bonus rather than total compensation. The results were almost identical.

reflect the attenuation of the data prior to 1940. The trend is hardly a very strong one, however, and is certainly not anywhere near the magnitude necessary to alone bring about a four-to-five-year change in average ages. Moreover, the 1960 figure is biased downward, and its true value would make any over-all trend look exceedingly mild. On the basis of these results, then, some other explanation must be found.

One thing that does stand out in the tabulations is the evidence that the typical top executive has a significantly longer term in office than any of his four closest subordinates. He holds his job, it seems, approximately half again as long as does the second-ranking executive and a little less than twice as long as any of the next three men—all of whom apparently have about the same tenure. This pattern is followed throughout the period under examination and shows no sign of lessening over time. The picture that emerges, therefore, is one of fairly rapid job turnover on the way to the top of the ladder but reasonable stability once it is attained.

By way of final comment, the fact that average top executive age has risen during the last quarter century has a further implication when it is considered in the context of the slow rate of growth of compensation observed over the same interval: not only have executives not experienced very substantial increases in pay, but it now seems to take each individual longer to reach a position where he can actually enjoy such increases as there are.

Differences in Rankings

The likelihood that the ranking of executives within a particular company by the size of their salary and bonus payments may not be the same as that which results from ordering them according to their *total* compensation has been alluded to earlier. The extent to which a difference in the two schedules does exist becomes apparent in the course of generating the cross-sectional comparisons just presented.

A sample consisting of the top five executives in each of fifty companies over a period of twenty-four years will contain at most 6,000 man-years of compensation data. By the nature of the available proxy statement information, 5,300 of those man-years were in fact able to be compiled and thus comprise the sample analyzed throughout the study.[9] The question therefore is: In how many instances would the individual occupying one of the 5,300 slots have been in a different position within his firm had the various rankings been constructed using direct cash payments as the relevant criterion [10] rather than aggregate remuneration? It turns out that there would have been a total of 2,484 such instances, implying that approximately 47 per cent of the time, salary and bonus figures are not good indexes of even the *relative* magnitude of an executive's rewards.

A second approach is to consider the number of "company-years" in which similar discrepancies occur. Out of a possible 1,200 such data units in the sample (fifty companies for twenty-four years each) a different ordering for some or all of the top five executives results in 810 cases, if current remuneration instead of total remuneration is used for the rankings.

There are a number of reasons for these differences. One that might be anticipated is that frequently a senior executive who is nearing retirement is not awarded stock option and incentive plan benefits to the same extent that his lower-salaried, and potentially more mobile, colleagues are. When the impact of those arrangements is considered, his total pay package may well emerge as less valuable than some of theirs.

Another situation is one in which a long-time top executive is kept on for several years past normal retirement age in order to lend his experience and counsel to the new generation. Since his pension benefits are by then fully determined and completely funded, there ceases to be any additional current income equivalent for him on that account,[11] and he is often passed over in the granting of new stock options and deferred compensation benefits. He may, however, continue to receive his firm's highest annual salary. Even if he is officially reclassified as a "consultant" and awarded a somewhat smaller annual retainer than his previous salary, he may still stand as one of the top men in the firm if judged on that basis alone, but not according to total compensation.

Differences in rankings can also arise if one executive has an espe-

[9] The process is discussed in Chapter 7. The population is that listed in Table 28 and Appendix J.

[10] As, of course, was done in the presentation of data on the five highest-salaried executives in each company over time.

[11] See the discussion of this point in Chapter 2.

cially favorable experience with his stock options, exercising them at a time when the market price of the shares involved is substantially higher than it was when other senior executives took similar action. The effect may be to raise him a notch or two in the total compensation hierarchy as compared with his position in terms of current remuneration. While it could be argued that this change is primarily a result of his investment skill—or good fortune—rather than an expression of the intent of the employer company, it is nonetheless a fact. Such executives do enjoy a higher level of remuneration than their less clever or less fortunate brethren. The value of a stock option necessarily depends in large part on the manner in which it is administered by its recipient and that attribute should be recognized in a scheme of compensation measurement and ranking.[12]

A fourth situation is that in which a difference in ages causes the aggregate remuneration of one executive to exceed that of another whose salary and bonus are somewhat greater. Suppose two individuals differ only slightly in the amount of salary and bonus they receive and in the size of the annual pension benefits they are promised, but the lower-salaried one is older by, say, five years. It is quite possible that, because the current income equivalent of the latter's pension will be spread over a shorter interval of time, it will be enough larger than the one constructed for his colleague to make the total value of his pay package greater. While again this may be considered a peculiarity of the circumstances, it is still true that the older executive, because he is closer to retirement, does in fact enjoy the larger effective reward.

Finally, of course, there is what might be termed the "normal" case: A particular individual's total remuneration turns out to be greater than that of several of his fellow executives having higher salaries and bonuses

---

[12] The possibility that unanticipated variations in stock option profits might account for certain changes in the rankings has a counterpart in terms of the collective experience of the men in the sample. The "plateau" in total remuneration reached in 1955 may well not have been an *intended* plateau. It could be, for example, that the rewards generated by stock options were unexpectedly large in 1955 and 1956 (see Charts 6 and 9) due to stock market conditions and that, in response, firms reduced the size not only of subsequent option grants but of other rewards in order to permit the remuneration of their top executives to average out over time to levels more like those originally aimed for. If this were the case, the historical record in terms of *desired* compensation might in fact be a steadily rising one during the 1950's even though the actual pattern exhibits a sudden increase followed by a leveling off.

simply because his firm quite intentionally—and for whatever reason—provides him with more in the way of deferred and contingent arrangements.[13] These are the instances which perhaps point up most clearly the desirability of adopting a comprehensive view of the pay package in attempting statements about its size and historical development. On the other hand, all the indicated possible causes of a different set of rankings are relevant and legitimate ones. They imply that every dimension of the pay package is important to an evaluation of its profile—and that this profile would be incorrectly drawn anywhere from one-half to two-thirds of the time if salary and bonus alone were used for the purpose.

Summary and Conclusions

Over the last quarter century, the annual salary-plus-bonus differentials between the top executives of large manufacturing firms and each of the men immediately below them in the corporate hierarchy have narrowed. In the case of before-tax current remuneration, this trend has occurred only in percentage terms, but after taxes both relative *and* absolute differentials have diminished. Throughout the period studied, the gap between the top executive and the second-ranking one has remained significantly greater than that between any of the other four positions recorded. In fact, the differentials increase steadily at successively higher levels of salary and bonus in every year.

When the value of the entire pay package is considered, a different history emerges. The total after-tax remuneration associated with each of the five highest-paid executive positions within the sample companies turns out to have grown at approximately the same rates since 1940. In this more meaningful sense, therefore, the senior executive compensation profile has not changed noticeably over time. Interestingly enough, that profile displays the same general characteristic as the salary and bonus schedule: the higher the executive position attained, the progressively greater the successive increases in total remuneration enjoyed.

The reason the two sets of time series differ in their historical implications is obviously the greater reliance on deferred and contingent com-

[13] Actually, the first two situations cited above really belong in this category as well.

pensation devices at higher levels of total reward. Since 1955, only 38 per cent of the highest-paid executive's aggregate after-tax remuneration has been provided by salary and bonus payments. The comparable figures for the other four top executive positions are 50, 56, 64, and 69 per cent, respectively. *Each* of the major supplements to current remuneration follows a similar pattern: The larger an individual's total compensation, the larger as a per cent of the total are every one of those supplements.

The conclusion these results suggest is that corporations seem to have made a deliberate effort to "undo" the differential effect of progressive personal income taxes on executives.[14] Indeed, that effort comes across in the data as not only deliberate but quite successful, since the persistent salary-and-bonus growth "lag" at the higher-paid executive positions has been very accurately taken care of by other devices.

A consequence of this phenomenon is the fact that the volatility of an executive's rewards increases as he attains successively higher positions within his firm. Stock options and many deferred compensation and profit-sharing plans utilize shares of the employer corporation's common stock as all or part of the compensation medium. The value of a man's pay package can therefore vary substantially from one year to the next depending on changes in investors' evaluations of his firm's performance. During the period 1955 to 1963, when such ownership-oriented rewards came into extensive use, annual changes of 16 to 32 per cent—both positive and negative—in the total remuneration associated with the same position within a firm were not uncommon, even when viewed in terms of the "average" occupant of that position. Stock options in particular accounted for much of this variability.

Information on executives' career experiences indicates that they are typically four to five years older now than were their predecessors of the early 1940's. It also appears that the higher the individual's position in his company, the longer he occupies it—the top executive in each firm enjoying by far the longest tenure of the five considered. In that connection, the size of a man's salary and bonus payments turns out to be a correct index of his standing in his firm in terms of aggregate remuneration in only about half the cases examined.

Several of the observed compensation patterns seem sufficiently well-

---

[14] Or have at least achieved results which are consistent with such an objective.

defined and reasonable that they may be extrapolated to lower management levels. A tendency toward less emphasis on deferred and contingent rewards the smaller the total remuneration to be provided is likely to appear throughout the corporation, since the need to side-step the impact of graduated personal income taxes diminishes accordingly. A steady decrease in the variability of the value of the pay package from year to year at those lower compensation levels should also follow, although the evidence for senior executives is somewhat ambiguous in this respect. Finally, a schedule of increasing total and current remuneration increments for the individual who climbs to successively higher management positions in his firm is consistent with the usual view of the compensation structure within a corporation. The rest of the story for less visible categories of executives, particularly with regard to the rates of growth of their remuneration over time, is more difficult to speculate about from the evidence available here and requires that their experience be examined directly. The compensation profile at the top of the corporate hierarchy, however, can now be spoken of with some confidence.

11

INTERCOMPANY COMPARISONS

An examination of the differences in top executive compensation policy among the corporations included in the sample rounds out the analysis. Is there a systematic relationship between the size of a firm and the rewards enjoyed by its senior executives? If so, which measure of size seems to be the most reliable predictor of compensation levels? Do large firms make more use of deferred and contingent forms of reward than small ones? Answers to such questions should serve to highlight at least some of the factors which have contributed to the generation of the collective experience described above.

Focus

Although data were not available on all five highest-paid executives in every one of the fifty companies studied in every year, this was not a significant problem when dealing with the aggregate compensation figures. There were enough observations at each executive level in each year to permit meaningful averages to be obtained. The regularity and consistency of the observed trends in remuneration within all five positions supports that contention. If the sample corporations are considered individually, however, gaps in the data do become an issue, since it is obviously inappropriate to attempt to compare the compensation of one firm's top five executives with that of the same group in a second firm, if for either or both companies a record for all five cannot be developed for the year to which the comparison is to apply.

Even though it was possible to provide data for 5,300 of the 6,000 man-years of remuneration experience that would comprise a complete sample between 1940 and 1963, the remaining 700 turn out to be widely distributed among the companies studied. As a consequence, a good many of the fifty would have to be excluded from consideration in certain years if the compensation differences among them were examined in terms of all five top executive positions.[1] That being the case, the comparisons here will concentrate on the remuneration of only the highest-paid individual in each firm. This will permit the maximum number of companies to contribute data to those comparisons, but it will not, importantly, mean that we will sacrifice much in the way of the reliability of the results obtained. The amount and the form of the rewards of a corporation's top executive are, in fact, a dependable guide to the experience of his colleagues in relation to executives in other firms.

For example, for thirty-nine corporations in the sample, information on all five top executive positions is available for 1940. If these firms are ranked first according to the total amount of after-tax compensation received by their highest-paid executive alone and then by the amount received by all five together, the Spearman rank correlation coefficient (ρ) between the two schedules turns out to be 0.934 and is easily significant at the .0001 level.[2] A similar conclusion applies to any year we might care to consider:

Year	ρ	Sample Size	Critical "t" at .0001 Level	Computed "t"
1940	0.934	39	4.129	15.890
1945	0.916	43	4.085	14.631
1950	0.922	45	4.067	15.571
1955	0.959	35	4.185	19.465
1963	0.971	25 [a]	4.415	19.470

[a] The 1963 computations are based on a comparison of rankings by (1) top executive total compensation and (2) total compensation of the top *three,* since there are only six firms in that year for which data on all five positions could be compiled.

For all practical purposes, therefore, the remuneration of the top executive in each firm should be a suitable proxy for the circumstances of his four closest subordinates. As such, it provides a convenient and efficient vehicle for the intercorporate analysis which is of concern here.[3]

---

[1] This, parenthetically, is an advertisement for the random nature of the missing data.

[2] Using a one-tailed "t" test for significance.

[3] A case could also be made for the proposition that, in any event, the experience of just the top executive is the most appropriate focus for such com-

Compensation and Company Characteristics: Distributions

A comparison of the attributes of the firms in the sample with the re-muneration enjoyed by their respective top executives indicates that there is a much greater degree of variation in characteristics among the companies themselves than there is in the amount of compensation they provide for their senior officers. This conclusion holds not only for the current structure of managerial rewards but for that which existed prior to World War II as well. Consider the following:

A. FOR 1940:

	Sample Mean (μ)	Standard Deviation (σ)	σ/μ
Company assets	$330.0	$351.0	1.064
Company sales	254.7	298.7	1.173
Before-tax profits	32.6	50.5	1.549
After-tax profits	22.0	31.8	1.445
Equity market value	243.7	383.8	1.574
Top executive's before-tax salary and bonus	137	95	0.693
Top executive's total after-tax compensation	102	80	0.787

B. FOR 1963:

	Sample Mean (μ)	Standard Deviation (σ)	σ/μ
Company assets	$1,583.0	$1,615.0	1.020
Company sales	1,910.5	2,337.9	1.223
Before-tax profits	248.5	495.1	1.992
After-tax profits	137.0	244.9	1.787
Equity market value	2,366.1	3,850.0	1.627
Top executive's before-tax salary and bonus	210	82	0.391
Top executive's total after-tax compensation	187	144	0.768

parisons because there is little question as to differences in the nature or scope of his job from one firm to the next. Problems of consistent job definition can become more acute in connection with lower-ranking individuals.

The figures pertaining to company characteristics are in millions of dollars, while those which refer to compensation are in thousands. Data from forty-nine companies are included in the calculations for 1940 and from forty-six companies for 1963—these being the number of firms out of the fifty studied for which full information about the remuneration of their top executive was available in those years.[4]

The significant column in the tabulations is that which records the ratio of the standard deviation of each distribution to its mean—the so-called "coefficient of variation." This parameter is a dimensionless index which measures the degree of dispersion of each item about its average value and thus provides a common basis for a comparison of variations in quantities which have quite different original dimensions. It is apparent from these calculations that both at the beginning and at the end of the time period covered there was a much wider diversity of characteristics among the corporations examined than there was in their compensation policies, at least at the top of the organization. If there is a secular trend in the figures, it seems to be in the direction of reinforcing this phenomenon. The coefficient of variation of all but one of the features of the companies in the sample increased between 1940 and 1963, while the corresponding values for their salary and total compensation awards decreased.[5]

A second noteworthy attribute of the data is the fact that the dispersion of the distribution of total after-tax compensation is considerably greater than that of the distribution of salary and bonus payments. This situation, of course, is a result of the impact of a wider range of factors on the value of the various deferred and contingent rewards enjoyed by executives than are relevant to their salaries and bonuses. In

[4] It should be noted that there is no reason to suspect that in this or any subsequent discussions a bias is introduced because several firms are excluded from the comparisons for lack of data. The inadequacy of some of the proxy statement information is not peculiar to any particular category or size of firm. The fact that we are unable in every case to include all fifty corporations in the analysis should therefore be of no more concern than if the original sample simply consisted of fewer firms to begin with.

[5] After-tax salary and bonus data were not included in the tabulations because the degree of variation in those figures is predictable from the given before-tax distribution, i.e., a progressive income tax schedule guarantees that the coefficient of variation of after-tax current remuneration will necessarily be less than that of its pretax counterpart. The contrast with the several company characteristics would therefore be even more marked on that basis.

addition to those parameters of company compensation policy and position attained which determine the amount of an individual's current remuneration each year, his aggregate earnings depend also on his age, his previous experience under whatever noncurrent compensation arrangements he enjoys, the market's most recent appraisal of the value of his firm's common stock, and his skill or good fortune in taking advantage of any stock option grants. It is reasonable to expect, therefore, that this aggregate would differ more substantially among executives than would the direct cash payments they enjoy. Because supplements to salary and bonus have become relatively more important over the years, it is also not surprising to find that the difference between the degree of dispersion in the total pay package and in current remuneration has widened since 1940. In that year the coefficient of variation for before-tax salary and bonus was 0.693 and for total compensation 0.787. In 1963 the figures were 0.394 and 0.768, respectively.[6]

Compensation Growth Rates

The rates of growth in the remuneration associated with the senior executive positions in the companies studied varied extensively around the average rate for the sample as a whole. The distribution of the relevant compound annual rates between 1940 and 1963 for the forty-five companies for which compensation data in both years were available is recorded in Table 30 and in Chart 26.[7] Those observations may be summarized as follows:

	Mean Growth Rate (per cent)	Standard Deviation of Distribution of Growth Rates (per cent)
Before-tax salary and bonus	2.6	2.0
After-tax salary and bonus	0.1	1.4
Total after-tax compensation	2.7	2.9

[6] Again, if after-tax salary and bonus were included in the comparisons, the contrast and its trend over time would be sharper still.

[7] The numerical designation of the individual firms in the table does not correspond to their alphabetic order as listed in Appendix I. The missing numbers denote the five companies for which either or both the 1940 and 1963 top-executive compensation figures could not be obtained.

TABLE 30

Distribution of Compensation Annual Growth Rates, 1940–63
(per cent)

Company Number	Before-Tax Salary	After-Tax Salary	Total Compensation	Company Number	Before-Tax Salary	After-Tax Salary	Total Compensation
1	1.5	−0.7	1.5	26	−0.1	−1.7	1.3
2	3.1	0.8	3.9	27	1.7	0.0	1.2
3	3.8	0.9	3.0	28	3.2	0.0	4.1
4	1.8	−0.1	1.0	30	3.5	0.2	5.8
5	3.3	0.5	5.7	31	2.9	0.4	3.9
6	4.4	1.0	−0.3	32	4.3	1.9	7.4
8	4.3	0.9	7.6	33	−0.7	−1.8	0.9
9	4.0	0.9	4.6	34	0.4	−1.3	1.3
10	0.8	−0.5	1.0	36	1.9	0.2	2.3
11	2.0	−0.6	−3.4	37	5.6	2.3	4.7
12	−1.4	−2.4	−0.2	38	1.6	−1.0	8.8
13	7.2	4.4	7.8	39	2.8	−0.2	7.1
15	−2.6	−3.8	4.9	40	2.6	0.2	1.7
16	4.0	0.3	4.7	41	3.6	1.1	2.5
17	1.8	0.0	4.9	42	6.0	2.2	2.4
18	4.6	1.5	1.6	43	1.7	0.0	−1.3
19	2.2	0.3	3.9	44	3.1	0.4	3.1
20	3.8	1.2	3.9	45	1.8	−0.1	−4.1
21	2.3	0.4	1.7	46	−2.7	−3.9	−3.1
22	3.6	0.6	3.9	48	4.5	1.7	2.6
23	1.4	−0.5	2.0	49	3.8	−0.2	3.8
24	0.0	−1.2	0.4	50	3.4	0.0	5.0
25	4.2	0.6	−2.2				

The mean values thus computed differ slightly from those determined in Chapter 8 because in this case each company's rate of growth is weighted equally, while earlier the weights were based on the absolute amount of compensation paid by each firm.

It is obvious both from this summary and from Chart 26 that executives had quite different experiences depending on the company they worked for. Particularly striking is the fact that in seven instances the total after-tax compensation received by the senior officer in the firm actually was *smaller* in 1963 than it was in 1940, i.e., the observed rate of growth is negative. The same is true of before-tax salary and bonus in

CHART 26

Distribution of Compensation Growth Rates, 1940–63

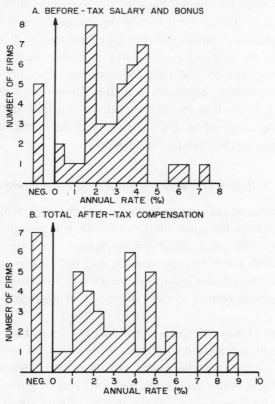

A. BEFORE - TAX SALARY AND BONUS

B. TOTAL AFTER–TAX COMPENSATION

five firms and of its after-tax counterpart in fully sixteen firms—over one-third of the indicated sample. It is worth noting, however, that while such situations certainly contribute to a poor collective historical performance of remuneration compared with the rates of growth of the employer companies, they do not by any means dominate or distort that comparison by affecting the aggregate figures disproportionately. In only one of the forty-five instances tabulated did all three measures of the compensation enjoyed by the top executive of a firm grow more rapidly than even the slowest-growing of the five indexes of the size of the firm itself. In two instances, two of the compensation measures grew more rapidly, and in four cases, one of them did so. Thus, for all but a small minority of companies in the sample, the assertions made in Chapters 8 and 9 on the basis of the aggregate data are unconditionally valid, and even for that minority the evidence is mixed.[8]

As judged by the standard deviations of the several distributions, the dispersion of the relevant growth rates is greatest in the case of total after-tax compensation and least for after-tax salary and bonus. That pattern is, of course, consistent with the "dampening" influence of a progressive tax structure on after-tax salary variations and with the fact that a broader range of factors has an impact on executives' total compensation than on their salaries and bonuses.

Growth Rate Comparisons: Salary vs. Total Compensation

Given the collection of data in Table 30 and the opportunity to compile similar tabulations for other intervals of time, it is possible to determine the extent to which differences among firms in the rates of growth of the most visible indexes of the rewards enjoyed by their senior officers —their salary and bonus receipts—are reliable indicators of differences among them with respect to rates of growth of aggregate remuneration as well.

A convenient way to examine this issue is provided by the rank correlation technique referred to above. If the corporations in the sample are ranked according to the rate of growth of their highest-paid executive's salary and bonus and according to the rate of growth of the same individual's total compensation, the degree of correspondence between the two schedules can be appraised by means of the Spearman rank correlation coefficient, ρ, where:

---

[8] Individual comparisons of the same sort are not possible in relating increases over time in executives' rewards to the rate of growth of the incomes of other professional groups, since collective data concerning the latter is all that is available here. However, it can be seen from Table 30 that the aggregate after-tax remuneration associated with the top executive position in thirty-seven of the forty-five firms grew more slowly between 1940 and 1963 than the 5.2 per cent per annum figure observed for physicians and dentists. In twenty-six of the forty-five cases, aggregate remuneration grew more slowly than the 3.9 per cent per annum increase experienced by lawyers. It seems fair to conclude, then, that in these comparisons as well the aggregate results apply also to the large majority of individual situations.

$$\rho = 1 - \frac{6 \sum_{i=1}^{n} d_i^2}{n^3 - n}$$

d_i refers to the difference between the two rankings assigned to firm i under the respective criteria, and n denotes the number of firms in the sample. This coefficient is designed in such a manner that when the two sets of rankings are identical, ρ has a value of plus 1; when one ranking is exactly the reverse of the other, ρ becomes minus 1. The possibility that the indicated degree of correspondence could have arisen by chance may be tested, for situations in which $n \geqq 10$, by calculating Student's "t," where in this context:

$$t = \rho \left[\frac{n-2}{1-\rho^2} \right]^{\frac{1}{2}}$$

with $n - 2$ degrees of freedom. A value for t greater than that associated with whatever level of confidence is chosen implies that the extent of the agreement between the two schedules suggested by ρ is significant at that level.[9]

The concern at the moment, then, is whether the firms in the sample which have awarded their top executives the most substantial increases in salary and bonus over time have displayed the same sort of leadership with regard to total compensation. In that connection, rates of growth during the postwar years seem as relevant as those covering the full period 1940 to 1963. As was indicated in Chapter 8, virtually all the observed appreciation in the several items tabulated occurred within the ten years subsequent to 1945. Therefore, the degree of correspondence between the rankings was examined for the intervals 1945 to 1955 and 1945 to 1963 as well. The results are shown in the tabulations on page 236. The difference in the correlation coefficients calculated for the before-tax and after-tax salary and bonus comparisons is, of course, accounted for by the differential impact of progressive income taxes on after-tax rates of growth.[10]

[9] For a complete discussion, see Sidney Siegel, *Nonparametric Statistics for the Behavioral Sciences,* New York, 1956, pp. 202–213.

[10] The problem of ties in the various rankings, which would necessitate a slight modification of the rank correlation computations, does not arise here. It turned out to be possible in almost every instance to resolve any apparent

A. BEFORE-TAX SALARY AND BONUS VS. TOTAL
AFTER-TAX COMPENSATION GROWTH RATES:

Interval	n	ρ	Computed t	Critical t at .01 Level
1940–63	45	0.428	3.104	2.416
1945–55	50	0.264	1.900	2.406
1945–63	46	0.164	1.102	2.414

B. AFTER-TAX SALARY AND BONUS VS. TOTAL
AFTER-TAX COMPENSATION GROWTH RATES:

Interval	n	ρ	Computed t	Critical t at .01 Level
1940–63	45	0.433	3.149	2.416
1945–55	50	0.284	3.053	2.406
1945–63	46	0.183	1.237	2.414

As is evident, the data suggest at best only a very loose connection over the time periods considered, especially from 1945 on. While two of the coefficients obtained are significant at the .01 level, they are still not really large enough to generate much confidence on the part of an observer that a rapid rate of growth in the level of salary and bonus awarded the top executive in a particular firm provides a good basis for assuming that the aggregate value of the compensation package associated with that position will have grown in like manner.

It could happen, however, that some peculiar feature of a single year's

equivalence between two or more of the observed rates of growth simply by carrying out the calculations to a greater number of significant digits. In those few cases in which the growth rates *were* precisely the same—e.g., a situation wherein salary and bonus exactly doubled in two different firms—the tie was broken by determining which of the two displayed the greater growth rate in payments to all five senior executive positions combined. Thus, one of the rationales for the appropriateness of confining the intercompany comparisons to only the highest-paid executive in each firm as a means of including as many of the fifty companies in the sample as possible in those comparisons was that the rewards enjoyed by such individuals were a very good index of the relative magnitude of the rewards received by their immediate subordinates. It is therefore consistent with the nature of our interest that the experience of lower-ranking executives be used to establish a difference between two firms when that difference is not apparent at the top of the organization alone.

data—extraordinary stock option profits realized by a few individuals, for example—might distort the growth rate figures on which the analysis is based and lead to an overly pessimistic appraisal of the degree of agreement between the several schedules. Such situations, if they exist, are most likely to occur in the later years of the study when, as we have seen, the volatility of executives' rewards increased substantially. Any adjustment of the data to eliminate possible problems of this sort should therefore focus on those years. Accordingly, the rates of growth between 1940 and 1963 and between 1945 and 1963 were recalculated, substituting for the original 1963 figures the average values for each item over the years 1960 through 1963. The new set of rankings generated did not, however, improve the correlation results. Thus:

A. BEFORE-TAX SALARY AND BONUS VS. TOTAL
AFTER-TAX COMPENSATION GROWTH RATES:

Interval	n [a]	ρ	Computed t	Critical t at .01 Level
1940 to 1960/63	44	.449	3.257	2.418
1945 to 1960/63	45	.209	1.401	2.416

B. AFTER-TAX SALARY AND BONUS VS. TOTAL
AFTER-TAX COMPENSATION GROWTH RATES:

Interval	n [a]	ρ	Computed t	Critical t at .01 Level
1940 to 1960/63	44	.363	2.525	2.418
1945 to 1960/63	45	.134	0.887	2.416

[a] The number of companies which can be included in the analysis is smaller in this case because we now require that compensation data be available in each of four years at the end of the relevant interval instead of just one.

Indeed, the various schedules seem to be rather less in agreement than before. The intervals which begin with 1940 still provide the better basis of comparison, but none of the relationships appear to be very strong.

The conclusion this suggests, then, is that increases in deferred and contingent rewards dominate the compensation policy differences among firms over time. Historical patterns of salary and bonus payments are not only in the aggregate poor indexes of the rate of growth in the total remuneration received by senior corporate executives—as Chapter 8 made clear—but are also unreliable as guides to relative growth rates in individual companies.

Salary vs. Total Compensation: Absolute Levels

A substantially better set of results is obtained from an examination of the absolute level of rewards. In each of six separate years spanning the time period under consideration, and on the basis of the annual averages computed for five different subperiods within that interval, the corporations in the sample were ranked according to the amount of salary and bonus paid their senior officers and according to the size of the same individuals' total pay packages.[11] The extent of the agreement between the schedules derived was then tested as above, with the following outcome:

SALARY AND BONUS VS. TOTAL COMPENSATION RANKINGS:

Year	n	ρ	Computed t	Critical t at .01 Level
1940	49	.793	8.916	2.408
1945	50	.433	3.327	2.406
1950	50	.599	5.186	2.406
1955	50	.343	2.533	2.406
1960	50	.588	5.038	2.406
1963	46	.625	5.308	2.414
1940–49 Average	49	.752	7.812	2.408
1951–55 Average	50	.455	3.540	2.406
1956–60 Average	50	.527	4.295	2.406
1955–63 Average	45	.594	4.840	2.416
1960–63 Average	45	.617	5.134	2.416

All the indicated coefficients are significant—most of them by a comfortable margin.[12]

---

[11] In this case, it was not necessary to compute two different sets of rankings for before- and after-tax salary and bonus, since on an absolute level scale, an executive will enjoy the same relative standing in the sample by either criterion.

[12] Except for that associated with the year 1955, they are significant even at the .001 level.

The pattern of the results, especially as summarized by the correlation coefficients for the five period-average rankings, is in accord with what one might expect from the compensation history outlined in the preceding chapters. The two schedules being compared correspond quite closely during the early years of the study when, of course, salary and bonus comprised the bulk of the executive pay package. This relationship drops off considerably in the interval 1951 through 1955 in response to the first really heavy use by corporations of the newer forms of deferred and contingent compensation. Thereafter, as firms' experience with such arrangements accumulates, as their employment becomes more widespread and systematic, and as the often sharp initial impact on certain individual executives' rewards starts to level off, the rankings begin steadily, if slowly, to converge again. By the early 1960's, the two schedules are in substantially greater agreement than they were ten years earlier.

Despite this improvement, however, a corporation's salary and bonus scale has not for some time been a truly satisfactory index of its overall compensation policy vis-à-vis other firms. Correlation coefficients on the order of .4 to .6 do not, after all, imply a very close relationship. Accordingly, while these results are markedly better than those generated by a comparison of rates of growth they still fall short of yielding a value for ρ—of, say, .9 or higher—which, in the view here, would suggest that the salary and bonus and total compensation rankings are in fact sufficiently alike that the former could confidently be used as a proxy for the latter.[13] Any empirical study which, either explicitly or implicitly, treats the two as interchangeable should therefore be suspect.

Company Growth and Compensation Growth

If, then, for many of the companies in the present sample, the policies which determine the direct current remuneration of the senior executive of the firm seem to create a rather different pattern of rewards than those which establish the amount of his aggregate remuneration, the next logical question is whether there may exist some systematic relationship between either of these items and the observable characteristics

[13] By, for example, the shareholders of a firm who were interested in appraising its executive compensation policy relative to other firms.

of the individual company. Consider this question first in terms of secular changes in the relevant quantities: Do the most rapidly growing corporations also provide their top executives with the most rapid increases in compensation?

For this purpose, the firms in the sample were ranked according to their respective rates of growth in each of the five dimensions of company size tabulated earlier: assets, sales, before-tax profits, after-tax profits, and the total market value of their common stock. That set of rankings—and corresponding ones for the rates of growth in top-executive before-tax salary and bonus, after-tax salary and bonus, and total after-tax compensation—were constructed for the intervals 1940 to 1963, 1945 to 1955, and 1945 to 1963. Once again, in order to eliminate any possible problems with unusual compensation data for a single year, separate rankings obtained by substituting for the 1963 figures the pertinent 1960 through 1963 averages were also compiled. The rank correlation coefficients between the schedules for each of the three measures of growth in compensation and those for each of the five indexes of company growth were then calculated. The results are recorded in Table 31 (see page 242).

As was true of the comparisons above, the paired rankings agree least over the period 1945 to 1955. Indeed, in two instances the correlation coefficients, even though not significant, turn out to be negative, suggesting that during these years the more vigorous the firm's expansion, the *slower* its senior officer's remuneration increased. Perhaps the most plausible explanation for such poor results can be found simply in the chronology of postwar compensation policy developments. It was at about this time that corporations began to take advantage of those deferred and contingent rewards whose value to the individual executive is particularly dependent not only upon his personal circumstances— e.g., his age—when they are initiated but also upon what were then rather rapidly changing stock market conditions. Since experience with these devices had not yet stabilized, it is not unusual that we observe an erratic pattern among firms in the late 1940's and early 1950's. Whatever permanent relationships may exist between company characteristics and executive rewards are unlikely to be reflected very accurately in the data for this period.

On the other hand, there seems to be only scattered evidence of such a relationship even in those comparisons which are concerned with rates of growth over what should be more suitable intervals of time. The remaining coefficients recorded display the "correct" sign, but just twelve of the sixty are significant at the .01 level. Averaging the data over several years again does not materially improve the comparisons. In the majority of cases, in fact, it reduces both the magnitude and the significance of the resulting coefficients. Apparently, any peculiarities that may be present in a particular year are not severe enough to require adjustment—or, perhaps more accurately, are not peculiarities at all.

The only generalizations worth attempting would seem to be the following:

1. The *total* compensation growth rankings correspond somewhat more closely to those of company growth rates than do either of the salary and bonus schedules.[14] Of the twelve correlation coefficients which are significant, eight are in the total compensation column.

2. All three indexes of compensation growth appear linked more to the rate of growth of a company's sales than to the other measures of its performance over time. In particular, a comparison with sales increases provides better results in every period than with the most frequently proposed alternative "explanatory" variable—company profits.

Even these conclusions, however, rest on fairly weak evidence, since the computations indicate at best only a very mild correspondence between the various rankings.

Company Size and Compensation Levels

The story in terms of absolute magnitudes is rather different, as Table 32 records. Virtually every coefficient of correlation between the several measures of a company's size and its senior officer's rewards in a given year or term of years is significant at the .01 level.[15] In the case of the salary and bonus comparisons there is not a single exception—all

---

[14] Exceptions occur primarily among the suspect 1945-to-1955 comparisons.

[15] As was noted previously, the before-tax and after-tax salary and bonus rankings are identical at a *point* in time, and it is not necessary to develop two separate schedules here as it was for the growth rate computations.

TABLE 31

Growth in Top Executive Compensation vs. Employer Company Growth: Rank Correlation Results

Interval	Company Characteristic	Correlation with Before-Tax Salary and Bonus		Correlation with After-Tax Salary and Bonus		Correlation with Total After-Tax Compensation		Sample Size (n)	Critical t at .01 Level
		ρ	Computed t	ρ	Computed t	ρ	Computed t		
1940 to 1963	Assets	.228	1.536	.244	1.655	.481 [a]	3.599		
	Sales	.449 [a]	3.292	.472 [a]	3.510	.477 [a]	3.558		
	Profits b.t.	.274	1.872	.294	2.015	.355 [a]	2.486	45	2.416
	Profits a.t.	.245	1.656	.260	1.764	.277	1.887		
	Market value	.180	1.199	.188	1.258	.290	1.988		
1940 to 1960/63	Assets	.174	1.146	.218	1.450	.475 [a]	3.500		
	Sales	.444 [a]	3.207	.466 [a]	3.416	.528 [a]	4.028		
	Profits b.t.	.287	1.941	.305	2.076	.354 [a]	2.453	44	2.418
	Profits a.t.	.209	1.386	.208	1.378	.248	1.665		
	Market value	.158	1.034	.183	1.205	.318	2.171		
1945 to 1955	Assets	.071	0.496	.063	0.436	.036	0.253		
	Sales	.084	0.583	.068	0.471	−.138	0.966		
	Profits b.t.	.143	0.998	.138	0.969	−.017	0.120	50	2.406
	Profits a.t.	.180	1.265	.170	1.193	.092	0.640		
	Market value	.178	1.255	.178	1.255	.145	1.017		

1945 to 1963	Assets	.248	1.701	.231	1.576	.376 [a]	2.688	46	2.414
	Sales	.280	1.932	.270	1.857	.322	2.258		
	Profits b.t.	.159	1.066	.163	1.098	.235	1.607		
	Profits a.t.	.139	0.933	.139	0.930	.283	1.958		
	Market value	.189	1.277	.186	1.258	.343 [a]	2.422		
1945 to 1960/63	Assets	.249	1.689	.183	1.223	.179	1.195	45	2.416
	Sales	.285	1.952	.224	1.504	.213	1.429		
	Profits b.t.	.253	1.712	.164	1.090	.155	1.028		
	Profits a.t.	.261	1.774	.141	0.933	.174	1.162		
	Market value	.276	1.883	.230	1.552	.213	1.433		

[a] Denotes significance at the .01 level.

TABLE 32

Top Executive Compensation vs. Employer Company Size: Rank Correlation Results

Year or Period	Company Character- istic	Correlation with Salary and Bonus		Correlation with Total Compensation		Sample Size (n)	Critical t at .01 Level
		ρ	t	ρ	t		
1940	Assets	.529	4.278	.602	5.165	49	2.408
	Sales	.626	5.502	.642	5.746		
	Profits b.t.	.600	5.135	.664	6.091		
	Profits a.t.	.619	5.406	.670	6.638		
	Market value	.536	4.348	.622	5.448		
1945	Assets	.415	3.164	.281	2.026	50	2.406
	Sales	.417	3.182	.111	0.773		
	Profits b.t.	.467	3.662	.241	1.723		
	Profits a.t.	.449	3.479	.228	1.618		
	Market value	.438	3.376	.301	2.183		
1950	Assets	.577	4.889	.484	3.828	50	2.406
	Sales	.535	4.389	.478	3.769		
	Profits b.t.	.629	5.600	.563	4.724		
	Profits a.t.	.595	5.133	.525	4.273		
	Market value	.531	4.343	.462	3.606		
1955	Assets	.495	3.948	.432	3.223	50	2.406
	Sales	.483	3.825	.317	2.316		
	Profits b.t.	.702	6.835	.506	4.063		
	Profits a.t.	.636	5.715	.529	4.322		
	Market value	.563	4.714	.457	3.560		
1960	Assets	.598	5.166	.300	2.175	50	2.406
	Sales	.486	3.851	.349	2.581		
	Profits b.t.	.687	6.547	.484	3.832		
	Profits a.t.	.666	6.187	.455	3.543		
	Market value	.674	6.324	.529	4.321		
1963	Assets	.544	4.301	.465	3.480	46	2.414
	Sales	.407	2.951	.530	4.143		
	Profits b.t.	.710	6.679	.570	4.605		
	Profits a.t.	.625	5.313	.560	4.483		
	Market value	.674	6.048	.591	4.855		

(*continued*)

TABLE 32 (concluded)

Year or Period	Company Characteristic	Correlation with Salary and Bonus		Correlation with Total Compensation		Sample Size (n)	Critical t at .01 Level
		ρ	t	ρ	t		
1940–49 Average	Assets	.559	4.622	.609	5.268	49	2.408
	Sales	.571	4.767	.453	3.480		
	Profits b.t.	.702	6.749	.638	5.686		
	Profits a.t.	.633	5.602	.638	5.673		
	Market value	.560	4.634	.567	4.721		
1951–55 Average	Assets	.563	4.721	.417	3.182	50	2.406
	Sales	.498	3.979	.322	2.357		
	Profits b.t.	.703	6.840	.503	4.029		
	Profits a.t.	.594	5.115	.538	4.425		
	Market value	.577	4.894	.473	3.717		
1956–60 Average	Assets	.514	4.153	.375	2.802	50	2.406
	Sales	.485	3.842	.366	2.721		
	Profits b.t.	.743	7.698	.497	3.965		
	Profits a.t.	.691	6.617	.506	4.060		
	Market value	.639	5.754	.569	4.789		
1960–63 Average	Assets	.578	4.641	.363	2.553	45	2.416
	Sales	.428	3.105	.423	3.058		
	Profits b.t.	.738	7.165	.563	4.465		
	Profits a.t.	.686	6.176	.512	3.904		
	Market value	.702	6.456	.586	4.736		
1955–63 Average	Assets	.574	4.594	.378	2.676	45	2.416
	Sales	.463	3.423	.298	2.046		
	Profits b.t.	.798	8.700	.478	3.572		
	Profits a.t.	.753	7.509	.469	3.483		
	Market value	.715	6.709	.493	3.717		

but four of the coefficients being significant at the .001 level.[16] It is, of course, inevitable that if the compensation rankings are in reasonable agreement with a schedule compiled on the basis of any one of the characteristics of the corporations in the sample, they will be found to agree with the schedules derived from each of the other four char-

[16] Which requires a value for t in excess of about 3.30 for samples of the size being considered here.

acteristics as well, since the latter are themselves highly correlated. It is therefore inappropriate in this context to attempt to single out a particular item as *the* explanatory variable for compensation policy. On the other hand, we do have available a substantial body of data from which it is possible to observe certain patterns. Without stretching the point too far, it should also be possible to suggest some conclusions from those patterns which provide at least a start in the direction of determining which of the attributes of the corporation seems the "best" predictor of the remuneration of its senior officer.

One feature of the calculations, for example, is the fact that, except in the year 1940, the degree of correspondence between the top executive salary and bonus rankings and those for each of the five indexes of company size is greater than between the latter and the same individuals' total compensation.[17] To the extent that there may be a causal relationship present, therefore, it seems to manifest itself more in terms of the current remuneration profile than as a determinant of over-all compensation levels.

A second, and complementary, phenomenon is the trend over time in the salary and bonus rankings toward somewhat greater agreement with the several company size schedules—reinforced by a similar shift in the opposite direction by the total compensation figures. In 1963, four of the five salary and bonus coefficients were higher than they were in 1940, but during the same interval, all five total compensation coefficients declined. While there are departures from both patterns in the intervening years, both appear valid in the long run.

Also of particular interest are the consistently better results obtained from a comparison of the two compensation measures with corporate profit rankings than with sales figures. For salary and bonus in ten of the eleven situations considered, both the before-tax and after-tax profit coefficients are greater than the sales coefficient, frequently by a wide margin. The exception again is in 1940, but the sales coefficients decline steadily thereafter. In the case of total compensation, *all* eleven pairs of profit coefficients exceed their sales counterparts. It is noteworthy that during the most recent years studied, however, the best set

[17] It does not make much difference either to this or succeeding conclusions whether we consider single years or averages over periods of years in the comparisons.

of figures in connection with total compensation is provided by a comparison of those data with the ranking of firms according to the aggregate market value of their common stock. Clearly, this trend is a consequence of the shift in emphasis within the pay package toward heavier reliance on rewards whose value to the executive depends on the market price behavior of his firm's shares.

Finally, the relationship between executive rewards and company size seems to have been weakest in 1945, with 1955 not far behind. Both outcomes can be explained by historical circumstances. In 1945 the effects of wartime restrictions on compensation increases were still being felt, even though the relative positions of the corporations in the sample in terms of sales, profits, assets, etc., had changed considerably because of wartime production. The problem in 1955, as we have seen, was the major change in corporate compensation policy which was then in the process of being consolidated. Despite these temporary discrepancies, however, it is clear that there *is* in general a strong connection between the size of a firm and its top executive's remuneration. The data further suggest, although more equivocally, that company profits are a somewhat better predictor of such payments, especially of salary and bonus levels, than are sales.

Evaluation

Such an analysis, of course, is only a very limited first step in this area, and no more is claimed for it here than that. A truly comprehensive appraisal of the sources of differences among firms would have to include in a unified multivariate regression format the influence of a host of factors which were ignored in the paired ordinal comparisons employed above. Among the more important of these are likely to be:

1. Differences in the degree of risk associated with different lines of business.

2. Differences in the degree of governmental regulation of the firm's activities.

3. Differences in the profit cycle in various industries.[18]

[18] That is, if an executive's decisions at any point in time set in motion forces whose impact on the corporation's success are not felt until five or ten years

4. Differences among firms in the extent to which top management has an ownership interest in the company.

5. Differences in the nature of the job responsibilities of the men at the top of the organization.

6. Differences in the collective bargaining environment—and, hence, in the degree of concern with the *appearance* of senior executive pay levels.

Taken together, these factors may very likely be as influential as employer company size and profitability in determining the patterns of remuneration we observe. They must either be recognized or controlled for in whatever model of the compensation process is constructed, if the net effect of company size is to be properly appraised. Because such an effort would require the collection and interpretation of a substantial body of evidence which is not central to the focus of the current study, it will not be undertaken here. The correlation results tabulated on the preceding pages suggest some rough qualitative conclusions, but are hardly adequate to the objective indicated.[19]

Composition of the Pay Package

Given information about the value of supplements to executive salaries and bonuses, it is also possible to seek an answer to a question which heretofore has been treated in only the most superficial manner: Is there a relationship between the size of a firm and the extent to which it

in the future, there is less reason for his remuneration to be linked to his firm's current performance than in situations where the payoff is more rapid.

[19] Among the attempts thus far made to "explain" executive compensation levels on the basis of company size and profitability are those of Roberts (*Executive Compensation,* Glencoe, Ill., 1959) and McGuire, Chiu, and Elbing ("Executive Incomes, Sales, and Profits," *American Economic Review,* September, 1962, pp. 753–761). In both cases, the phenomenon of a high degree of correlation among the possible independent variables in the regression equations caused difficulties in deciding upon the "best" predictor of compensation. A more fundamental problem in connection with the usefulness of their analysis, however, is that neither effort dealt with any measures of the remuneration provided by deferred and contingent rewards. Only executive salaries and bonuses were considered—and, as has been made clear here, the latter constitute less than half the value of the relevant earnings.

utilizes deferred and contingent compensation arrangements to reward its executives? A mere census of the relative popularity of such devices among small and large firms is of little use, since not just their existence but their benefit structures are of concern. As it turns out, the data suggest that the larger and more profitable the firm, the more heavily it does in fact rely on supplemental compensation. The evidence is not overwhelming, however, and its interpretation is subject to certain qualifications.

The raw data themselves are worth calling attention to. Table 33 records the percentages which salary and bonus provided of the aggregate after-tax remuneration enjoyed, during the periods 1940 through 1949 and 1955 through 1963, by the men who were the highest-paid executives in each of the fifty companies in the sample. The two distributions are summarized in Chart 27. As can be seen, the percentages in the earlier period vary from 40.9 to 100, with a mean of 75.6 and a standard deviation of 16.9. The distribution is mildly bimodal, observations clustering both in the area of 55 to 65 and 90 to 100 per cent. In recent years the figures run from as low as 13.7 up to 82.5 per cent. The mean of the latter distribution, which has a pronounced mode in the region of 35 to 45 per cent, is 44.4, and its standard deviation 16.4 per cent.

The policy differences among the firms depicted are therefore quite substantial within both intervals, the dispersion being slightly less in absolute terms in the later period but considerably larger in relation to the then-lower mean. In each case, the range of values tabulated is sufficient to make a comparison with company size meaningful, and the fact that the data represent aggregate figures over two decade-long intervals, at opposite ends of the time during which most firms' compensation policies seemed to be in transition, should permit some confidence that the long-run objectives of those policies are accurately characterized.

When the corporations listed are ranked according to the percentage of total after-tax compensation which supplements to salary and bonus provided for their executives during the two time periods, and these rankings are compared with those derived from each firm's average assets, annual sales, etc., over the same periods, the following results are obtained:

Interval	Index of Company Size	Correlation with Relative Importance of Supplements to Salary and Bonus		Critical t at .01 Level
		ρ	t	
1940–49	Assets	.395	2.950	
	Sales	.222	1.561	2.408
	Profits, b.t.	.323	2.340	(n = 49)
	Profits, a.t.	.356	2.612	
	Market value	.275	1.962	
1955–63	Assets	.263	1.788	
	Sales	.133	0.880	2.416
	Profits, b.t.	.326	2.263	(n = 45)
	Profits, a.t.	.314	2.171	
	Market value	.351	2.460	

While only three of the coefficients are significant at the level indicated, all are comfortably positive, and it does appear likely that there is a direct, if not very strong, relationship present.

One feature of the comparisons which duplicates the pattern observed in connection with absolute levels of remuneration is the evidence that both measures of employer-company profits are better guides to the composition of the pay package than are company sales. The differences in the coefficients are quite sizeable in each of the two time periods considered. A second, and not unexpected, phenomenon is the improvement over time in the performance of the market value of a firm's common stock as a predictor of the extent to which it makes use of deferred and contingent rewards. This trend, of course, is simply a reflection of the fact that nowadays the value of many of those rewards depends directly on stock price movements.

Our interpretation of these results, however, must be hedged. Even if we believe that the degree of correspondence shown between the several sets of rankings implies causation somewhere along the line, it could well be that the underlying stimulus is not company size or profitability per se, but another attribute of the firm which happens to be related to both. An example might be the possibility that the larger the corporation, the less likely is an individual executive to be among its major shareholders. In order to counter that situation and encourage

TABLE 33

Salary and Bonus as a Per Cent of Total After-Tax Compensation,
by Company

Company Number	Salary and Bonus		Company Number	Salary and Bonus	
	1940–49	1955–63		1940–49	1955–63
1	52.8	69.9	28	74.9	29.2
2	93.6	43.0	29	60.6	–
3	80.3	39.4	30	63.2	24.8
4	86.4	28.1	31	57.4	39.4
5	56.8	25.9	32	91.1	50.7
6	53.9	55.7	33	85.9	35.8
7	88.6	–	34	100.0	35.0
8	64.1	–	35	51.7	–
9	91.5	45.5	36	79.0	82.5
10	62.5	74.2	37	94.8	57.2
11	60.7	41.6	38	100.0	19.2
12	74.1	50.5	39	64.9	27.2
13	100.0	66.7	40	97.6	40.5
14	100.0	–	41	94.0	43.2
15	100.0	16.4	42	65.7	39.1
16	79.4	37.4	43	58.3	77.8
17	55.5	24.2	44	58.7	52.3
18	61.2	57.9	45	47.5	36.4
19	76.8	38.0	46	91.1	56.1
20	90.7	39.5	47	–	33.1
21	93.1	13.7	48	81.3	62.4
22	93.8	44.2	49	71.4	52.6
23	64.6	35.4	50	71.6	44.5
24	94.6	62.2			
25	40.9	37.2	μ	75.6	44.4
26	58.4	37.2	σ	16.9	16.4
27	70.1	77.0	σ/μ	.223	.370

a closer identification by him with shareholder interests, the large firm may feel more impelled to include in its compensation package such instruments as stock options and profit-sharing plans through which a substantial ownership position can be attained by the executive.

Perhaps another possibility is that the larger firm may simply be

CHART 27

*Distribution of Salary and Bonus as a Percentage of Total
After-Tax Compensation, 1940–49 and 1955–63*

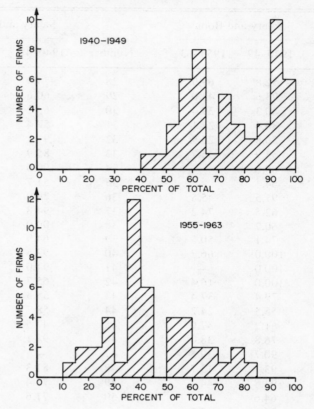

more sophisticated in its compensation planning and more alert to the
desirability of the various supplements which our tax laws have come
to sanction.[20] Whether this argument is as credible in the context of
a sample consisting entirely of very large corporations as it would be
if we were dealing with a broader range of company sizes is, of course,
questionable.

The mechanics of certain aspects of the compensation process suggest

[20] See Appendix M for a related discussion.

still a third explanation. If, as is usually the case, the formula for establishing the benefits due an executive under, say, his firm's pension plan is expressed in terms of his before-tax salary, the after-tax value of those benefits will be more important to him in relation to after-tax salary at successively higher salary levels. The same will be true of any supplemental compensation items that are awarded in proportion to current remuneration but taxed at lower rates.[21] If, then, it turns out that top executive salaries and bonuses are directly related to company size, the proportion of total after-tax compensation supplied by deferred and contingent rewards can be expected to follow suit, even though every firm in the sample might adopt similar benefit *formulas* for those devices. Clearly, every firm does not do so, and we find a much greater degree of agreement between the salary and bonus and company size rankings than between the latter and salary and bonus percentages.[22] To the extent that pensions and other supplemental pay plans do tend to become standardized among firms, however, the pattern indicated will develop, and it may explain at least part of the relationship we observe.[23]

The real issues in this connection may therefore involve a variety of factors, only some of which are manifestations of intentional policy decisions by the firm. Whatever the cause, it does appear that the relative importance of deferred and contingent rewards increases with company size and profitability, but that tendency also appears to be rather mild.

The "Best" Predictor of Compensation Levels

In examining the data for these rankings it became evident that there *is* one attribute of the firm which provides an extremely good basis for

[21] The number of shares granted under a stock option, for example, is often a function of the optionee's salary.

[22] Differences in such factors as the ages of the executives involved and the manner in which they exercise their stock options also give rise to variations in the value of noncurrent rewards which are not present in connection with salaries.

[23] Another possibility which should not be neglected is that cause-and-effect may run in just the opposite direction from that implied here. It might be argued that those firms with high sales, profits, and equity market values enjoy that status *because* they make extensive use of deferred and contingent rewards of the type whose value to the executive depends on favorable stock market reaction to management's decisions. Officials in such firms are therefore given a particular incentive to perform their duties effectively, and they react accordingly.

predicting its standing in the sample in terms of the aggregate remuneration enjoyed by its top executive. Unfortunately, however, this discovery does not really help much in understanding *why* things are as they are, and for that reason the relationship observed is more a curiosity than a useful analytical tool. The item referred to is simply the percentage of the total value of the firm's top executive compensation package which is accounted for by supplements to salary and bonus. A ranking of the corporations in the sample according to that percentage for any given period—especially recent ones—corresponds almost exactly to the schedule obtained by ranking them in order of the absolute magnitude of their senior officers' aggregate remuneration. Consider the following correlation results:

RANK BY SUPPLEMENTS TO SALARY AND BONUS AS A
PER CENT OF ALL COMPENSATION VS. RANK BY SIZE
OF TOTAL PAY PACKAGE

				Critical t	
Interval	n	ρ	Computed t	.01 Level	.00001 Level
1940–49	49	.756	7.929	2.408	4.744
1951–55	50	.893	13.726	2.406	4.733
1956–60	50	.889	13.422	2.406	4.733
1960–63	45	.963	23.557	2.416	4.793
1955–63	45	.932	16.809	2.416	4.793

The importance of deferred and contingent arrangements is well illustrated by these comparisons. The firms that have the highest over-all pay scales are precisely those which emphasize supplements to salary and bonus most heavily. In fact, if one were going to ignore certain payments in a study of intercorporate patterns of managerial remuneration he would be better advised to forget about salary and bonus and concentrate on the rest of the pay package rather than the reverse. While intriguing, this conclusion of course leaves us somewhat short of being able to explain or even predict why the firm chooses, or feels compelled, to employ deferred and contingent rewards to the extent it does. We can, in effect, now state with great confidence that corporations which have provided their top officials with high levels of earnings have done so almost entirely by means other than salary and bonus, but we still are not in a position to rationalize that result.

Extrapolating the Results

As was indicated at the beginning of the chapter, the cross-sectional comparisons we have been considering are based on compensation data which describe the experience of only the highest-paid executive in each of the corporations studied. The focus was so limited out of a desire to include in those comparisons as many of the fifty companies in the original sample as possible. Given the necessity of operating under that constraint, the question arises as to whether the various patterns we observe would have been duplicated had it been possible to extend the analysis to the full five-man senior executive group from which the historical profile recorded in previous chapters was drawn.

Some evidence to support an affirmative answer was cited above. We saw that the correlation coefficients obtained by comparing the ranking of the firms in the sample according to the total after-tax compensation of their highest-paid official and according to that for their five highest-paid together were on the order of .95 and significant at the .0001 level. A similar comparison of the other pertinent dimensions of the pay package yields correspondingly high coefficients, as Table 34 records. In the great majority of cases it does seem that the experience of a firm's top executive vis-à-vis that of his peers in other companies is also a reliable indicator of the relative standing of his four closest subordinates. It therefore seems likely that the conclusions suggested here would have been changed very little if the analysis could have been broadened to encompass the latter's rewards as well.

Summary

An examination of the differences in top executive compensation policy among the firms in the sample reveals that there exist within the composite historical experience depicted earlier significant variations in the size and structure of the relevant pay packages. The magnitude of these variations is, however, proportionately less than the range of size and profitability exhibited by the firms themselves—a phenomenon which appears to be growing stronger over time. As might be expected, there is a greater dispersion in the distribution of executives' total compensation than in that of their salaries and bonuses.

TABLE 34

Compensation of Highest-Paid Executive vs. Compensation of Five Highest-Paid Together: Rank Correlations Across Firms

	Year or Period	n	ρ	Computed t	Critical t	
					.01 Level	.0001 Level
	1940	39	.878	11.168	2.432	4.129
	1945	42	.924	15.236	2.423	4.094
Rank by salary and bonus levels	1950	44	.938	17.534	2.418	4.076
	1955	34	.942	15.984	2.449	4.201
	1960	19	.933	10.719	2.518	4.493
Rank by rate of growth of before-tax salary and bonus	1940–60	16	.894	7.470	2.552	4.648
	1945–55	29	.904	10.983	2.473	4.299
Rank by rate of growth of after-tax salary and bonus	1940–60	16	.768	4.482	2.552	4.648
	1945–55	29	.894	10.344	2.473	4.299
Rank by rate of growth of total after-tax compensation	1940–60	16	.871	6.621	2.552	4.648
	1945–55	30	.948	15.825	2.467	4.275

Note: Rankings not carried through 1963 because of small sample size which results.

A comparison on a company-by-company basis of the rate of growth of executive rewards and the rate of growth of corporate assets, sales, profits, and common stock market values reinforces the conclusion drawn from the aggregate data that top executive remuneration has not kept pace with increases in employer-company size. We are able to find only scattered instances in which the compensation associated with the highest-paid position in a firm grew as rapidly as even the most sluggish index of its own expansion.

A second contention offered previously is also strengthened. Much was made of the point that an executive's salary and bonus were not likely to be very useful in predicting the amount of his total compensation. The low correlation coefficients obtained by comparing the aggregate and current remuneration rankings for the sample provide clear support for that hypothesis. The difference between the two criteria is especially marked in connection with rates of growth over the time period studied. Those corporations in which executive salaries and bonuses are at a high level are very frequently not among the more generous in terms of total compensation.

There is, on the other hand, considerable evidence that top executive rewards and employer-company size are directly related. We find that the firm's profits are a somewhat better guide to its pay scale than are its sales—an advantage which has become more marked in recent years. Because of the possibly significant influence of a series of external factors which could not feasibly be included in the analysis, however, this conclusion must be regarded as suggestive rather than definitive. While the extent to which a firm makes use of deferred and contingent remuneration for its senior executives also appears to increase with company size, that increase is fairly mild and can, in part at least, be explained by certain "technical" aspects of the compensation process.

12

SENSITIVITY ANALYSIS

The question of the extent to which the results described in the preceding chapters depend upon the particular values chosen for such key parameters as executives' discount rates, outside income, and nontaxable deductions and exemptions has been raised in a number of connections. Each time, the argument has been that the techniques employed to measure the worth of the various deferred and contingent compensation devices under consideration are such that the outcome of an empirical application of those techniques should be affected very little by rather substantial changes in the parameters involved. It is the task of this chapter to document that assertion.

Procedure

The approach will be to cast up, from the body of data compiled for the study, a profile of the career of a "typical" executive, and then to test the impact on an analysis of his compensation of a series of changes in assumptions as to the conditions under which that compensation was received. The alternative would be to redo the calculations for the entire sample some fifteen or twenty times, changing one or two parameters for each trial—a strategy which is rejected as not only impractical but unnecessary. The results of the investigation have been presented throughout in terms of the collective experience of executives in fifty corporations, and a sensitivity analysis which concentrates on the rewards of an "average" individual as derived from the careers of those executives should provide as useful an appraisal of the influence of the several parameters chosen as would a full reconstruction of the various calculations.

Since the procedures employed in valuing the components of the pay package made it possible to separate the computations related to executives' stock options from those for their other rewards,[1] the same separation will be effected here. The typical experience under an option plan will be examined independently and will be concerned only with those individuals who were granted options rather than with the entire sample studied. This will serve to highlight the features of the valuation techniques constructed for an instrument which we have seen to be almost as important a source of remuneration as salary and bonus for top corporate executives during the late 1950's and early 1960's. Those techniques and the nature of the contingencies involved are sufficiently distinctive that some extra concentration on them seems appropriate.

The Typical Executive: A Profile

Because most of the conclusions presented above have been based on the *mean* values of the compensation provided by the fifty corporations studied, a similar viewpoint will be adopted in reconstructing the experience of a typical executive. The magnitude of his rewards and the timing of their receipt will be specified simply by summing the relevant dimensions of the careers of the some 550 individuals for whom data were compiled and dividing by the total number of observations applicable to each. For example, the mean length of time an executive appears in the sample is almost exactly fourteen years: There are 7,802 man-years of data and a total of 558 executives. Of those fourteen years, the last ten—or 5,300 of the total 7,802—were spent among the five highest-paid positions in the man's firm and are our most direct concern.[2] Information on the compensation he enjoyed during the four earlier years is, however, necessary to a proper valuation of his subsequent rewards and must therefore be taken into account. Finally, since all or part of the data for some 20 per cent (1,561 man-years) of the history analyzed could not be gathered from proxy statements and had to be estimated, the figures for the first three years of an executive's career will normally be of this type.[3]

---

[1] See the numerical example presented in Chapter 6.

[2] See Chapter 7.

[3] With few exceptions, it *was* during the early years of the executive's career wherein such extrapolation was necessary.

Given the indicated framework, the size and the pattern over time of the pertinent rewards are easily obtained. We find that the mean age of the 558 executives when they initially appeared in the sample was just over 49 years.[4] During that first year they averaged $61,750 in before-tax salary and bonus, were promised $4,040 in annual noncontributory pension benefits, and were required to contribute an average $510 toward financing of a prospective annual contributory pension benefit amounting to $3,600. A minority were, in addition, the beneficiaries of deferred compensation and profit-sharing plans, the anticipated annual post-retirement payments under which come to $130 when averaged over the entire sample. Nine years was the mean term of such plans; i.e., payments were to begin at age 65 and continue through age 73.[5] Similar calculations were made using the data observed for the second and subsequent years of each executive's experience, the compensation totals being divided by the number of individuals contributing to them in every instance.

On that basis, the "typical" compensation history shown in the tabulation on p. 261 emerges.[6] In order to analyze this history, it is necessary to specify the calendar-year period covered, since the tax rates relevant to the various computations have fluctuated over time. The mean year in which the individuals under consideration first appeared in the sample turns out to be 1942, and that year is therefore adopted as a reference point, i.e., the career of our typical executive will be said to have begun in 1942 and ended in 1955. The tax schedules employed in the subsequent analysis reflect this convention.

Parameter Changes

The assumptions about the nature of the compensation environment which were built into the empirical results described above took the form

---

[4] All such averages will be rounded to the nearest full year for purposes of the following computations.

[5] As a matter of convenience, the few profit-sharing plans confronted—all of which provided for a single large payment at age 65—were included in this category by assuming that the lump sum expected was instead to be paid out in nine equal annual installments as if it were a deferred compensation arrangement. This assumption permits a single computation to suffice here for both rewards even though the two devices were evaluated separately in the main body of the study.

[6] Excluding for the moment any stock option grants.

Age	Before-Tax Salary and Bonus	Expected Annual Non-Contributory Pension Benefit	Expected Annual Contributory Pension Benefit	Executive's Annual Contributions	Expected Annual Deferred Compensation Benefit [a]
49	$ 61,750	$ 4,040	$ 3,600	$ 510	$ 130
50	65,290	4,940	4,340	610	170
51	68,210	5,490	4,990	700	210
52	72,790	5,930	5,270	760	310
53	74,660	6,790	5,730	860	500
54	76,710	6,980	6,200	910	690
55	83,130	7,430	6,740	980	730
56	84,880	7,830	7,260	1,100	1,140
57	91,000	8,740	8,220	1,270	1,710
58	97,950	9,520	9,250	1,460	2,290
59	107,620	11,070	10,350	1,610	2,670
60	114,630	11,830	11,370	1,770	3,360
61	121,560	11,810	12,330	1,910	4,600
62 [b]	132,180	12,960	12,870	1,940	5,890

[a] The average duration of the benefit promise is nine years throughout.

[b] The fact that the mean age of the executives when they disappear from the sample is below 65—the normal retirement age—should not seem surprising. For one thing, even if they all did retire "on time," they would be only 64 years old during the last year of their careers, and that would be the figure we would observe. Some, of course, died prior to retiring, others retired early, and a few resigned along the way to take a job with a company not in the sample. In addition, one firm studied set retirement at age 60 for its executives, thereby contributing to a lower average. The most important factor, however, is a purely technical one: Because the compensation data examined end in 1963, there are a number of executives whose histories necessarily are terminated in midstream and who were rather younger than 65 when they were last seen.

of choices as to the values of three parameters: the discount rate used in measuring the present value to the executive of any deferred payments, the fraction of his annual earnings which were claimed as deductions and exemptions, and the amount of income he received from sources other than his corporate employer. An annual rate of 2½ per cent after taxes was taken to be the relevant discount rate for pension and deferred compensation benefits; executives' deductions and personal exemptions were put at 10 per cent of gross income through 1950 and 15 per cent thereafter; and outside income was assumed to come to 15 per cent of before-tax salary and bonus receipts. As a test of the impact of these choices, our typical executive's career will be evaluated using first the indicated parameters and then a series of alternative assumptions. In particular, the discount rate will be doubled to 5 per cent, deductions and exemptions figures of zero and 20 per cent will be tried, and the executive's outside income set equal to zero, 25, and 50 per cent of his annual salary and bonus. Since some portion of the data listed for the first three years of his career is likely to have been estimated, additional calculations in which those estimates are varied by as much as 50 per cent will be undertaken. The results of these trials should encompass as wide a range of possibilities as need occupy us here.

Outcome of the Tests

A total of thirteen sets of computations were made. The first incorporated the environmental assumptions adopted in the main body of the study. The next nine assumed different values, one at a time, for each of the three parameters at issue and for the executive's early compensation data. The last three tested several combinations of such changes designed to identify the extent to which they offset or reinforce each other. A list of the sequence of the various assumptions is presented in Table 35 and a sampling of the outcome of the calculations in Table 36.[7]

Changes in the absolute magnitude of the numbers generated are, of course, not our real concern since the conclusions arrived at in previous chapters have dealt with the relationships *between* the components of

[7] The figures used for the first three years' compensation data in trial No. 8 require some explanation. The objective was to consider the impact on the analysis of overestimates of those figures. There is, however, a limit to the amount of overstatement that can occur if we observe a steadily rising trend in the man's earnings. Once we know the actual figures for his salary, prospective pension benefits, etc., for any given year, we can be fairly confident that those which were associated with previous years were lower. Therefore, if we wish to test the effect of larger numbers than the ones listed for ages 49, 50, and 51 for our typical executive, they should not exceed their counterparts at age 52 if the test is to be meaningful. In keeping with that constraint, the decision here was simply to split the difference and adopt the resulting figures as a "50 per cent overestimate" of the data. The salary and bonus figure for age 49, for example, was set at $67,270—halfway between the original (estimated) $61,-750 and the $72,790 recorded for age 52. A similar procedure was adopted for the other items of compensation observed in the first three years.

TABLE 35

Sequence of Assumptions Used in the Sensitivity Analysis
Computations

Trial Number	Discount Rate (per cent)	Deductions and Exemptions (per cent of income)	Outside Income (per cent of salary and bonus)
1	2½	10% through 1950; 15% thereafter	15
2	5	Same as Trial 1	15
3	2½	Same as Trial 1	None
4	2½	Same as Trial 1	25
5	2½	Same as Trial 1	50
6	2½	None	15
7	2½	20%	15
8	All parameters as in Trial 1, but first three years' compensation data raised by one-half the difference between the recorded figures and those listed for year four (see footnote 7).		
9	All parameters as in Trial 1, but first three years' compensation data reduced by 20 per cent.		
10	All parameters as in Trial 1, but first three years' compensation data reduced by 50 per cent.		
11	5	Same as Trial 1	50
12	2½	None	None
13	2½	None	50

the pay package and with their *rates of growth*. For that reason, the results of the thirteen trials indicated may be summarized for interpretation simply by recording for each year (1) the percentages of our typical executive's total after-tax compensation which are attributable to his salary and bonus, on the one hand, and his pension and deferred compensation benefits on the other, and (2) the pattern of increases in the value of all three over time. These figures provide as much information about the influence of changes in parameters and errors in estimation as we require. The relevant comparisons are presented in Tables 37 and 38. The numbering of the trials corresponds to that of Table 35.

TABLE 36

Sample Results: Sensitivity Analysis Computations
(dollars)

Age	Before-Tax Salary and Bonus	After-Tax Salary and Bonus	Pension After-Tax Current Equivalent	Deferred Compensation After-Tax Current Equivalent	Total After-Tax Compensation
			Trial Number 1		
49	61,750	30,870	2,910	30	33,810
50	65,290	28,550	3,480	40	32,070
51	68,210	29,320	3,910	50	33,280
52	72,790	30,440	4,170	80	34,690
53	74,660	34,990	4,770	140	39,900
54	76,720	35,620	5,120	210	40,950
55	83,130	49,770	5,890	220	55,880
56	84,880	50,560	6,630	430	57,620
57	91,000	53,190	8,470	770	62,430
58	97,950	53,970	10,360	1,150	65,480
59	107,620	53,850	13,470	1,410	68,730
60	114,630	56,270	15,850	2,020	74,140
61	121,560	62,640	17,330	3,500	83,470
62	132,180	66,250	21,100	6,820	94,170
			Trial Number 2		
49	61,750	30,870	2,640	20	33,530
50	65,290	28,550	3,170	30	31,750
51	68,210	29,320	3,560	30	32,910
52	72,790	30,440	3,790	50	34,280
53	74,660	34,990	4,360	100	39,450
54	76,720	35,620	4,680	150	40,450
55	83,130	49,770	5,400	160	55,330
56	84,880	50,560	6,110	310	56,980
57	91,000	53,190	7,870	560	61,620
58	97,950	53,970	9,690	850	64,510
59	107,620	53,850	12,730	1,060	67,640
60	114,630	56,270	15,050	1,540	72,860
61	121,560	62,640	16,470	2,760	81,870
62	132,180	66,250	20,150	5,530	91,930

(*continued*)

TABLE 36 (concluded)

Age	Before-Tax Salary and Bonus	After-Tax Salary and Bonus	Pension After-Tax Current Equivalent	Deferred Compensation After-Tax Current Equivalent	Total After-Tax Compensation
			Trial Number 5		
49	61,750	28,150	2,480	30	30,660
50	65,290	25,490	2,960	40	28,490
51	68,210	26,080	3,320	40	29,440
52	72,790	26,950	3,510	70	30,530
53	74,660	31,570	4,040	120	35,730
54	76,720	32,060	4,330	190	36,580
55	83,130	46,310	4,920	200	51,430
56	84,880	47,020	5,580	390	52,990
57	91,000	49,450	7,150	690	57,290
58	97,950	49,650	8,670	1,030	59,350
59	107,620	49,620	11,240	1,260	62,120
60	114,630	51,740	13,250	1,790	66,780
61	121,560	57,310	14,410	3,100	74,820
62	132,180	60,440	17,440	6,010	83,890
			Trial Number 7		
49	61,750	35,370	3,000	30	38,400
50	65,290	33,830	3,620	40	37,490
51	68,210	34,860	4,090	50	39,000
52	72,790	36,470	4,370	80	40,920
53	74,660	40,710	5,030	150	45,890
54	76,720	41,530	5,420	220	47,170
55	83,130	54,810	6,210	230	61,250
56	84,880	55,710	7,010	450	63,170
57	91,000	58,860	8,940	790	68,590
58	97,950	57,500	10,920	1,180	69,600
59	107,620	57,980	14,230	1,450	73,660
60	114,630	60,690	16,790	2,080	79,560
61	121,560	67,200	18,360	3,620	89,180
62	132,180	71,400	22,490	7,060	100,950

TABLE 37

After-Tax Salary and Bonus as a Per Cent of Total After-Tax Compensation: Sensitivity Analysis for a Typical Executive

Trial Number	Executive Age													
	49	50	51	52	53	54	55	56	57	58	59	60	61	62
1	91	89	88	88	88	87	89	88	85	82	78	76	75	70
2	92	90	89	89	89	88	90	89	86	84	80	77	76	72
3	91	89	88	87	87	86	88	87	84	82	77	74	73	68
4	92	89	88	88	88	87	90	88	86	83	79	77	76	71
5	92	89	89	88	88	88	90	89	86	84	80	78	77	72
6	90	87	86	86	86	86	89	87	85	80	76	73	73	68
7	92	90	89	89	89	88	90	88	86	83	79	76	75	71
8	90	89	88	88	88	87	89	88	85	83	78	76	75	70
9	92	90	89	87	87	87	89	88	85	82	78	76	75	70
10	92	90	90	87	87	86	88	87	85	82	78	76	75	70
11	93	91	90	89	89	89	91	90	88	85	81	79	78	74
12	90	87	86	85	86	85	88.	86	84	79	74	71	70	65
13	91	88	87	86	87	86	90	88	86	81	77	74	74	69

Looking first at Table 37, we see that there is remarkably little change in our assessment of the significance of deferred and contingent rewards in the pay package regardless of the values chosen for the several parameters. The percentages observed fall within a very narrow range in all cases where only one parameter is changed from its original value (trials 2 through 7), and the figures recorded for trial 1, which incorporates the assumptions actually used in the study, consistently fall midway between the extremes of that range. A similar conclusion emerges from the calculations (trials 8 through 10) which involve revisions in the compensation data listed for the first three years of the man's career: the percentage composition of the pay package is virtually unaffected.

The circumstances which produce the most noticeable change in the percentages are exemplified by trials 11 and 12. For the former, the assumptions built into trials 2 and 5 were combined and for the latter, those from trials 3 and 6—the objective in each instance being to put

TABLE 38

Growth in After-Tax Rewards: Sensitivity Analysis for a Typical Executive

Trial Number	Salary and Bonus			Pension and Deferred Compensation			Total Compensation		
	Value at Age 53	Value at Age 62	Ratio	Value at Age 53	Value at Age 62	Ratio	Value at Age 53	Value at Age 62	Ratio
1	$34,990	$66,250	1.89	$4,910	$27,920	5.68	$39,900	$ 94,170	2.36
2	34,990	66,250	1.89	4,460	25,680	5.76	39,450	91,940	2.33
3	36,720	69,280	1.89	5,470	32,230	5.89	42,190	101,510	2.41
4	33,940	64,500	1.90	4,630	25,970	5.61	38,570	90,470	2.35
5	31,570	60,440	1.91	4,160	23,440	5.63	35,730	83,880	2.35
6	29,100	50,470	1.73	4,620	23,940	5.18	33,720	74,410	2.20
7	40,710	71,400	1.75	5,170	29,540	5.71	45,880	100,940	2.20
8	34,990	66,250	1.89	4,850	27,860	5.75	39,840	94,110	2.36
9	34,990	66,250	1.89	5,070	28,070	5.53	40,060	94,320	2.35
10	34,990	66,250	1.89	5,350	28,330	5.29	40,340	94,580	2.34
11	31,570	60,440	1.91	3,730	21,480	5.75	35,300	81,920	2.32
12	31,050	54,040	1.74	5,280	28,970	5.49	36,330	83,010	2.28
13	25,260	43,420	1.72	3,800	19,200	5.05	29,060	62,620	2.15

together a set of conditions whose effects on the analysis seemed likely to be in the same direction. Even at that, the numbers generated are not significantly different from those of trial 1, and the assumptions involved describe a pair of compensation environments which must certainly be near the fringes of reasonableness. In the one case, the executive is assumed to have outside income equal to fully half his pretax salary and bonus and to be able to realize 5 per cent per annum *after taxes* on investments which are in the same category of risk as government bonds; in the other, there is no outside income of any kind and the man claims no deductions or exemptions from taxable income in computing his personal tax liability. Finally, trial 13 was made as a test of the degree to which changes in parameters which have opposite effects on the analysis when taken singly will operate to offset each other when combined. The assumptions adopted for trials 5 and 6 (no deductions and exemptions but outside income amounting to 50 per cent of salary and bonus) were superimposed. As would be expected, the results are much like those obtained in trial 1.

In comparing the various sets of figures to trial 1, it is worth noting that in those instances where a change in assumptions does give rise to a slight difference in our appraisal of the percentage composition of the pay package, the difference is almost invariably maintained *throughout* the fourteen-year period examined. Therefore, even if there are some minor discrepancies in the data due to errors in estimation or in choosing the values of the relevant parameters, those errors will have little impact on perhaps the most important conclusion suggested by the present study: the extent to which there has been a shift in emphasis within the executive compensation package over time toward a greater reliance on deferred and contingent rewards. That shift is clearly identified in all thirteen trials and has essentially the same dimensions in each. Chart 28 summarizes the comparisons.

Further support for these assertions is offered in Table 38, which indicates the rate of growth in the value of the typical executive's after-tax remuneration under the assumptions listed above. The calculations use as a base the compensation figures for the year when the executive is age 53 in order to make it possible to compare the results of the thirteen trials, since several of them specify changes in the magnitude of the man's rewards during the early years of his career. Obviously, if the

CHART 28

Sensitivity Analysis Results: Salary and Bonus as a
Percentage of Total After-Tax Compensation

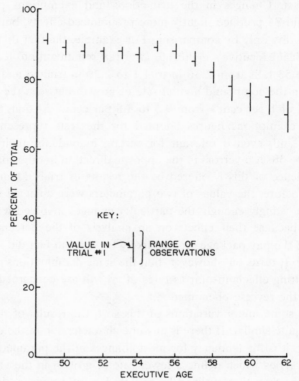

original data for ages 49, 50, and 51 are revised, any time series based
thereon will be affected. Our interest, however, is in the impact of such
revisions on an evaluation of the man's compensation over the *last ten*
years depicted because, as we saw, it was during that period that he
occupied one of the five highest-paid executive positions in his firm.
The interval from age 53 through age 62 is therefore the pertinent one.

It is clear from the tabulations that the pattern of growth in the value
of the several rewards changes very little in response to the indicated
changes in assumptions. Variations in the discount rate (trial 2), in the
amount of outside income (trials 3 through 5), and in the early com-

pensation data (trials 8 through 10) have a negligible impact. They apparently alter the value of all three elements of the pay package to just about the same extent in every year and thereby leave the historical profile intact. Changes in the deductions and exemptions percentage (trials 6 and 7) produce slightly more pronounced effects, but the latter are noteworthy only by comparison. For example, the fact that the ratio of our typical executive's aggregate after-tax remuneration at age 62 to that at age 53 falls from 2.36 in trial 1 to 2.20 in trials 6 and 7 implies a decline in the compound annual rate of growth between the two years of just $7/10$ of 1 per cent—from 9.5 to 8.8 per cent.[8] At that, the deductions and exemptions figures adopted for the tests represent extreme situations, and, even if relevant for certain individuals, their influence may well be offset by errors in the opposite direction in other parameters. Some evidence of this is offered by the results of trials 11 and 12, for which, as before, the values of two parameters were changed simultaneously. Interestingly enough, the particular changes involved were chosen originally because their effects on an analysis of the percentage composition of the pay package seemed likely to—and in fact did—reinforce each other. It turns out, however, that the same combinations of changes have offsetting effects insofar as rates of growth are concerned. Trial 13 illustrates the reverse phenomenon.

Despite some minor variations of this sort, the results of the thirteen trials are quite similar. If there is any one characteristic of the data which stands out, it is the tendency for most changes in the parameters to produce time series which define a lower rate of growth in the value of the pay package than that outlined by trial 1. It would appear, then, that if there have been errors made in specifying the magnitude of those parameters, they have been predominantly in the direction of *overstating* the secular increase in the compensation of the executives who comprise

[8] The difference between these rates and the approximately 3 per cent per annum recorded in Chapter 8 for the entire sample is, of course, due to the concentration here on a single individual's career. During the ten years when he is one of his firm's top five officers, he is likely to be moving to a succession of higher positions, and his remuneration can be expected to grow more rapidly than that associated with any one of the offices he holds. Since the data in Chapter 8 were cast in terms of the developments within the same position over time, it is not surprising to find that the rates of growth observed there were lower.

the sample. Such errors would only strengthen the majority of the conclusions which were drawn above from the experience of that sample.[9]

Stock Options

The same arguments can be made in connection with executive stock options. Of the 558 individuals whose compensation histories were examined, 221 (40 per cent) were granted at least one option. Since there were a total of 518 different grants observed, the average was slightly in excess of two per person. All but a very small percentage occurred after 1950. The aggregate after-tax remuneration produced amounted to some $80.5 million, or approximately $364,000 for each recipient.

It will be recalled that one feature of the valuation techniques employed in generating these figures was a stipulation that negative current equivalents were ruled out. Even if the pattern of annual changes in the value of a particular individual's option(s) was such as to dictate that in a given year an assessment should be made against his salary and bonus in order to "recoup" some portion of the current equivalents previously credited to him, that assessment was not recorded. Instead, the combined current equivalent of his options for the year was set equal to zero, the argument being that in practice this would almost certainly be the lower limit of any such arrangement.[10] Since it requires a fairly severe decline in common stock prices to create situations of this sort, the contention was that the results of an empirical analysis of executives' experiences with options would not be affected very greatly if the procedure described were adopted. A tabulation of the number of cases in which a negative current equivalent for an executive was indicated, but ignored, supports this claim: The total of $80,505,000 in stock option current equivalents would have been reduced by only $650,000—by $\frac{8}{10}$ of 1 per cent—had negative values actually been taken into account.[11]

[9] See especially, Chapters 8 and 9.
[10] See Chapter 4.
[11] It should be stressed, however, that this result depends heavily on the particular time period under consideration. Had the general trend of stock prices since 1950 not been so favorable, negative stock option current income equivalents would have been much more of a problem here.

A "TYPICAL" STOCK OPTION HISTORY

As was true of pensions and deferred compensation arrangements, the most efficient method for determining the impact of changes in tax rates and opportunity costs on stock option rewards is to concentrate on an appraisal of the experience of a "typical" executive. In addition, stock options have been such an important—and controversial—source of managerial remuneration in recent years that a description of the circumstances surrounding the average recipient among the senior officers of large manufacturing firms is of more than passing interest in its own right. That profile will once again be drawn in terms of the *mean* values for the sample.

The typical optionee was granted an option on two different occasions. The first such occasion was in 1954 and the age of the executive just under 54 years. The mean option price was exactly $52, a figure which represented approximately 97 per cent of the then-market price of the optioned stock. The arrangement conferred the right to purchase a total of 7,337 common shares of the employer corporation, and the average term of the option was seven years.[12] A second grant typically followed three years later. It covered 4,444 shares at a mean option price $35.18 higher than that of its predecessor, but was also seven years in duration.

In over 90 per cent of the cases studied, the executive exercised each of his options in full within four years of the date of granting. This pattern did not vary significantly among successive grants to the same individual. The usual situation consisted of the exercise of approximately 62 per cent of the option during the third year of the contract and the remainder during the subsequent year. By combining these observations with the history of stock price movements under the various arrangements, we may describe the experience of a typical option recipient as follows:

---

[12] The last figure is somewhat lower than might be anticipated on the basis of the nominal option term of ten years which was chosen by most firms in the sample. The difference is explained primarily by the fact that a great many options were granted to individuals who at the time had fewer than ten years of employment remaining until retirement. For them, the effective term of the option was shorter than the nominal period specified, since their rights expired at age 65.

OPTION NUMBER 1

Granted	1954
Executive age	54 years
Number of shares	7,337
Option price	$52 per share
Term	7 years

Stock Price and Exercise Data:

Year	End-of-Year Stock Price	Number of Shares Exercised	Market Price at Exercise
1954	$ 56.80	—	—
1955	65.10	—	—
1956	72.15	—	—
1957	91.98	4,549	$ 81.79
1958	100.61	2,788	100.55

OPTION NUMBER 2

Granted	1957
Executive age	57 years
Number of shares	4,444
Option price	$87.18 per share
Term	7 years

Stock Price and Exercise Data:

Year	End-of-Year Stock Price	Number of Shares Exercised	Market Price at Exercise
1957	$ 91.98	—	—
1958	100.61	—	—
1959	107.33	—	—
1960	127.16	2,755	$116.97
1961	135.79	1,689	135.73

If some of the later stock prices listed seem high as compared with the range in which most corporations' shares are traded, it is because the data incorporate an adjustment for stock splits and stock dividends. All prices are expressed in terms of the equivalent of one share of stock outstanding as of the date of the *first* option grant.

SENSITIVITY ANALYSIS

The issue, then, is whether the results of an analysis of the compensation provided by these options are affected very greatly by changes in assumptions about executives' personal tax circumstances and market opportunities. As we saw, such assumptions take the form of specifying just two parameters: the tax rate applicable to the profits realized, and the discount rate used in calculating the present value of the appropriate stream of "current income equivalent" payments.[13] A figure of 15 per cent was chosen for the former. This was an estimate of the extent to which the statutory 25 per cent capital gains rate would be softened in practice by the deferral of the tax, by the tax savings attributable to the additional deductions and exemptions which option profits seemed likely to give rise to, and by the possibility that some executives would avoid the tax entirely by passing on the shares acquired in their estates. Similarly, historical evidence as to the average rates of return obtained from investments in common stocks suggested 5 per cent per annum after taxes as a reasonable discount rate.

With only these two parameters to contend with, a sensitivity analysis of the option experience depicted is easily accomplished. The task is made easier by the fact that the impact of changing one of the parameters can be predicted exactly: because the tax rate chosen enters into all computations of the actual and prospective rewards associated with options as a scale factor, the numbers generated by the valuation procedures adopted are simply a linear function of that choice. Thus, if the 15 per cent rate actually employed were changed to 20 per cent, the current income equivalents of the stock options received by every executive in the sample would be reduced to 80/85 of their original values.[14] The implication for a sensitivity analysis therefore is clear. The higher the tax rate assumed, the lower the remuneration credited to options.

It is also true, however, that the range of meaningful assumptions is sufficiently narrow that the possible effects of changes therein on the empirical results cannot be very great. For example, it was reported in Chapter 8 that stock options accounted for some 27 per cent of the aggregate after-tax remuneration enjoyed during the years 1955 through

[13] See Chapter 4.
[14] See below, Table 39, for confirmation.

1963 by the five highest-paid executives in each of the fifty corporations studied. Had the tax rate on option profits been set at 20 instead of 15 per cent, their share of the total pay package would have fallen to 26 per cent over the same period [15]—a decline which does not seem large enough to cast much of a shadow on any conclusions reached above. Similarly, the resulting change in tax assessments would have lowered the compound annual rate of growth in total after-tax compensation between 1940 and 1963 only from 3.34 to 3.27 per cent. A decrease in the tax rate to 10 per cent would, of course, produce equal but opposite effects. Since the "true" rate must lie somewhere between zero and 25, the numbers generated by the 15 per cent figure chosen for the study cannot be far wrong.

The consequences of changing the discount rate used in the calculations are less predictable, but turn out to be no more pronounced. Table 39 records the current income equivalents derived from our typical executive's stock option experience under the assumption first of a 5 per cent per annum after-tax opportunity cost and then a figure of 10 per cent. The differences between the two "total" columns each year indicate that doubling the discount rate increases the calculated value of the remuneration provided by the option some 6 per cent. Since this is about the extent of the change that would ensue were the tax rate raised to 20 per cent, the level of our concern with the sensitivity of the empirical results should be similar. Indeed, if both parameters are revised simultaneously, their effects pretty well cancel, as the third set of figures in Table 39 illustrates.[16] In any event, it would require a greater change in the relevant discount rate than that considered here to significantly alter the outcome of the computations. Figures in excess of 10 per cent per annum after taxes do not, however, appear very meaningful.

Summary

Insofar as assumptions about corporate executives' personal circumstances have been required by the valuation techniques developed in

---

[15] That is, to the fraction $(80/85)/[0.73 + (80/85)(0.27)]$ of the original figure of 27 per cent.

[16] Consistent with the arguments made above, each of these numbers is precisely 80/85 the size of its counterpart in the second trial.

TABLE 39

Sensitivity Analysis of Stock Option Rewards

Executive Age	After-Tax Current Income Equivalents (dollars)		
	Option No. 1	Option No. 2	Total

Trial number 1: Discount rate = 5 per cent;
Tax rate = 15 per cent

55	5,095	–	5,095
56	15,100	–	15,100
57	25,020	–	25,020
58	47,238	3,114	50,352
59	52,461	9,466	61,927
60	52,461	15,232	67,693
61	52,461	28,690	81,151
62	–	31,755	31,755
63	–	31,755	31,755
64	–	31,755	31,755
Totals	249,836	151,767	401,603

Trial number 2: Discount rate = 10 per cent;
Tax rate = 15 per cent

55	5,767	–	5,767
56	16,877	–	16,877
57	27,678	–	27,678
58	50,693	3,522	54,215
59	54,385	10,572	64,957
60	54,385	16,848	71,233
61	54,385	30,766	85,151
62	–	32,875	32,875
63	–	32,875	32,875
64	–	32,875	32,875
Totals	264,170	160,333	424,503

Trial number 3: Discount rate = 10 per cent;
Tax rate = 20 per cent

55	5,428	–	5,428
56	15,884	–	15,884
57	26,050	–	26,050
58	47,711	3,315	51,026
59	51,186	9,950	61,136
60	51,186	15,857	67,043
61	51,186	28,956	80,142
62	–	30,941	30,941
63	–	30,941	30,941
64	–	30,941	30,941
Totals	248,631	150,901	399,532

preceding chapters, the contention has been that the results of applying those techniques should not depend heavily on the particular assumptions made. An appraisal of a representative compensation history supports this claim. Wide variations in the values of the parameters which characterize the compensation environment do not produce important changes in the conclusions reached. The impact of those variations is cushioned by the design of the current income equivalents offered and by the emphasis throughout on the relationships between rewards rather than on their absolute magnitudes.

13

SUMMARY

Both the size and the structure of the senior corporate executive's compensation package have undergone substantial and important changes over the last quarter century. While this is perhaps not an unanticipated conclusion, neither the dimensions nor the pace of these changes have been thus far adequately stressed. The objective here has been to remedy this deficiency by developing and applying techniques of valuation which provide an accurate and comprehensive measure of the worth of the pay package to its recipient at any point in time. Because of their key role in the business community in general, and their influence on patterns of compensation policy in particular, the senior officers of fifty of the country's largest manufacturing corporations were chosen as the focus for the study. In all, the sample included data on the experience of approximately 550 executives and covered some 8,000 man-years' worth of compensation history, giving rise to a record of secular changes which begins in 1940 and continues through 1963.

The Findings

While top executives' salary and bonus income has increased by 83 per cent before taxes and 33 per cent after taxes since 1940, their aggregate after-tax remuneration has approximately doubled. Deferred and contingent rewards, which now comprise about half the compensation package, have accounted for the major portion of this increase. The restricted stock option, created by tax legislation in the early 1950's, has been an especially important item, providing nearly one-third of all after-tax remuneration enjoyed by senior executives in recent years. As a result of this development and the concomitant growth in the popular-

278

ity of other forms of reward that utilize shares of the employer corporation's common stock as the compensation medium, the year-to-year volatility of the value of the managerial pay package has increased substantially over time, and the individual executive's earnings have become more closely linked to the market fortunes of his firm's shareholders. Because such rewards began to come into wide use primarily in the late 1940's and early 1950's, most of the growth in pay we observe occurred within the ten years immediately following World War II.

That growth has not, however, been very impressive in comparison with most historical indexes. In the aggregate, the sales, assets, profits, and market value of the corporations for which the executives in the sample worked grew much more rapidly than either the salaries and bonuses or the total compensation of those executives. Other important professional groups—physicians, lawyers, and dentists—have also done better over time; their 1963 after-tax incomes ranged from 2.4 to 3.2 times the corresponding 1940 figures as compared with 2.1 for top executives. Manufacturing production workers earned 3.6 times as much after taxes in 1963 as in 1940, and the take-home pay of the individuals at the bottom of the corporate managerial hierarchy—recent MBA graduates—increased by approximately 400 per cent. Upon adjusting for price changes, in fact, it turns out that the senior executives in our sample were no better off in 1963 than in 1940 in terms of *real* after-tax income. In large part, these developments can be attributed to a sharp rise in personal tax rates, which has had a particularly severe impact on high-income groups such as executives. It seems likely, however, that the nature of the compensation bargaining process and the publicity given top executive rewards by the proxy statement reporting requirements of the SEC have also contributed downward pressures.

Looking in cross section at the remuneration enjoyed by the five highest-paid executives in each of the firms in the sample, we find that the salary and bonus differentials between the top executive and his four closest subordinates have narrowed considerably over the last twenty-five years. The typical second- through fifth-ranking executives in large manufacturing corporations now receive, respectively, 75, 64, 57, and 53 per cent as much before-tax salary and bonus as their firm's senior officer. In 1940–41 the figures were 62, 50, 44, and 39 per cent. Despite these changes, it remains true that both the absolute and percentage gaps between successive positions increase steadily as the individual climbs the executive ladder.

The history of the more pertinent aggregate remuneration profile is quite different. When the values of the various supplements to salary and bonus are considered, the percentage compensation differentials among the top five executive positions prove to be almost exactly the same in recent years as they were in the early 1940's. In relation to the total after-tax earnings of the highest-paid executive, those for the other four positions studied came to 67, 56, 45, and 38 per cent for the interval 1955–63 as compared with 64, 53, 45, and 40 per cent in 1940–41. Taken in conjunction with the salary and bonus time series, this phenomenon suggests strongly that the corporations in the sample not only plan their compensation packages in a comprehensive manner, but have been guided in so doing by a desire to maintain the after-tax structure of rewards in the senior executive ranks intact in the face of substantial increases in personal tax rates. The remarkable stability of the structure during a period in which the rewards in question doubled in size seems to attest either to the skill or the good fortune connected with that effort.

This result was, of course, achieved by a policy of utilizing more extensively at higher executive levels the less heavily taxed deferred and contingent compensation arrangements as adjuncts to salary and bonus payments. The value of each of the major instruments in that category— pensions, stock options, deferred compensation, and profit-sharing plans —increased steadily in importance from the fifth-ranking to the top executive position in every year considered. Between 1955 and 1963, for example, 31, 36, 44, 50, and 62 per cent of all after-tax remuneration associated with the five positions—in ascending order—was generated by means other than direct cash payments. Since many of these arrangements depend for their value on the market price behavior of the corporation's common stock, the volatility of the pay package also increased correspondingly. Not surprisingly, stock options accounted for most of the fluctuations observed.

In collecting the data for these comparisons, information as to the ages of the executives and their terms in office necessarily became available. It was found that the individuals who occupied each of the top five positions in the sample corporations in the early 1960's were approximately five years older on average than were their predecessors of the early 1940's. The mean length of time the various positions were held by the same individual also appears to have diminished slightly.

When the cross-sections are viewed in terms of intercompany patterns of reward, we discover that executive compensation practices vary much less widely than do the measurable attributes of the employer corporations themselves. The dispersion in the sample of both salary and bonus and aggregate remuneration levels among senior executives is substantially smaller than that displayed by the assets, sales, profits, and market values of their firms—a phenomenon which is more pronounced now than it was twenty-five years ago. In addition, the conclusion arrived at earlier, that over time the earnings of top executives have not kept pace with the expansion of the corporations for which they work, is reinforced when that comparison is made on a company-by-company basis. In only about 10 per cent of the cases examined did the compensation associated with the senior executive position in a given firm grow as rapidly between 1940 and 1963 as even the most sluggish index of the company's growth.

The dominant role of deferred and contingent rewards in the pay package is underlined by the poor performance of corporate salary and bonus scales as predictors of total compensation levels. There are sharp and consistent differences between the schedules obtained by ranking firms according to the amount of direct current remuneration received by their top executives and those constructed from the corresponding aggregate remuneration figures. The resulting rank correlation coefficients are typically on the order of .4 to .6, and have declined over the years as supplements to salary and bonus have increased in popularity and value. A similar story emerges from a comparison of salary and bonus and total compensation growth rates since 1940. The coefficients calculated by matching those two sets of rankings run anywhere from .1 to .4 and satisfy significance tests at the .01 level only in scattered instances.

There is considerable evidence, on the other hand, that top executive earnings and employer-company size are directly related. Insofar as there is a difference in the degree to which such a relationship appears among the various criteria tabulated, a firm's profits seem a somewhat better predictor of the probable magnitude of its senior officers' rewards than do either its assets, its sales, or the market value of its common stock. The connection between executive salaries and bonuses and each of those items is consistently stronger than between the latter and the same individuals' total after-tax remuneration. We also have some indication that the larger and more profitable the corporation, the more it makes use of supplements to salary and bonus for its senior executives— a phenomenon which, while persistent, is sufficiently mild that it could be as much a result of certain technical features of the compensation process as a policy decision in its own right. It is clear, however, that the firms in the sample which provide their top management with the highest levels of aggregate remuneration are precisely those which utilize such supplements most extensively.

The Current Equivalents

The key to the analysis, of course, is the concept of a "current income equivalent" for each deferred and contingent compensation arrangement in the pay package. Upon the design and implementation of these indexes of the worth of such instruments as pension plans, stock option grants, and deferred compensation contracts rests the validity of the conclusions summarized above. The principles underlying their development throughout have been that (1) it is possible to cast up as an alternative to every noncurrent form of reward a stream of salary payments between which and the reward itself the executive would be indifferent, and (2) that "indifference" is most appropriately defined in terms of after-tax present values. An attempt has been made in each instance to duplicate in the current equivalent not only the compensatory achievements but the volatility and incentive features of the device being evaluated. The early chapters of the study spell out the particulars of that effort. The contention is that a corporation could, if it chose, substitute for any one of the arrangements considered the hypothetical series of salary payments which constitute its indicated current equivalent without diminishing either the earnings or the dedication of the firm's executives. In that sense the total of these equivalents provides an accurate and meaningful measure of the value of a compensation package which consists in fact of a wide variety of quite dissimilar components. Fortunately, this total turns out—at least insofar as the present sample is concerned—to be affected very little by rather broad changes in assumptions as to the characteristics of the environment in which rewards are received and the nature of executives' market alternatives. It therefore should be possible to have some confidence that the numbers generated permit an accurate appraisal of the historical record.

Additional Research

As has been suggested at several points along the way, the analysis presented falls considerably short of exhausting the opportunities for research in this area. For example, the question of the relationship between employer-company size and top executive pay was examined only tentatively here. Because of the likely impact on the compensation decision both of other characteristics of the individual firm and certain features of its environment, the attempts thus far made to isolate the influence of corporate size or profitability per se have not been very successful. Moreover, they have dealt only with salary and bonus awards rather than with the total pay package. Now that it is possible to speak in terms of the latter, the way is open to collect and process the additional data which will permit these other factors to be recognized and a more meaningful analysis undertaken.

A second item of interest is the compensation experience of executives who occupy positions in the corporate managerial hierarchy below those which comprise the current sample. There is reason to believe that many of the conclusions which emerge from the historical record of senior executives' rewards may not hold for lower-level administrators. The major obstacles to further research in this area are the difficulty in obtaining comprehensive and reliable data and the question of accurate job definition. Since the information available in proxy statements covers just the top few men in each firm, the economic circumstances of subordinate officials can be investigated only by securing the cooperation of a group of interested companies and acquiring the necessary data directly from them. This having been done, the problem then is to make sure that the data provided relate to the same sort of positions in each firm and that those positions remain intact throughout the time period studied. While not impossible, this is plainly a harder task than that tackled here.

An issue raised in connection with the incentive aspects of various forms of reward—the pattern of stock holdings among top executives—also deserves further attention. The extent to which such individuals normally maintain a significant ownership interest in their respective firms is important to the argument that compensation arrangements utilizing shares of the employer corporation's common stock should be made available in order to encourage a greater degree of identification with shareholder objectives—and to the argument that there is not now sufficient such identification. Fortunately, data pertaining to stock holdings *are* published annually in corporations' proxy statements and are supplemented monthly by an SEC record of their officers' transactions. A sample of executives like that compiled for the present study is a natural starting point.

A somewhat different but equally compelling problem concerns the attitudes and reactions of the two parties to the compensation bargain. Whether in most cases the executive and the employer company both have an accurate appreciation of the value of the various deferred and contingent rewards in the pay package is clearly going to have an effect on the nature of the settlements they produce. Given the techniques developed above for making such appraisals for a broad range of devices, it would be of interest to determine how close the perceptions of executives and compensation administrators actually are to these figures, to what extent and in what manner ex ante estimates of compensatory value are made, whether either party attributes differential incentive features to the several instruments employed, and how large a factor cost comparisons are in the decisions. In short, we need a better understanding of the compensation process as it is viewed from the inside in order to test the external evaluation presented here.

Finally, the same sort of historical and cross-sectional analysis performed for large manufacturing corporations should be expanded to encompass other important categories of business activity. The compensation experience of the top executives of public utility companies, of financial institutions, of firms engaged in retail trade, of transportation companies, and of a sample of smaller manufacturing enterprises may or may not differ significantly from that depicted above but, in any event, is relevant to a comprehensive appraisal of the secular growth and current pattern of managerial remuneration in the community. The techniques employed in the present study are directly transferable to such an investigation.

The twofold objective here, therefore, has been to develop a flexible conceptual framework in which the value to an individual executive of the many disparate components of his pay package can be measured and to apply that framework empirically in order to determine the manner in which corporations have recast their compensation policies over time in response to changes in the tax laws and in the economic environment. It is hoped that both the approach taken and the findings presented provide a basis and an incentive for additional research.

APPENDIXES

APPENDIX A

DEDUCTIONS AND EXEMPTIONS
AS A PER CENT OF INCOME

Information on the personal exemptions and the deductions from taxable income claimed by individuals having incomes of the same order of magnitude as those enjoyed by the executives in the sample was obtained from the *Statistics of Income* data published by the Internal Revenue Service for the six years 1944, 1947, 1950, 1953, 1956, and 1959. The ratio of the total of deductions and exemptions to the aggregate income received by all taxpayers with adjusted gross incomes greater than $25,000 in each of those years was computed. Aggregate income was defined as the sum of the reported adjusted gross income and the amount of net long-term capital gains not already included in AGI. The results were as follows (the underlying figures are recorded in Table A-1).

DEDUCTIONS AND EXEMPTIONS AS A PER CENT OF ALL INCOME

AGI Class ($000's)	1944	1947	1950	1953	1956	1959
25–50	10.8	11.9	13.7	18.3	16.4	18.1
50–100	9.9	10.8	11.3	15.7	14.1	15.8
100–150	10.1	11.0	10.7	14.3	14.8	15.6
150–200	10.7	11.5	10.4	14.6	15.3	16.2
200–500	10.9	11.0	11.1	16.0	15.4	16.0
500–1000	9.9	11.6	9.8	14.5	14.1	14.5
Over 1000	12.5	10.0	9.7	15.1	13.5	15.0

Clearly, the ratios within each year are quite uniform across a broad range of income classes, and they encourage the assumption of a single

TABLE A-1

Income Data

(dollar figures in millions)

AGI Class (thousand dollars)	Total AGI	Capital Gains (50%)	Total Income	Personal Exemptions	Deductions	Exemptions Plus Deductions	Exemptions and Deductions as % of Total Income
			1944 Data				
25–50	3,388.7	118.5	3,507.2	118.7	261.1	379.7	10.8
50–100	1,926.0	98.3	2,024.3	31.7	168.6	200.2	9.9
100–150	584.7	43.4	628.1	4.9	58.7	63.6	10.1
150–200	267.6	26.4	294.0	1.5	29.9	31.3	10.7
200–500	419.7	57.2	476.9	1.4	50.7	52.1	10.9
500–1000	149.0	31.7	180.7	0.2	17.7	17.9	9.9
Over 1000	109.6	19.8	129.4	0.1	16.1	16.2	12.5
			1947 Data				
25–50	4,923.4	201.5	5,125.0	180.2	431.3	611.5	11.9
50–100	2,525.7	176.3	2,702.0	41.9	250.4	292.3	10.8
100–150	759.9	89.4	849.3	6.3	87.3	93.5	11.0
150–200	352.6	51.0	403.6	1.9	44.6	46.5	11.5
200–500	573.6	127.1	700.7	1.7	75.0	76.7	11.0
500–1000	201.8	53.0	254.8	0.2	29.3	29.6	11.6
Over 1000	214.9	73.2	288.2	0.1	28.8	28.9	10.1
			1950 Data				
25–50	7,425.5	376.3	7,801.7	445.0	620.9	1,065.9	13.7
50–100	4,192.5	304.6	4,497.1	123.4	386.3	509.7	11.3
100–150	1,386.5	156.6	1,543.1	21.9	143.8	165.8	10.7
150–200	676.8	98.3	775.0	7.4	73.6	81.0	10.4
200–500	1,141.2	229.9	1,371.2	7.3	144.9	152.2	11.1
500–1000	419.5	132.4	551.8	1.1	52.8	53.8	9.8
Over 1000	433.4	131.3	564.7	0.3	54.3	54.7	9.7

(*continued*)

TABLE A-1 (concluded)

AGI Class (thousand dollars)	Total AGI	Capital Gains (50%)	Total Income	Personal Exemptions	Deductions	Exemptions Plus Deductions	Exemptions and Deductions as % of Total Income
			1953 Data				
25–50	6,355.7	191.2	6,546.9	546.5	651.8	1,198.3	18.3
50–100	5,682.1	212.7	5,894.8	310.7	612.8	923.5	15.7
100–150	3,994.6	239.3	4,233.9	120.2	484.2	604.5	14.3
150–200	1,638.7	184.0	1,822.6	23.6	243.3	266.9	14.6
200–500	753.1	148.1	901.2	4.9	138.7	143.7	16.0
500–1000	252.4	69.5	321.9	0.6	46.2	46.8	14.5
Over 1000	275.3	70.8	346.1	0.2	52.0	52.2	15.1
			1956 Data				
25–50	11,638.4	673.0	12,311.4	753.3	1,262.5	2,015.9	16.4
50–100	5,900.3	582.2	6,482.5	189.4	721.8	911.2	14.1
100–150	1,679.3	291.8	1,971.1	28.9	262.1	291.0	14.8
150–200	659.1	138.2	797.3	7.9	114.3	122.2	15.3
200–500	1,138.0	320.0	1,458.1	8.1	216.5	224.6	15.4
500–1000	396.6	154.2	550.8	1.2	76.3	77.5	14.1
Over 1000	549.6	241.1	790.8	0.5	106.0	106.5	13.5
			1959 Data				
25–50	14,148.9	919.6	15,068.5	956.3	1,766.7	2,723.0	18.1
50–100	7,549.5	799.6	8,349.1	255.5	1,060.4	1,315.9	15.8
100–150	2,080.6	394.2	2,474.8	37.0	348.0	385.0	15.6
150–200	764.3	192.0	956.2	9.5	145.2	154.7	16.2
200–500	1,361.9	457.4	1,819.4	9.9	281.3	291.1	16.0
500–1000	478.2	220.9	699.0	1.4	100.1	101.6	14.5
Over 1000	545.6	258.0	803.6	0.5	120.1	120.6	15.0

flat rate for all individuals. Moreover, there is a rather clear-cut difference between the experience of the years 1944, 1947, and 1950 and that observed thereafter. Almost all the figures in the earlier years fall between 9.5 and 11.5 per cent and in the later ones, between 14.5 and 16.0 per cent. Accordingly, the convention adopted in the study, that deductions and exemptions together amounted to 10 per cent of income through 1950 and 15 per cent from then on, seems not only a convenient but a fairly accurate characterization of the actual historical pattern. As long as corporate executives' behavior did not differ markedly from that suggested by the aggregate figures for all individuals with similar incomes, this convention should be a suitable approximation of their experience.

The supporting data from the *Statistics of Income* tabulations for the six years indicated consist of: (1) total adjusted gross income on all returns in each AGI class (2) the amount of net long-term capital gains included in the AGI figures; (3) total personal exemptions claimed by the taxpayers in each class; (4) total deductions claimed in each class.

Since just one-half of aggregate net long-term capital gains are counted in the reported AGI figures, the sum of items (1) and (2) represents the total income enjoyed by each AGI category.

APPENDIX B

MORTALITY EXPERIENCE TABULATIONS

Insurance companies compile, from their policy underwriting experience, a record of the rate at which their policyholders of various ages die. This information is organized and presented in the form of a "mortality table." Since the classes of people who purchase different kinds of insurance policies typically exhibit different longevity characteristics, there exist not one but several such tables, each of which is relevant to a particular type of insurance contract. All are revised periodically to reflect new information on longevity as it becomes available.

The tabulations are most commonly organized in the following manner: An arbitrary group of individual policyholders all of a particular—and equally arbitrary—age initially is hypothesized. The number out of this group who will, on the basis of current experience, attain successively higher ages is then recorded. For example, if the table is begun at age 5 with 10,000 persons, it might look like:

Age x	l_x
5	10000.00
6	9994.41
7	9989.22
8	9984.29
9	9979.49
10	9974.74
·	·
·	·
·	·

(Continued)

293

Age x	l_x
50	9371.75
.	.
.	.
.	.
75	5173.47
.	.
.	.
.	.
110	0.01
111	0.00

where l_x denotes the number of individuals who are expected to live to at least age x. According to this table, of every 10,000 policyholders who are now age 5, 9994.41 are expected to attain age 6, 9989.22 to attain age 7, 5173.47 age 75, 0.01 age 110, but none age 111.

From these figures, the probability that an individual of any given age at the present time will live to any other given age can readily be computed. Thus the probability that a child now age 5 will live at least one more year is

$$\frac{9994.41}{10000.00} = 0.999441.$$

Similarly, the chances of his attaining age 50 are

$$\frac{9371.75}{10000.00} = 0.937175.$$

And, of course, age 5 need not be the reference point in every case. The probability that a man age 50 will live to see his seventy-fifth birthday is

$$\frac{5173.47}{9371.75} = 0.552028.$$

In general, therefore, if we let $_np_x$ denote the probability that an individual of age x now will attain age $x + n$, we have

$$_np_x = \frac{l_{x+n}}{l_x},$$

which permits us to utilize the raw data of the mortality table to analyze

in any situation an executive's prospects for actually receiving the payments promised him under his company's pension plan.

For certain calculations—in particular, those concerned with the
value of whatever death benefits may be associated with the compensation arrangement in question—it is useful to derive a second set of
mortality tabulations from the information listed above: the number
of individuals out of the original 10,000 who are, on average, expected
to *die* after having attained various ages. Thus we may define the
quantity d_x where

$$d_x = l_x - l_{x+1}$$

and construct an additional column in the mortality table:

Age x	l_x	d_x
5	10000.00	5.59
6	9994.41	5.19
7	9989.22	4.93
8	9984.29	4.80
.	.	.
.	.	.
.	.	.
50	9371.75	60.68
51	9311.07	66.92
.	.	.
.	.	.
.	.	.
75	5173.47	322.97
76	4850.50	331.52
.	.	.
.	.	.
.	.	.
110	0.01	0.01
111	0.00	—

The probability that an individual now age 5 will die after attaining
age 7 but before attaining age 8 therefore is

$$\frac{4.93}{10000.00} = 0.000493.$$

If he reaches age 8, the likelihood that he will die between his fiftieth and fifty-first birthday is

$$\frac{60.68}{9984.29} = 0.006078.$$

In general, then,

$$_nq_x = \frac{d_{x+n}}{l_x}$$

where $_nq_x$ denotes the probability that a man presently age x will die within a year after attaining age $x + n$.

APPENDIX C

1951 GROUP ANNUITY
MORTALITY TABLE FOR MALES

Age x	l_x	d_x	Age x	l_x	d_x
5	9999.9999	5.5900	31	9837.6874	10.3689
6	9994.4099	5.1871	32	9827.3185	11.0263
7	9989.2228	4.9347	33	9816.2922	11.7599
8	9984.2881	4.8024	34	9804.5323	12.5596
9	9979.4857	4.7502	35	9791.9727	13.4542
10	9974.7355	4.7579	36	9778.5185	14.4233
11	9969.9776	4.8454	37	9764.0952	15.4956
12	9965.1322	4.9427	38	9748.5996	16.6799
13	9960.1895	5.0399	39	9731.9197	17.9943
14	9955.1496	5.1468	40	9713.9254	19.4279
15	9950.0028	5.2735	41	9694.4975	21.2503
16	9944.7293	5.4099	42	9673.2472	23.6995
17	9939.3194	5.5660	43	9649.5477	26.7196
18	9933.7534	5.7318	44	9622.8281	30.2830
19	9928.0216	5.9072	45	9592.5451	34.3413
20	9922.1144	6.1120	46	9558.2038	38.8541
21	9916.0024	6.3462	47	9519.3497	43.7795
22	9909.6562	6.5998	48	9475.5702	49.0835
23	9903.0564	6.8628	49	9426.4867	54.7396
24	9896.1936	7.1648	50	9371.7471	60.6821
25	9889.0288	7.4959	51	9311.0650	66.9186
26	9881.5329	7.8657	52	9244.1464	73.3800
27	9873.6672	8.2741	53	9170.7664	80.0700
28	9865.3931	8.7309	54	9090.6964	86.9343
29	9856.6622	9.2160	55	9003.7621	93.9633
30	9847.4462	9.7588	56	8909.7988	101.0906

(Continued)
297

Age x	l_x	d_x	Age x	l_x	d_x
57	8808.7082	108.3295	84	2152.3957	295.0353
58	8700.3787	115.7324	85	1857.3604	272.7571
59	8584.6463	123.4386	86	1584.6033	248.5228
60	8461.2077	131.6141	87	1336.0805	223.2858
61	8329.5936	140.4869	88	1112.7947	197.8404
62	8189.1067	150.2947	89	0914.9543	172.8523
63	8038.8120	161.3229	90	0742.1020	148.8612
64	7877.4891	173.8326	91	0593.2408	126.0963
65	7703.6565	188.1079	92	0467.1445	105.1827
66	7515.5486	204.3703	93	0361.9618	086.3366
67	7311.1783	220.1542	94	0275.6252	069.6684
68	7091.0241	233.9045	95	0205.9568	055.2016
69	6857.1196	246.4654	96	0150.7552	042.8831
70	6610.6542	259.8185	97	0107.8721	032.6014
71	6350.8357	274.2481	98	0075.2707	024.2007
72	6076.5876	288.4291	99	0051.0700	017.4928
73	5788.0955	301.4672	100	0033.5772	012.2712
74	5486.6283	313.1603	101	0021.3060	008.3208
75	5173.4680	322.9641	102	0012.9852	005.4275
76	4850.5039	331.5174	103	0007.5577	003.4017
77	4518.9865	339.5205	104	0004.1560	002.0331
78	4179.4660	345.5875	105	0002.1229	001.1413
79	3833.8785	348.6759	106	0000.9816	000.5866
80	3485.2026	347.4015	107	0000.3950	000.2653
81	3137.8011	341.0978	108	0000.1297	000.0988
82	2796.7033	329.9523	109	0000.0309	000.0269
83	2466.7510	314.3553	110	0000.0040	000.0040

APPENDIX D

PRESENT VALUE COMPUTATIONS

Illustrative Case

Consider the case of an executive who is now age 50 and who is promised under his corporation's pension plan a retirement benefit of $20,000 per year to begin at age 65 and continue for life. Let us assume that our best estimate of the tax bracket he will be in upon retirement suggests that, after personal taxes, this benefit will amount to $10,000 each year. If the annual discount rate which expresses the time value of money to the executive—his relevant "opportunity cost"—is r, the present value to him as of age 50 of the payment he expects to receive during the first year of his retirement is

$$PV(65) = (\$10,000)(_{15}p_{50})(1 + r)^{-15}$$

where $_{15}p_{50}$ denotes the probability that he will in fact attain age 65 and is equal to the ratio l_{65}/l_{50} from the appropriate mortality table.[1] Thus this present value is really a present *expected* value. It represents the (discounted) mean payoff associated with a discrete probability distribution, which, as it applies to each potential retirement benefit, has but two possible outcomes: the man in question attains the age at which the benefit is to be paid; or he dies beforehand. The complete expression for $PV(65)$ in this case therefore is

$$PV(65) = (\$10,000)(_{15}p_{50})(1 + r)^{-15} + (0)(1 - {}_{15}p_{50})(1 + r)^{-15}.$$

But since the value of the second term is—and, clearly, always will be —zero, it may be neglected.

Similarly, the present value of the benefit due at age 66 is

$$PV(66) = (\$10,000)(_{16}p_{50})(1 + r)^{-16}.$$

[1] See Appendix B.

299

And, for the entire series of benefits:

$$PV = \sum_{n=65}^{w} PV(n)$$

where w refers to the highest age which, according to the relevant mortality table, the executive can possibly attain. In the instance of the mortality table depicted in Appendix B, for example, w is equal to 110.

The Noncontributory Pension

Since the only benefits due an employee under a noncontributory corporate pension plan are a series of equal annual payments beginning at retirement and continuing until he dies, the present value expression for such an arrangement is quite simple. It will be assumed here and in each of the subsequent appendixes dealing with the value of these plans that retirement is expected to occur at age 65. The actuarial symbols defined in Appendix B will be used throughout.

If the annual before-tax retirement benefit promised is $1 and the applicable effective tax on it is denoted by t, the present value to a man now age x of the payment he expects to receive in the first year of his retirement (at age 65) is

$$PVRB(65) = (1 - t)\left(\frac{l_{65}}{l_x}\right)\left(\frac{1}{1+r}\right)^{65-x};$$

that of the payment anticipated in the following year is

$$PVRB(66) = (1 - t)\left(\frac{l_{66}}{l_x}\right)\left(\frac{1}{1+r}\right)^{66-x};$$

and, in general,

$$PVRB(65 + n) = (1 - t)\left(\frac{l_{65+n}}{l_x}\right)\left(\frac{1}{1+r}\right)^{65-x+n}$$

for $0 \leq n \leq 35$, since age 110 is the ultimate age tabulated in the mortality table employed here. If we then define

$$v = \frac{1}{1+r}$$

$$D_x = v^x l_x$$

and multiply both numerator and denominator of the expressions above by v^x, they can be rewritten as:

$$PVRB(65) = (1 - t)\left(\frac{v^x}{v^x}\right)\left(\frac{l_{65}}{l_x}\right)(v^{65-x}) = (1 - t)\left(\frac{D_{65}}{D_x}\right)$$

$$PVRB(66) = (1 - t)\left(\frac{D_{66}}{D_x}\right)$$

$$PVRB(65 + n) = (1 - t)\left(\frac{D_{65+n}}{D_x}\right).$$

This is a rather less cumbersome form with which to work.

The present value of the entire pension promise, comprised as it is of only the indicated payments, is, therefore,

$$PV = \sum_{n=1}^{35} PVRB(65 + n)$$

$$= (1 - t)\left(\frac{D_{65} + D_{66} + \cdots + D_{110}}{D_x}\right).$$

And, finally, defining the symbol

$$N_x = \sum_{n=x}^{110} D_n = D_x + D_{x+1} + \cdots + D_{110},$$

we can write, as the relevant after-tax present value formula per dollar of before-tax prospective retirement benefit,

$$PV = (1 - t)\left(\frac{N_{65}}{D_x}\right).$$

A tabulation of the values for N_x and D_x over the appropriate range of ages then permits a rapid and convenient computation of the worth of any noncontributory pension considered.

The Contributory Pension

The benefit format and tax treatment of a contributory corporate pension plan are considerably more complex than those of its noncontributory counterpart. There are three different sets of prospective payments under such a plan:

1. The annual retirement benefit itself, due to begin at age 65 and continue thereafter for the life of the employee;

2. A death benefit payment consisting of a return of the interest-accumulated value of the employee's contributions if he dies prior to retirement;

3. A death benefit payment equal to the difference between the interest-accumulated value of the employee's contributions as of age 65 and the aggregate retirement benefits he has received if he should die after retiring.

The three will be considered separately here. The analysis again will be cast in terms of a $1 annual before-tax retirement benefit promise to the employee.

THE ANNUAL RETIREMENT BENEFIT

Depending on the amount the employee contributes to the pension plan over the years, either of two tax rules applies to his retirement benefits. If the aggregate amount of his contributions is less than the total benefits he expects to receive during the first *three* years of retirement, the full amount of each receipt is tax-free until those contributions have been recouped. All subsequent payments are taxable in their entirety at regular personal income rates.

If the aggregate contributions exceed three years' worth of retirement benefits, the "life-expectancy" tax rule applies. Under that alternative, a portion of each benefit receipt is considered tax-free regardless of how long the employee lives to collect his pension. The relevant portion is determined as follows: [2] The maximum postretirement death benefit payable under the plan is divided by the amount of the annual retirement benefit due. The result denotes the number of years it takes to "earn out" that benefit—to reduce it to zero—given that every dollar of pension received automatically diminishes the prospective death benefit by $1. This figure is then rounded off to the nearest integer and an adjustment percentage obtained by entering Table III of IRS regulation 1.72-9 under the indicated number of years. This adjustment percentage is applied to the aggregate amount of the employee's lifetime contributions to the pension plan in order to reduce that total as the basis

---

[2] This is the procedure referred to in footnote 30 of Chapter 2.

for calculating the tax-free percentage according to the "life-expectancy" rule.

To illustrate: assume that an executive, now age 50, is required to contribute $5,000 per year to his firm's pension plan and is promised thereunder an annual retirement benefit of $20,000. By age 65, he will have contributed $75,000 to the plan. Since he stands to receive only $60,000 in benefits during the first three years of his retirement, the life-expectancy tax rule applies.[3] Suppose, further, that the $75,000 in contributions will accumulate, at the rate of interest specified in the pension agreement,[4] to $90,000 by age 65 if all fifteen payments are made. This amount then is the maximum postretirement death benefit payable under the plan and is the pertinent figure for our computations. Thus, the length of time it will take to recoup that sum in pension benefits is

$$\frac{\$90,000}{\$20,000/\text{yr.}} = 4.5 \text{ years.}$$

Rounding this off to five years and entering the designated IRS table for retirement at age 65 and a five-year recoupment period, the "adjustment factor" turns out to be 7 per cent. This means that the remainder, i.e., 93 per cent, of the executive's aggregate (unaccumulated) contributions of $75,000 are the basis for determining the tax-free portion of his annual pension benefit. Because the IRS also specifies that fifteen years is the average life expectancy for a man age 65, the assumption for tax purposes is that our executive stands to receive a total of $300,000 in pension benefits before he dies. Therefore, $\frac{(.93)(75,000)}{300,000}$, or .232, of each annual payment will be considered tax-free.

By way of general notation, then, we may express the after-tax present value to a man age x of a $1 per year before-tax retirement benefit promise under a contributory pension plan as

[3] If his contributions amounted to $2,000 per year instead, the total would come to $30,000 by age 65. Thus the alternative tax treatment would take effect, all $20,000 of the first pension receipt and $10,000 of the second being tax-free.

[4] This rate will be assumed here to be equal to 2½ per cent. The rates for most pension plans are in fact very close to this figure.

$$PVRB = (1 - t_1)\left(\frac{l_{65}}{l_x}\right)(v^{65-x}) + (1 - t_2)\left(\frac{l_{66}}{l_x}\right)(v^{66-x})$$

$$+ (1 - t_3)\left(\frac{l_{67}}{l_x}\right)(v^{67-x}) + (1 - t_4)\sum_{n=68}^{110}\left(\frac{l_n}{l_x}\right)(v^{n-x})$$

where t_1 = effective tax rate on first year's benefit,
$\quad\quad t_2$ = effective tax rate on second year's benefit,
$\quad\quad t_3$ = effective tax rate on third year's benefit,
$\quad\quad t_4$ = effective tax rate on fourth and subsequent years' benefits.

These are determined by obtaining the appropriate tax-free portions from the procedures described above and calculating the regular personal income tax levies on the remainder. In the case of the life-expectancy rule, of course, $t_1 = t_2 = t_3 = t_4$.

If both numerator and denominator of each term on the right-hand side of the equation are multiplied by v^x, and the symbols D_x and N_x are introduced as above, this standard formula reduces to

$$PVRB = (1 - t_1)\left(\frac{D_{65}}{D_x}\right) + (1 - t_2)\left(\frac{D_{66}}{D_x}\right)$$

$$+ (1 - t_3)\left(\frac{D_{67}}{D_x}\right) + (1 - t_4)\left(\frac{N_{68}}{D_x}\right),$$

or, for a life-expectancy rule situation,

$$PVRB = (1 - t)\left(\frac{N_{65}}{D_x}\right)$$

which, except for the value for t which will pertain, is the same result as for a noncontributory pension.

POSTRETIREMENT DEATH BENEFITS

If the annual contributions to the pension plan by the employee per dollar of before-tax retirement benefit are K, and they accumulate interest at a rate i under the terms of the plan, a man now age x will have amassed, at age 65, a sum equal to

$$K(1 + i)^{65-x} + K(1 + i)^{65-(x+1)} + K(1 + i)^{65-(x+2)}$$

$$+ \cdots + K(1 + i) = MDB.$$

As indicated in the preceding section, this figure represents the maximum death benefit payable to the employee's estate if he should die after retiring.

Using

$$S_n = \sum_{a=1}^{n} (1 + i)^a$$

to denote the accumulated value of a series of n payments as of the end of the nth period, we have: $MDB = KS_{65-x}$.[5] Every dollar of pension benefit received in retirement then reduces the amount of the prospective payment to the estate until the entire sum is recouped, at which time the death settlement provision ceases. Thus, if the employee should die after attaining age 65 and receiving the first annual installment of his pension ($1 in the situation chosen as standard here) but before attaining age 66, his estate will be paid the amount: $(KS_{65-x}) - 1$. If he dies the following year, the payment will be $(KS_{65-x}) - 2$, and so on. A portion of any such payments—that amount deemed by the IRS to consist simply of a return of the employee's contributions—is taxed at whatever estate tax rates apply and the remainder—the interest earnings imputed to those contributions—is taxed as a long-term capital gain. On the assumption suggested in Chapter 2, that 25 per cent is a reasonable approximation of over-all effective estate tax rates for executives, the division of these death benefits into the two components is a matter of indifference to the present calculations. A 25 per cent rate is taken to apply to both portions and therefore to the total, whatever its breakdown.

Since the probability that an employee, now age x, will die during the first year of his retirement is denoted by the ratio d_{65}/l_x,[6] the after-tax present value of that first possible postretirement death benefit is

$$PVDB(65) = (KS_{65-x} - 1)(.75)\left(\frac{d_{65}}{l_x}\right) v^{66-x}.$$

This benefit is discounted back $66 - x$ years on the conventional actuarial assumption that such payments are made at the *end* of the year in which death occurs. The present value of the following year's benefit is

$$PVDB(65) = (KS_{65-x} - 2)(.75)\left(\frac{d_{66}}{l_x}\right) v^{67-x}.$$

[5] Which was equal to $90,000 in the illustration cited above.
[6] See Appendix B.

The aggregate present value of the entire series of these potential receipts may therefore be represented as

$$PVDB = \sum_{n=65}^{m} PVDB(n)$$

where m refers to the age at which the sum (KS_{65-x}) is finally drawn down to zero.

PRERETIREMENT DEATH BENEFITS

If the executive should die *before* reaching age 65, his estate stands to receive the interest-accumulated value of the contributions he has made up to that time. Thus, if our man, age x, should die within the coming year, he will have contributed an amount K and his estate will receive $K(1 + i)$ in return—again assuming payment at the end of the year. Of this amount, K is taxed at estate tax rates and iK at capital gains rates. Continuing the assumption that the two percentages are equal, a flat rate of 25 per cent applies to the entire benefit in the calculations here. After taxes, then, the benefit payable upon death at age x is

$$DB(x) = (.75)(K)(1 + i)$$

and its present value is

$$DBPV(x) = (.75)(K)(1 + i)(v)\left(\frac{d_x}{l_x}\right).$$

If the employee dies the following year, he will have made two contributions to the plan, and the resulting after-tax death benefit will be

$$DB(x + 1) = (.75)(K)[(1 + i) + (1 + i)^2] = (.75K)(S_2).$$

This has a present value equal to

$$DBPV(x + 1) = (.75K)(S_2)(v^2)\left(\frac{d_{x+1}}{l_x}\right).$$

In general, therefore,

$$DBPV(x + n) = (.75K)(S_{n+1})(v^{n+1})\left(\frac{d_{x+n}}{l_x}\right)$$

and, for the complete set of such payments,

$$DBPV = \sum_{n=0}^{64-x} DBPV(x + n).$$

This last is the total present value of the preretirement death benefit feature.

THE CONTRIBUTIONS

The employee's obligation to contribute to the financing of the pension plan, of course, represents to him a negative present value that must be subtracted from the aggregate value of the indicated benefits in order to obtain the appropriate net figure for the whole package. For a man now age x, that negative present value can be expressed as

$$NKPV = K\left(\frac{l_x}{l_x}\right) + Kv\left(\frac{l_{x+1}}{l_x}\right) + Kv^2\left(\frac{l_{x+2}}{l_x}\right) + \cdots + Kv^{64-x}\left(\frac{l_{64}}{l_x}\right).$$

Each term is the product of the probability that he will live to make the required contribution and the discounted amount of that contribution. This expression ultimately reduces to

$$NKPV = \left(\frac{N_x - N_{65}}{D_x}\right)(K)$$

following the notation introduced above.

THE TOTAL

The combined present value of the various benefit provisions of the contributory pension, therefore, is simply: $PV = PVRB + PVDB + DBPV - NKPV$. The necessary computations can be programmed with little difficulty, given the appropriate mortality data and discount rates.

The Individual Retirement Annuity

The form of individual annuity chosen as the executive's market alternative to both types of pension arrangements has two component benefit provisions: the retirement benefit itself; and a preretirement death benefit. Their tax treatment generally resembles that of the contributory pension.

THE RETIREMENT BENEFIT

The annual retirement benefit is to begin at age 65 and continue for the life of the employee. According to the IRS, that portion of each receipt represented by the ratio of total premiums paid to total benefits anticipated is exempt from the personal income tax. Thus, if the annual premium quoted to a man, age x, for the purchase of a $1 per year retirement annuity is denoted by P_x, he will have to pay a total of $(P_x)(65 - x)$ dollars in premiums through age 64. Given a fifteen-year life expectancy at age 65—the IRS' figure—he is assumed to have fifteen $1 annuity benefits in store. Therefore, the tax-free portion of each such benefit will be

$$f = \frac{(P_x)(65 - x)}{15}$$

and the after-tax present value of that benefit stream will be

$$PVB = (1 - t)\left(\frac{l_{65}}{l_x}\right)(v^{65-x}) + (1 - t)\left(\frac{l_{66}}{l_x}\right)(v^{66-x})$$
$$+ \cdots + (1 - t)\left(\frac{l_{110}}{l_x}\right)(v^{110-x})$$

or, ultimately,

$$PVB = (1 - t)\left(\frac{N_{65}}{D_x}\right)$$

where the effective tax rate, t, depends on the value of f.

THE PRERETIREMENT DEATH BENEFIT

If the prospective annuitant should die before reaching age 65, his estate receives as a settlement the "cash surrender value" of the contract as of the time of death. The applicable schedule of these cash values is specified in the annuity agreement, and it is necessary to have that schedule in order to perform the present value computations.[7] When and if payment is made, the entire amount is taxed to the man's estate at the normal rates—25 per cent by assumption here—and, in addition, any excess over the aggregate premiums paid up to that time is

[7] See Appendix K for the schedule used in the empirical portion of the current study.

taxed as a long-term capital gain. In determining the latter assessment, however, the estate tax on the relevant portion is deducted in defining the tax base.

To illustrate: If a man who has paid ten $500 annual premiums toward the purchase of a retirement annuity dies, and his estate receives a $6,000 death benefit, the tax thereon is: (a) 25 per cent of $6,000, or $1,500 in estate taxes and (b) 25 per cent of ($6,000 − $5,000)(.75), or $187.50 in capital gains taxes. This comes to $1,687.50 in all. The $250 in estate tax payable on the $1,000 difference is excluded from additional taxation.

In general, then, if P_x is the annual premium required and CV_{x+n} the cash value/death benefit payable at age $x + n$, the after-tax amount of that benefit is

$$DB(x + n) = (.75)(CV_{x+n}) - (.25)(.75)[(CV_{x+n}) - (n + 1)(P_x)].$$

Its present value is:

$$DBPV(x + n) = [DB(x + n)] \left[\frac{d_{x+n}}{l_x} \right] (v^{n+1}).$$

And the present value of the complete set of such payments is:

$$DBPV = \sum_{n=0}^{64-x} DBPV(x + n).$$

THE ANNUITY AS A WHOLE

The total present value of a $1 per year individual retirement annuity arrangement to a man, age x, is therefore: $PV = PVB + DBPV$, since no postretirement death benefits are included in the package specified here.

APPENDIX E

ELIGIBILITY REQUIREMENTS FOR "QUALIFIED" CORPORATE RETIREMENT PLANS

The annual payments a corporation makes either to its own trust fund or to an insurance company in order to meet the anticipated cost of its employee pension plan are tax deductible if that plan satisfies the following requirements:

1. The plan is permanent.
2. The plan is for the exclusive benefit of employees and their beneficiaries.
3. The distribution of benefits under the plan is on the basis of an explicit and predetermined formula.
4. Contributions by the corporation and benefit payments do not discriminate in favor of the firm's officers, shareholders, supervisory employees, or highly paid employees.
5. The plan benefits either (a) 70 per cent of all employees, (b) 80 per cent of all eligible employees, provided at least 70 per cent of all employees are eligible, or (c) all employees within a classification which does not discriminate in favor of highly paid employees.

Deductions for such plans are limited to 15 per cent of the direct annual payroll cost of the employees covered by the plan, except where a larger amount is required to provide for the funding of past service credits.

If the plan does not meet the indicated requirements, the employer company may deduct contributions to it only if the covered employees' rights to the benefits promised are nonforfeitable. Otherwise, no tax

310

deduction at all is allowed, either at the time contributions to the fund are made or when retirement benefits to the employees are ultimately paid. See Internal Revenue Code, Sections 401 and 404 as summarized in Joint Economic Committee, Congress of the United States, *The Federal Tax System: Facts and Problems* (Washington: 1964), pp. 120–121.

APPENDIX F

PRESENT VALUE AND CURRENT EQUIVALENT OF A DEFERRED COMPENSATION CONTRACT

As was indicated in the text, the type of contract adopted here as a standard for computational purposes is probably the most common deferred compensation instrument in use today. It consists, as does a contributory pension, of three benefit provisions: postretirement deferred payments to the executive, a preretirement death benefit, and a postretirement death benefit. It was possible to fit just about every arrangement actually confronted into the analytical mold developed for this benefit package, even if the deferred payments were to be made in shares of the corporation's stock rather than in cash. The methodology for doing so is discussed in Chapter 5 and in Appendix H below. Both discussions build on the basic framework to be outlined here.

The Deferred Payments to the Executive

The central feature of deferred compensation contracts is, of course, the promise by the corporation to pay a specified sum to the executive each year for a given number of years following his retirement. Unlike the benefits under a pension plan, these payments are to cease after that given period, even though the executive may continue to live. Since the executive himself is not required to contribute any of his own funds to the arrangement, the full amounts of any payments he eventually receives are taxable to him at regular personal income tax rates.

The after-tax present value to a man, now age x, of the deferred payments he stands to receive may therefore be expressed as

$$PVDP = (A)(1 - t)\left(\frac{l_{65}}{l_x}\right)(v^{65-x}) + (A)(1 - t)\left(\frac{l_{66}}{l_x}\right)(v^{66-x})$$

$$+ \cdots + (A)(1 - t)\left(\frac{l_{65+R-1}}{l_x}\right)(v^{65+R-1})$$

or:

$$PVDP = (A)(1 - t)\left(\frac{N_{65} - N_{65+R}}{D_x}\right)$$

where A denotes the annual before-tax payment in prospect, t the effective personal tax rate thereon, and R the number of years for which payments are to be made.

The Preretirement Death Benefit

If the executive dies before age 65, a lump-sum settlement with his estate in the amount of the aggregate payments due if he had lived is typically made. Thus his heirs would receive $(A)(R)$ dollars in the situation just depicted, all of which is taxable at whatever estate tax rates apply. By assumption here, 25 per cent is taken to be a reasonable estimate of the latter. Thus the after-tax present value of the preretirement death benefits under the contract for a man now age x comes to

$$PVDB1 = (.75AR)\left[\left(\frac{d_x}{l_x}\right)(v) + \left(\frac{d_{x+1}}{l_x}\right)(v^2) + \cdots + \left(\frac{d_{64}}{l_x}\right)(v^{65-x})\right].$$

The Postretirement Death Benefit

A similar settlement is made after retirement as well, if the executive does not survive to claim all R payments promised him. The only difference is that the amount of those installments already received is deducted from the total contracted for in determining the size of the death benefit—which again is taxed in full at estate tax rates. If he should die after attaining age 65 and receiving the first annual payment, but before reaching age 66, for example, his estate would be awarded $(A)(R - 1)$ dollars and would net, in the view here, 75 per cent of that amount after taxes. If he died in the following year, the payment would be $(A)(R - 2)$ dollars, and so on. The after-tax present value of all such receipts as of age x is, then,

$$PVDB2 = (A)(R - 1)(.75)\left(\frac{d_{65}}{l_x}\right)(v^{66-x}) + (A)(R - 2)(.75)\left(\frac{d_{66}}{l_x}\right)(v^{67-x})$$

$$+ \cdots + (A)(.75)\left(\frac{d_{65+R-2}}{l_x}\right)(v^{65+R-1}).$$

By convention, the executive if he lives receives his deferred pay at the *beginning* of each year but any death benefits are remitted at the *end* of the year.

The present value of the whole deferred compensation package is, of course, simply the total of the three expressions developed above: $DCPV = PVDP + PVDB1 + PVDB2.$

The Current Income Equivalent

Given this present value, the stream of salary payments which are defined here as the "after-tax current income equivalent" of the arrangement in question can be computed. Those payments are specified to begin at age x and continue through age 64, being payable only to the executive and therefore of sufficient size that they connote the requisite present value when discounted for mortality as well as for time deferral. In the case at hand, therefore, the relevant condition is that

$$(ATCEQ)\left[\left(\frac{l_x}{l_x}\right) + \left(\frac{l_{x+1}}{l_x}\right)(v) + \cdots + \left(\frac{l_{64}}{l_x}\right)(v^{64-x})\right] = DCPV$$

where $ATCEQ$ denotes the necessary annual salary payment. Rearranging and substituting the shorthand actuarial symbols used previously, we find that

$$ATCEQ = \frac{(D_x)(DCPV)}{(N_x - N_{64})}.$$

Were the executive's annual after-tax salary raised by this amount, he would be as well off, looking ahead at age x, as he is in fact with the deferred compensation arrangement described.

APPENDIX G

EXECUTIVE STOCK OPTIONS

Section 218 of the Revenue Act of 1950 added "Section 130A: Employee Stock Options" to the Internal Revenue Code. It established rules for the favorable tax treatment of what were termed "Restricted Stock Options" granted to employees of corporations. In order to qualify for that designation, the option was required to satisfy the following conditions:

1. It must have been granted after February 26, 1945, to an individual for a reason connected with his employment.

2. It must have been granted by the employer corporation or its parent or subsidiary to purchase stock of such corporations.

3. The option price must have been at least 85 per cent of the fair market value of the optioned stock at the time the option was granted.

4. The option must be nontransferable except by will or by the laws of descent and distribution.

5. It could be exercisable, during the lifetime of the optionee, only by him.

6. The optionee, at the time the option was granted, could not have owned stock possessing more than 10 per cent of the combined voting power of all classes of stock of the employer corporation.

If the option met those requirements, and if the optionee: (1) was an employee of the corporation granting the option or of its parent or subsidiary at the time he exercised the option—or had been one within three months beforehand—and (2) did not dispose of the stock acquired under the option until at least two years after the date the option was granted or until at least six months after the date the option was exercised, he was eligible for the following special tax treatment:

1. If the option price was 95 per cent or more of the market value of the stock at the time the option was granted, any gain from the subsequent sale

315

of the optioned stock was considered a capital gain and taxed accordingly.

2. If instead the option price was between 85 and 95 per cent of the market value of the stock at the time the option was granted, any profit realized upon subsequent resale was taxed as follows: (a) if, at the time of the sale, the market price of the stock was less than the market price when the option was granted, the difference between the option price and the sale price was treated as ordinary income at the time of the sale; (b) if, at the time of the sale, the market price of the stock was greater than the market price when the option was granted, the difference between the option price and the market price at the date of granting was treated as ordinary income; the excess of sale price over that market price was considered a capital gain.

The law also provided that, in the event of a stock split or a stock dividend payable to the employer corporation's shareholders, the number of shares under option to the executive, and the option price, could be adjusted to reflect that change. No deduction from taxable income pursuant to either the granting or the eventual exercise of the option was allowed the corporation itself.

The revision of the Internal Revenue Code undertaken by Congress in 1954 made several modifications in these rules. Chief among them were:

1. The restriction as to those individuals who owned more than 10 per cent of the employer corporation's stock was removed. It was specified, however, that any options granted to such persons had to be issued at a price not less than 110 per cent of the market price on the date of granting if they were to qualify as "Restricted" stock options.

2. Variable-price options were sanctioned. According to this provision, it became possible to reduce the price of an option previously granted under certain conditions if it turned out that the market price of the optioned stock declined subsequent to the granting of the option and the new, lower price persisted for a significant period of time.

3. A limit of ten years was placed on the term of a single option.

The rest of the 1950 legislation was retained substantially intact, and the entire set of regulations became Section 421 rather than Section 130A of the Revenue Code.

In 1964, however, a major change in the relevant statutes occurred.

A much less favorable view of the privileges that should be associated with the option was adopted by Congress, and the attractiveness of that device diminished noticeably. The revised legislation (now Sections 421–425 of the Revenue Code) specified that, in order for an option to be awarded special tax treatment under the new designation "Qualified Stock Option":

1. The option price must equal or exceed the market value of the stock involved at the time the option is granted.

2. The option must be exercised within five years of the date of its granting.

3. The shares of stock acquired under the option must not be resold within three years of the date it is exercised.

4. The option must be granted pursuant to a plan which specifies the number of shares of stock to be issued and the employees or class of employees who are to receive the options. This plan must be approved by the shareholders of the corporation within twelve months of its adoption and cannot extend for more than ten years.

5. The option price cannot be reduced in the face of declining stock market conditions nor can the option, by its terms, be exercisable while there is outstanding an option which was granted to the same employee at an earlier time.

6. The optionee, immediately before the option is granted, must not own stock representing more than 5 per cent of the voting power or value of all classes of stock of the issuing corporation (up to 10 per cent in the case of certain specified small businesses).

If these conditions are met, the difference between the market price of the stock acquired under option at the time it is eventually resold and the original option price is considered to be a long-term capital gain and is taxed accordingly.

If instead the optionee disposes of the stock less than three years but more than six months after exercise, the spread between the option price and the market price on the date of *exercise* is taxed as ordinary income at the time the stock is sold. The difference between the market price at the time of the sale and that at the time of exercise is taxed as a capital gain.

Finally, if the stock acquired is resold within six months of exercise, any profits are taxable in full as ordinary income.

Valuation Under the New Tax Law

Despite these rather substantial changes in the tax treatment of options, the procedures described in Chapter 4 of the text for measuring the compensatory value of—and constructing "current income equivalents" for—options granted before 1964 can be applied directly to those issued under the new legislation as well. It is true that, as a result of that legislation, executives are likely to enjoy somewhat more modest option profits in the future than they have in the past, but the basic character of the instrument has not been altered, and our approach to its valuation should require no important adjustments.

For example, the fact that the maximum term of the option has been shortened to five years and the minimum option price raised to 100 per cent of market on the date of granting merely implies that these parameters will now determine the duration and magnitude of the executive's stock option current equivalent instead of the ten-year, 95 per cent combination most frequently encountered prior to 1964. Similarly, the restriction that employees who own stock representing more than 5 per cent of the voting power or value of all classes of stock of the employer corporation cannot now qualify for favorable tax treatment on any options they are granted simply means that a slightly smaller number of executives may end up receiving such options in the years to come than might otherwise have been the case. There is, however, no reason to view those who do still qualify and differently than we have in the past.

The one provision of the new tax law which might suggest a revision of our valuation procedures is that which specifies a holding period of three years from the date of exercise of an option as a requirement for capital gains tax treatment of any profits realized upon resale of the shares thus acquired. It was argued in Chapter 4 that under the original stock option legislation the compensation implicit in the optionee's opportunity to purchase shares of stock at a discount from the prevailing market price could be measured very precisely by the size of that discount at the time it was claimed, i.e., on the date of the option's exercise. From that point on the optionee stood in the same position as any investor who might have purchased a like number of shares on the open market; the only difference between his opportunities and everyone else's was the initial purchase discount itself. Under those conditions, the gap between option price and market price at exercise completely defined the optionee's net market advantage and supplied us with an accurate index of the compensation he obtained from his option.

According to the rules currently in effect, however, the executive who exercises an option is subject to a constraint which is not imposed on other investors: he must wait a full three years before reselling the shares he has purchased in order to avoid having his profits taxed as ordinary income. The question therefore arises as to whether there should be some downward adjustment in our appraisal of the value of that option to reflect this requirement. The position taken here is that the indicated constraint is more apparent than real and that no such adjustment is necessary, since the optionee's market activities are not in practice limited by the additional holding period per se and he is not put at any meaningful disadvantage by it.

For one thing, most executives retain the shares acquired pursuant to the exercise of stock options in their portfolios for a substantial period of time, even in the absence of formal sanctions for not doing so.[1] They seem to consider an option a convenient vehicle for obtaining on favorable terms a long-run ownership interest in their firms rather than a speculative opportunity to realize quick profits. Few of them are therefore likely in practice to feel themselves differentially "locked in" to the shares thus purchased even in the face of a three-year waiting period. It may well be, of course, that those shares simply take the place of some the optionee would otherwise have acquired in the normal course of affairs, and that on balance his aggregate holdings of the stock of his employer are not increased over time. That is quite a different issue, however, and one which deserves to be treated on its own merits. The fact remains that executives have not in the past typically resold optioned stock for several years, even though they could have done so without a tax penalty.[2]

---

[1] For evidence on this point, see: George E. Lent and John A. Menge, "The Importance of Restricted Stock Options in Executive Compensation," *Management Record*, June 1962.

[2] Clearly, other types of implicit or informal sanctions threatened by the organizations to which such executives belong may, in part at least, account for

There is also evidence that, in general, top corporate executives maintain a fairly sizeable ownership interest in their respective firms apart from any shares acquired through the exercise of stock options. Thus, if an optionee should decide to liquidate a portion of his holdings in order to free funds for consumption or other investments, he can almost certainly do so by selling off shares which were purchased in the normal manner and which have been held long enough to qualify for capital gains tax treatment. In this manner, optioned stock is effectively insulated from the tax penalties of short-term trading.

Both of these arguments are, of course, empirical.[3] The contention is that a long holding period requirement is not a real constraint for the great majority of executives who are granted options because they can and will ordinarily hold for several years anyway. Nonetheless, for certain individuals this will not—or would not by preference—be true, and in their case the worth of the option will be somewhat overstated by utilizing the pre-1964 valuation procedures and current income equivalent format for options granted thereafter. Even for some of these individuals, however, there is a way out which still preserves the validity of the position taken here. If the optionee's problem is only one of liquidity, he need not accept a tax penalty in order to raise funds. He can simply borrow against the value of his stock and repay the loan later by liquidating his holdings after the three-year period expires. It is only in situations where the optionee would, but for tax considerations, dispose of the shares he has acquired within three years because he anticipates a decline in price or perceives a more favorable alternative investment opportunity that he does in fact find himself at a disadvantage vis-à-vis the market.[4] As was suggested above, this problem should not

this phenomenon. Thus, the executive might hesitate to dispose of shares he has acquired under option for fear of having that action interpreted by his superiors or by the firm's shareholders as an expression of his lack of confidence in its future prospects.

[3] And, as such, clearly require more documentation than they have been given here, if they are actually to be used as a basis for valuation.

[4] It is worth noting that, were it possible for top corporate executives to *sell short* shares of their firms' stock, the adverse tax consequences associated even with these situations could be circumvented. Thus the optionee would, instead of selling off stock acquired under option, go short in an equal number of shares at what seemed to him the opportune time. He would then cover that short sale with the proceeds of the sale of the optioned shares as soon as they were eligible for capital gains tax treatment. Unfortunately—for us, that is—

arise frequently. When applied to executive stock options issued under the new tax law, therefore, the techniques developed in Chapter 4 will no more than slightly overstate their "true" value.

the senior officers and directors of large publicly held corporations are prohibited by the SEC from engaging in such activities (Securities and Exchange Act, Section 9).

APPENDIX H

PRESENT VALUE AND CURRENT EQUIVALENTS OF OTHER COMPENSATION ARRANGEMENTS

Deferred Stock Bonuses

The analytical framework for measuring the compensatory value of a postretirement deferred stock bonus arrangement is essentially the same as that developed for cash deferred pay contracts. The benefit structures and tax treatment of the two instruments are virtually identical, the only difference being the form in which benefits are ultimately transmitted. Thus a deferred stock bonus provides for: (1) a series of annual payments to the employee in retirement, each consisting of a specified number of shares of the employer corporation's common stock; (2) The immediate transferral of all the shares set aside under that arrangement to the employee's estate if he dies prior to retirement; and (3) an immediate settlement with the estate in the amount of the remaining installments due if the employee dies after retiring but before enjoying the full series of annual payments designated.

The shares received are taxed to the employee at regular personal income tax rates or to his estate at the applicable estate tax rates—in both cases according to the market value of those shares at the time of *receipt*. The one peculiarity of the valuation procedure required for such an arrangement is the necessity to make a new appraisal of the worth of the benefit package periodically as stock prices change, even if no additional shares are allotted to it.

THE ANNUAL RETIREMENT PAYMENTS

If an executive, age x, is promised a deferred stock bonus consisting of a series of R annual payments of K shares each, to begin upon his retirement at age 65, and if the current market price of those shares is

322

P_x dollars each, the after-tax present value of the prospective payments may be written as

$$PVRP(x) = (K)(P_x)(1 - t)\left[\left(\frac{l_{65}}{l_x}\right)(v^{65-x}) + \left(\frac{l_{66}}{l_x}\right)(v^{66-x})\right.$$
$$\left. + \cdots + \left(\frac{l_{65+R-1}}{l_x}\right)(v^{65+R-1})\right];$$

or, more conveniently,

$$PVRP(x) = (K)(P_x)(1 - t)\left(\frac{N_{65} - N_{65+R}}{D_x}\right)$$

where t denotes the over-all effective personal tax rate associated with an annual income of size $(K)(P_x)$.[1]

If, by the time the executive reaches age $x + 1$, the market price of the shares involved has changed, it is necessary to adjust our estimate of the value of his deferred bonus to reflect this change in his circumstances. Thus we have

$$\Delta PVRP(x + 1) = (K)(P_{x+1} - P_x)(1 - \Delta t)\left(\frac{N_{65} - N_{65+R}}{D_{x+1}}\right).$$

This represents the after-tax present value as of age $x + 1$ of the increase (or decrease) in the worth of the bonus agreement occasioned by the stock price rise (or fall) experienced during the preceding year. The notation Δt refers to the effective personal tax rate on the *increment*. This procedure is then repeated every year until the man retires, the result being a *series* of present value computations for each deferred bonus observed.[2]

PRERETIREMENT DEATH BENEFITS

Assuming 25 per cent to be a fair approximation of the relevant estate tax levy for executives, the present value as of age x of the pre-

[1] As indicated in the discussion of these instruments in Chapter 5, footnote 11, 5 per cent per annum is deemed the appropriate discount rate for purposes of calculating present values. Therefore, the symbol v in the equations above is defined as $(1/1.05)$ rather than the $(1/1.025)$ figure used for pension and cash deferred compensation arrangements.

[2] As noted in the text in connection with stock option valuation, the change in stock price could be recorded every month or every quarter if a more frequent appraisal and revision of the worth of the particular arrangement were considered desirable. Since the analysis throughout the present study has been in terms of annual data, however, that orientation will be maintained here.

retirement death benefits payable under the arrangement described above is

$$PVDB1(x) = (.75)(K)(P_x)(R)\left[\left(\frac{d_x}{l_x}\right)(v)\right.$$

$$\left.+ \left(\frac{d_{x+1}}{l_x}\right)(v^2) + \cdots + \left(\frac{d_{64}}{l_x}\right)(v^{65-x})\right].$$

Except for the substitution of the product $(K)(P_x)$ for the annual cash payment A, this is a duplicate of the expression derived in Appendix F for a regular deferred compensation contract.

Every year in which the market price of the stock changes, then, the incremental death benefit present value *as of that year* is computed. Thus,

$$\Delta PVDB1(x + 1) = (.75)(K)(P_{x+1} - P_x)(R)\left[\left(\frac{d_{x+1}}{l_{x+1}}\right)(v)\right.$$

$$\left.+ \left(\frac{d_{x+2}}{l_{x+1}}\right)(v^2) + \cdots + \left(\frac{d_{64}}{l_{x+1}}\right)(v^{65-x-1})\right]$$

and, in general,

$$\Delta PVDB1(x + n) = (.75)(K)(P_{x+n} - P_{x+n-1})(R) \sum_{m=n}^{64-x}\left(\frac{d_{x+m}}{l_{x+n}}\right)(v^{m-n+1})$$

for $1 \leq n \leq (64 - x)$.

POSTRETIREMENT DEATH BENEFITS

A similar analysis applies to the postretirement death benefits. If the executive, now age x, should die during the first year of his retirement, his estate stands to receive the $(K)(R - 1)$ shares of stock that will not yet have been distributed to him by the corporation in annual deferred bonus payments. Given a current per-share stock price of P_x, that death benefit is estimated to have a before-tax value equal to $(P_x)(K)(R - 1)$ dollars and therefore implies an after-tax present value as of age x of

$$(.75)(P_x)(K)(R - 1)\left(\frac{d_{65}}{l_x}\right)(v^{66-x}).$$

If he dies the following year, the resulting death settlement will consist of $(K)(R - 2)$ shares having a present value now of

$$(.75)(P_x)(K)(R - 2)\left(\frac{d_{66}}{l_x}\right)(v^{67-x}).$$

And, for the whole series of such prospective payments, we have

$$PVDB2(x) = (.75)(P_x)(K) \sum_{n=1}^{R-1} (R - n)\left(\frac{d_{64+n}}{l_x}\right)(v^{65-x+n}).$$

Each time stock prices rise or fall, the change in this present value is determined as before. Thus,

$$\Delta PVDB2(x + 1) = (.75)(P_{x+1} - P_x)(K) \sum_{n=1}^{R-1}(R - n)\left(\frac{d_{64+n}}{l_{x+1}}\right)(v^{65-x+n-1})$$

and

$$\Delta PVDB2(x + m) = (.75)(P_{x+m} - P_{x+m-1})(K) \text{ multiplied by}$$

$$\sum_{n=1}^{R-1} (R - n)\left(\frac{d_{64+n}}{l_{x+m}}\right)(v^{65-x+n-m})$$

for each $1 \leq m \leq (64 - x)$. The increment is evaluated in every instance as of the year it occurs.

THE TOTAL PACKAGE

The aggregate after-tax present value of the deferred stock bonus at the time it is established is, then,

$$PVDSB(x) = PVRP(x) + PVDB1(x) + PVDB2(x).$$

The total change therein in each subsequent year is

$$\Delta PVDSB(x + n) = \Delta PVRP(x + n) + \Delta PVDB1(x + n) + \Delta PVDB2(x + n),$$

which must be computed through age 64 for the executive in question.

THE CURRENT EQUIVALENT

The stream of annual after-tax salary payments beginning at age x, continuing up to and including age 64, and having a present value as of age x equal to $PVDSB(x)$ is the first element in the "current income equivalent" of the deferred bonus. Thus, where $ATCEQ(x)$ is the necessary annual payment,

$$PVDSB(x) = [ATCEQ(x)]\left[\left(\frac{l_x}{l_x}\right) + \left(\frac{l_{x+1}}{l_x}\right)(v) + \cdots + \left(\frac{l_{64}}{l_x}\right)(v^{64-x})\right]$$

defines the relevant equality. Rearranging:

$$ATCEQ(x) = \frac{[PVDSB(x)](D_x)}{(N_x - N_{65})}.$$

And, in each subsequent year, the appropriate increment to that stream of payments is

$$\Delta ATCEQ(x + n) = \frac{[\Delta PVDSB(x + n)](D_{x+n})}{(N_{x+n} - N_{65})}.$$

As a result, the total in any given year for the deferred stock bonus which was initially established at age x comes to

$$ATCEQ(x + n) = ATCEQ(x) + \sum_{m=1}^{n} [\Delta ATCEQ(x + m)].$$

The current equivalents for additional bonuses of this type can then simply be added to this figure to arrive at an aggregate which reflects not only the initial value of each but any later changes in that value.

Profit-Sharing Plans

A corporate profit-sharing plan which provides that the funds allocated to it be invested in shares of the firm's common stock and those shares distributed to the employee immediately upon his retirement is simply a special case of a deferred stock bonus and may be analyzed in a similar manner. The only benefits payable under such an arrangement are the indicated retirement distribution and a preretirement death benefit which specifies that the shares credited to the employee's account be awarded to his estate if he should die before attaining age 65. Both are taxable on the basis of the market value of the shares involved on the date they are distributed, the retirement payment at the capital gains tax rate and the death benefit at estate tax rates. As with a deferred stock bonus, it is necessary to keep track of changes over time in stock prices in order to update the value of the arrangement and ensure that its current income equivalent adequately reflects that value.

THE RETIREMENT BENEFIT

An employee now age x who has credited to his profit-sharing account in the current year M shares of the employer corporation's common stock having a market price equal to P_x dollars per share has in prospect a lump-sum retirement benefit of $(M)(P_x)$ dollars. The after-tax present value of that benefit is therefore

$$PVRB(x) = (.75)(M)(P_x)\left(\frac{l_{65}}{l_x}\right)(v^{65-x})$$

where again in this case, $v = (1/1.05)$. If, over the following year, the market price of the shares changes, the employee will have experienced a change in the prospective value of his remuneration amounting to

$$\Delta PVRB(x + 1) = (.75)(M)(P_{x+1} - P_x)\left(\frac{l_{65}}{l_{x+1}}\right)(v^{65-x-1})$$

and, in general

$$\Delta PVRB(x + n) = (.75)(M)(P_{x+n} - P_{x+n-1})\left(\frac{l_{65}}{l_{x+n}}\right)(v^{65-x-n})$$

for all $1 \leqq n \leqq (64 - x)$.

PRERETIREMENT DEATH BENEFITS

The benefit format and present value of these payments are simply duplicates of those applicable to deferred stock bonuses. Thus

$$PVDB(x) = (.75)(M)(P_x)\left[\left(\frac{d_x}{l_x}\right)(v) + \left(\frac{d_{x+1}}{l_x}\right)(v^2)\right.$$
$$\left. + \cdots + \left(\frac{d_{64}}{l_x}\right)(v^{65-x})\right]$$

and

$$\Delta PVDB(x + n) = (.75)(M)(P_{x+n} - P_{x+n-1})\sum_{m=n}^{64-x}\left(\frac{d_{x+m}}{l_{x+n}}\right)(v^{m-n+1})$$

for the yearly present value increments.

THE PACKAGE AND ITS CURRENT EQUIVALENT

The combined present value of the two benefits is $PV(x) = PVRB(x) + PVDB(x)$ and the annual change in that value $\Delta PV(x + n) = \Delta PVRB(x + n) + \Delta PVDB(x + n)$. Following our previous notation, the after-tax current income equivalent of the arrangement is

$$ATCEQ(x) = \frac{[PV(x)](D_x)}{(N_x - N_{65})}$$

$$ATCEQ(x + n) = ATCEQ(x) + \sum_{j=1}^{n} [\Delta ATCEQ(x + j)]$$

where

$$\Delta ATCEQ(x + j) = \frac{[\Delta PV(x + j)](D_{x+j})}{(N_{x+j} - N_{65})}.$$

A profit-sharing plan under which benefits were payable in cash instead would be analyzed in the same way, the only difference being that adjustments for changes in stock prices would, of course, be unnecessary.

Savings Plans

Since the typical corporate "savings plan" or "thrift plan" closely resembles a profit-sharing arrangement, the framework for its valuation is almost identical. The only new element is the presence of contributions to the plan by the employee, whose value must be deducted in arriving at the relevant *net* present value.

THE RETIREMENT BENEFIT

A savings plan commonly specifies that the total of the employee's and the corporation's contributions, along with the accumulated investment income earned on them, be distributed to the employee in a lump sum upon his retirement. The capital gains tax applies to the excess of such distributions over the aggregate contributions by the employee. Therefore, if the firm adds a dollars to the man's savings plan account for every dollar he contributes each year, the total prospective retirement benefit which results from a contribution of size K out of current salary by an employee now age x is $(K)(1 + a)$. After taxes, this implies a future receipt of

$$K(1 + a) - (.25)(aK) = K(1 + .75a)$$

having a present value, as of age x, equal to

$$PVRB(x) = (K)(1 + .75a)\left(\frac{l_{65}}{l_x}\right)(v^{65-x})$$

adopting the usual notation.

If, then, each dollar placed in the savings plan in that year is invested so as to have a capital value—including the reinvestment of any dividend or interest income—equal to I_{x+1} dollars at the end of the year, the present value of the anticipated retirement benefit must be revised to reflect this change. Accordingly, the employee would, as of age $x + 1$, expect to receive upon retirement $(I_{x+1})(K)(1 + a)$ dollars before taxes as a result of his participation in the plan during the previous year. Of this amount, K dollars will be tax-free, and the new prospective after-tax benefit comes to

$$(I_{x+1})(K)(1 + a) - (.25)[(I_{x+1})(K)(1 + a) - K]$$
$$= K[1 + (.75)(I_{x+1})(1 + a)].$$

This represents an increase of

$$K[1 + (.75)(I_{x+1})(1 + a)] - K[1 + (.75)(a)]$$
$$= (.75)(K)[(I_{x+1})(K)(1 + a) - a]$$

pursuant to the year's investment experience. The after-tax present value of that increment is

$$\Delta PVRB(x + 1) = (.75)(K)[(I_{x+1})(1 + a) - a]\left(\frac{l_{65}}{l_{x+1}}\right)(v^{65-x-1})$$

If, in the following year, each dollar of capital value at the beginning of the year becomes I_{x+2} dollars at the end, the before-tax retirement benefit rises to $(I_{x+2})(I_{x+1})(K)(1 + a)$. After taxes it is

$$(I_{x+2})(I_{x+1})(K)(1 + a) - (.25)[(I_{x+2})(I_{x+1})(K)(1 + a) - K]$$
$$= K[1 + (.75)(I_{x+2})(I_{x+1})(1 + a)]$$

and the increment is

$$K[1 + (.75)(I_{x+2})(I_{x+1})(1 + a)] - K[1 + (.75)(I_{x+1})(1 + a)]$$

$$= (.75)(K)(I_{x+1})(1 + a)(I_{x+2} - 1)$$

with an after-tax present value of

$$\Delta PVRB(x + 2) = (.75)(K)(I_{x+1})(1 + a)(I_{x+2} - 1)\left(\frac{l_{65}}{l_{x+2}}\right)(v^{65-x-2}).$$

In general, then,

$$\Delta PVRB(x + n) = (.75)(K)(1 + a)(I_{x+n} - 1)\left(\frac{l_{65}}{l_{x+n}}\right)(v^{65-x-n})\prod_{i=1}^{n-1}(I_{x+n})$$

for all $2 \leq n \leq (64 - x)$.

PRERETIREMENT DEATH BENEFITS

Should the employee die before attaining age 65, the usual arrange-ment provides that his estate receives the then-accumulated value of both his and the firm's contributions to the plan. As in the case of a con-tributory pension,[3] the portion of that receipt which consists of a return of the man's own contributions is taxed to the estate at the regular estate tax rates and the rest as a long-term capital gain. By convention here, of course, this implies a 25 per cent rate for both portions and therefore for the total.

Thus, the amount of the prospective death benefit, as perceived at age x, is $K(1 + a)$ dollars and its after-tax present value is

$$PVDB(x) = (.75)(K)(1 + a)\left[\left(\frac{d_x}{l_x}\right)(v) + \left(\frac{d_{x+1}}{l_x}\right)(v^2)\right.$$

$$\left. + \cdots + \left(\frac{d_{64}}{l_x}\right)(v^{65-x})\right].$$

As a result of the investment income credited to the account during the first year, the potential benefit increases to $(I_{x+1})(K)(1 + a)$ dollars, a gain of $(I_{x+1} - 1)(K)(1 + a)$ over the initial figure and an addi-tional after-tax present value of

$$\Delta PVDB(x + 1) = (.75)(I_{x+1} - 1)(K)(1 + a)\sum_{j=1}^{64-x}\left(\frac{d_{x+j}}{l_{x+1}}\right)(v^j).$$

[3] See Appendix D.

In general

$$\Delta PVDB(x + n) = (.75)(I_{x+n} - 1)(K)(1 + a) \text{ multiplied by}$$

$$\left[\prod_{i=1}^{n-1} (I_{x+i}) \right] \sum_{j=n}^{64-x} \left(\frac{d_{x+j}}{l_{x+n}} \right) (v^{j-n+1})$$

again for $2 \le n \le (64 - x)$.

THE PACKAGE AND THE CURRENT EQUIVALENT

The rest of the story, then, follows exactly the pattern above. Thus, $PV(x) = PVRB(x) + PVDB(x) - K$ and $\Delta PV(x + n) = \Delta PVRB(x + n) + \Delta PVDB(x + n)$ for the present values, the employee's initial contribution, K, being subtracted in order to obtain the appropriate *net* value to him of the indicated benefits. For their current income equivalent

$$ATCEQ(x) = \frac{[PV(x)](D_x)}{(N_x - N_{65})}$$

$$ATCEQ(x + n) = ATCEQ(x) + \sum_{j=1}^{n} [\Delta ATCEQ(x + j)]$$

where

$$\Delta ATCEQ(x + j) = \frac{[\Delta PV(x + j)][D_{x+j}]}{(N_{x+j} - N_{65})}.$$

The current equivalents of the benefits from the plan resulting from subsequent years' participation by the employee can then simply be added to these figures.

APPENDIX I

COMPANIES IN THE SAMPLE

Allied Chemical Corporation
American Can Company
American Cyanamid Company
American Metal Climax, Incorporated
American Tobacco Company
Anaconda Company
Bendix Corporation
Bethlehem Steel Corporation
Boeing Company
Borden Company
Caterpillar Tractor Company
Cities Service Company
Continental Can Company
Continental Oil Company
Douglas Aircraft Company
Dow Chemical Company
E. I. DuPont de Nemours and Company
Eastman Kodak Company
Firestone Tire and Rubber Company
General Electric Company
General Foods Corporation
General Motors Corporation
General Tire and Rubber Company
B. F. Goodrich Company
Goodyear Tire and Rubber Company
Gulf Oil Corporation

Inland Steel Company
International Business Machines Corporation
International Harvester Company
International Paper Company
International Telephone and Telegraph Corporation
Jones and Laughlin Steel Corporation
Lockheed Aircraft Corporation
National Dairy Products Corporation
North American Aviation, Incorporated
Phillips Petroleum Company
Procter and Gamble Company
Radio Corporation of America
Republic Steel Corporation
R. J. Reynolds Tobacco Company
Shell Oil Company
Sinclair Oil Corporation
Standard Oil Company (Indiana)
Swift and Company
Texaco, Incorporated
Tidewater Oil Company
United Aircraft Corporation
United States Rubber Company
United States Steel Corporation
Westinghouse Electric Corporation

APPENDIX J

SAMPLE SIZE EACH YEAR

Executive Rank, by Total After-Tax Compensation

Year	Highest-Paid	Second Highest-Paid	Third Highest-Paid	Fourth Highest-Paid	Fifth Highest-Paid
1940	49	48	44	45	44
1941	49	48	47	46	45
1942	49	49	47	45	46
1943	49	49	47	47	45
1944	50	50	48	47	46
1945	50	50	48	46	45
1946	50	49	49	47	44
1947	50	49	49	47	46
1948	50	50	50	48	43
1949	50	50	50	48	43
1950	50	50	49	49	46
1951	50	50	49	46	47
1952	50	50	47	47	46
1953	50	50	46	47	40
1954	50	50	47	45	41
1955	50	50	46	43	38
1956	50	48	46	42	31
1957	50	48	45	40	29
1958	50	49	40	38	29
1959	50	48	38	32	29
1960	50	46	33	32	24
1961	49	44	32	27	23
1962	48	40	30	24	19
1963	47	37	30	21	13

NOTE: A complete sample in each case would be 50.

333

APPENDIX K

DERIVATION OF THE INDIVIDUAL RETIREMENT ANNUITY PREMIUM RATE SCHEDULE

Historical premium rate quotations were obtained from two leading insurance companies: Connecticut General Life Insurance Company and The Travelers Insurance Company. The quotations represented the annual premiums required for the purchase of a nonparticipating straight life annuity to begin at age 65 and providing for a full cash refund (of the interest-accumulated net premiums) in the event of the death of the prospective annuitant prior to that time. This is the individual annuity form specified in Chapter 2 as the executive's relevant market alternative to his employer's pension plan.

Even though the compensation data presented throughout the study cover the period 1940 through 1963, it was necessary to secure premium rate information back to 1938 in order to handle properly those cases in which executives came under pension plans as early as that year. Both insurance companies have had several premium schedules in effect since then, indicating that for completeness separate tabulations for each of the various subperiods should be compiled here. In the interest of efficiency, however, the number of such subperiods was arbitrarily restricted to three: 1938 through 1948, 1949 through 1958, and 1959 through 1963. These intervals roughly coincide with those covered by the schedules offered by the two firms, which were not entirely congruent, and give expression to the more significant changes in premium rates which have occurred since 1938. They should, therefore, provide both a manageable and an acceptable representation of the recent history of individual annuity costs.

Each of the various premium rate quotations was supplied in the form of a schedule of end-of-year "cash values" and an accompanying annuity conversion factor for age 65. For example, the following schedule applied to annuity contracts sold from 1938 through 1948 by one of the two insurance companies:

Number of Years Premiums Paid	Cash Value at End of Year Per $100 Annual Premium
1	$ 52
2	142
3	244
4	352
5	464
6	581
7	704
8	832
.	.
.	.
.	.
28	4,723
29	5,009
30	5,307

Annuity payable at age 65 per $1,000 of cash value = $6.68 per month.

According to these quotations, then, a man who, at age 57, contracted to purchase a retirement annuity and paid eight annual premiums of $100 each would, at age 65, stand to receive

$$\left(\frac{832}{1000}\right)(6.68) = \$5.558$$

per month, or a total of $66.69 in annuity benefits per year, since he would have accumulated $832 in cash value by that time. Similarly, had he begun to pay premiums when he was 35 years old, his annual benefit at age 65 would have been

$$\left(\frac{5307}{1000}\right)(6.68)(12) = \$425.41$$

as a result of paying thirty annual premiums of $100.

It is, of course, a simple matter to transform this schedule of cash values into a schedule of premium rates per dollar of annuity benefit as a function of age at the time premium payments begin. Thus, if a $100 annual premium starting at age 35 and continuing through age 64 will purchase $425.41 in annuity benefits, a $1 annuity benefit would require

$$\frac{100}{425.41} = \$0.235$$

in premiums per year. In general, the cash-value-to-premium rate conversion formula is

$$P(x) = \frac{(100)(1000)}{(12)(6.68)[C(65 - x)]}$$

where $P(x)$ denotes the annual premium payable beginning at age x for the purchase of a $1 per year annuity which is to start at age 65, and $C(65 - x)$ is the cash value tabulated above for $(65 - x)$ years' worth of premium payments. In the example just cited, an age of 35 at the time of the initial premium payment implied a total of $(65 - 35)$, or thirty years of premiums. Therefore,

$$P(35) = \frac{(100)(1000)}{(12)(6.68)(5307)} = \$0.235.$$

Because the computations involved in arriving at the "current income equivalent" of a pension make it convenient to have the premium quotations stated in this form, each of the schedules provided by the insurance companies was transformed accordingly. In the case of the schedule above, the result was:

Age at Time of Purchase	Annual Premium Per Dollar of Annuity at Age 65
64	23.9044
63	8.7852
62	5.1127
61	3.5440
60	2.6885
59	2.1471

(Continued)

Age at Time of Purchase	Annual Premium Per Dollar of Annuity at Age 65
58	1.7720
57	1.4994
.	.
.	.
.	.
37	0.2641
36	0.2490
35	0.2350

These are, therefore, the relevant figures for the years 1938 through 1948 for this particular firm. A similar schedule was derived for the other insurance company and the average of the two taken to be the "typical" premium rate per dollar of retirement annuity confronted by executives during that period.

The procedure was then repeated for the intervals 1949–58 and 1959–63. The complete set of averaged premium rates which was obtained is the following:

Age at Time of Purchase	Annual Premium Per Dollar of Annuity		
	1938–48	1949–58	1959–63
64	$20.9453	$18.8166	$16.1630
63	8.0126	7.8305	7.2040
62	4.7947	4.8864	4.6011
61	3.3821	3.5314	3.3708
60	2.5841	2.7526	2.6541
59	2.2784	2.2392	2.1550
58	1.7252	1.8844	1.8113
57	1.4666	1.6183	1.5545
56	1.2687	1.4149	1.3570
55	1.1157	1.2544	1.2006
54	0.9899	1.1206	1.0720
53	0.8856	1.0109	0.9668
52	0.7985	0.9182	0.8779
51	0.7248	0.8399	0.8019
50	0.6614	0.7720	0.7363

(Continued)

| Age at Time | Annual Premium Per Dollar of Annuity | | |
of Purchase	1938–48	1949–58	1959–63
49	0.6063	0.7130	0.6796
48	0.5578	0.6614	0.6297
47	0.5154	0.6155	0.5852
46	0.4777	0.5748	0.5460
45	0.4438	0.5380	0.5106
44	0.4135	0.5052	0.4795
43	0.3861	0.4753	0.4515
42	0.3613	0.4481	0.4259
41	0.3386	0.4234	0.4025
40	0.3180	0.4007	0.3811
39	0.2991	0.3799	0.3609
38	0.2817	0.3606	0.3423
37	0.2657	0.3428	0.3250
36	0.2508	0.3263	0.3091
35	0.2371	0.3109	0.2943

A schedule for ages 35 through 64 was sufficient to encompass all the executives there was occasion to treat empirically, since most of them were already quite high up in their firms' hierarchy by the time pension plans came into common use.[1]

The second feature of individual annuity contracts which is pertinent to the calculations is their provision for a refund of the potential annuitant's premiums if he should die before attaining the age at which his annuity is to begin.[2] That provision specifies that his estate shall receive the amount of the *gross* premiums paid up to the time of his death *or* the cash value listed for that year, whichever is greater.[3] If an individual who contracted to purchase an annuity under the terms of the first schedule tabulated in this appendix died after making, say, three $100 annual premium payments, his estate would have received $300, since the cash value indicated for year 3 is only $244. If he had died after making eight payments, his estate would have received $832, which exceeds the $800 in total gross premiums paid to that point. In effect, the listed cash values represent the sum to which the individual's *net*

[1] See Chapter 7.

[2] No death benefits are payable after the annuity begins according to the form of that instrument chosen here as a standard of comparison for the pension. See Chapter 2.

[3] See also Appendix D.

premiums—net of sales commissions and administrative expenses—accumulate at the rate of interest guaranteed by the contract as of the end
of each successive year of premium payments. Thus, the insurance
company agrees to refund at least the absolute amount of the policyholder's gross premiums in the event of his premature death, and will
pay the accumulated amount of his net premiums if that figure is
greater.

This feature, of course, has a significant value to an individual who
might contemplate the purchase of an annuity and is, as was outlined in
Appendix D, an important element in the determination of that particular contract which is as valuable as his pension. It is desirable to tabulate
the present value of the possible death benefits per dollar of prospective
annuity along with the applicable premium rates in order to eliminate
the need to recompute those present values each time a measurement of
the annuity's *total* present value is required. This can be accomplished
by first converting the original schedule of cash values per $100 annual
premium into one expressed in terms of cash value per dollar of anticipated annuity receipt, and then using those figures as the inputs to the
death benefit present value formula developed in Appendix D.

To illustrate: A man, age 57, who contracted to pay eight $100 an-
nual premiums to the insurance company whose cash value schedule is
listed above would, as part of the bargain, be assured that his estate
would receive the following schedule of death benefits depending on the
time of his death:

If Death Should Occur at Age: [a]	The Estate Will Receive: [a]
57	$100
58	200
59	300
60	400
61	500
62	600
63	704
64	832

[a] Assumes premiums are paid at the
beginning of each year and that, if
death occurs, it is at some point subsequent to that payment.

If he paid instead the $1.4994 annual premium required for a $1 annuity, the associated schedule of death benefits would look like:

Age at Time of Death	Death Benefit
57	$ 1.4994
58	2.9988
59	4.4982
60	5.9976
61	7.4970
62	8.9964
63	10.5559
64	12.4750

Each of these values is simply (1.4994/100) of the corresponding figures above. This, then, is the relevant tabulation for age 57 for a schedule of per-dollar annuity present values for this particular insurance company. As indicated in Appendix D, death benefits are tax-free to the policyholder's estate if they represent merely a return of his gross premiums—as would be the case if he should die at any time prior to attaining age 63 in the example here—but a capital gains tax is assessed on any excess above the gross premiums. Thus, if our $1 annuity purchaser should die when he is age 63, his estate would receive, after taxes, $(10.5559) - (0.25)(10.5559 - 10.4958) =$ $10.5409, since $10.4958 represents the total amount of seven $1.4994 annual premiums. Similarly, if he should die the following year, his estate would receive $(12.4750) - (0.25)(12.4750 - 11.9952) =$ $12.3630 net of taxes.

When this series of potential after-tax death benefits is discounted for mortality and time deferral back to age 57 (as discussed in Appendix D), the result is the aggregate present value of those payments per dollar of retirement annuity purchased—the form in which it is most convenient to express the relationship for purposes of "current equivalent" calculations. Similar values can be obtained for each of the ages 35 through 64 at which executives might begin the purchase of an annuity, and the outcome for the insurance company whose cash value schedule has been used as an illustration here is:

Age at Time of Initial Premium Payment	Present Value of Death Benefit Per Dollar of Annuity
64	$0.3873
63	0.4002
62	0.4392
61	0.4794
60	0.5165
59	0.5476
58	0.5729
57	0.5968
.	.
.	.
.	.
37	0.6457
36	0.6360
35	0.6258

When these figures and the corresponding ones for the years 1938–48 for the other insurance company are averaged, a composite schedule of death benefit present values for that period similar to the composite premium rates derived earlier is obtained. When the process is repeated for the other two time periods of interest, the following tabulation results:

Age at Time of Initial Premium Payment	Present Value of Death Benefits Per Dollar of Annuity		
	1938–48	1949–58	1959–63
64	$0.3381	$0.3038	$0.2609
63	0.3650	0.3567	0.3281
62	0.4118	0.4197	0.3952
61	0.4575	0.4777	0.4560
60	0.4964	0.5288	0.5098
59	0.5310	0.5711	0.5496
58	0.5571	0.6085	0.5849
57	0.5808	0.6388	0.6152
56	0.6020	0.6646	0.6421
55	0.6218	0.6866	0.6656
54	0.6376	0.7041	0.6849
53	0.6503	0.7196	0.7020

(Continued)

Age at Time of Initial Premium Payment	Present Value of Death Benefits Per Dollar of Annuity		
	1938–48	1949–58	1959–63
52	0.6608	0.7321	0.7158
51	0.6692	0.7428	0.7269
50	0.6753	0.7509	0.7355
49	0.6795	0.7571	0.7422
48	0.6816	0.7614	0.7468
47	0.6825	0.7638	0.7492
46	0.6818	0.7647	0.7502
45	0.6795	0.7637	0.7495
44	0.6762	0.7619	0.7486
43	0.6718	0.7584	0.7464
42	0.6665	0.7538	0.7428
41	0.6601	0.7485	0.7381
40	0.6530	0.7420	0.7324
39	0.6453	0.7349	0.7250
38	0.6369	0.7268	0.7168
37	0.6281	0.7184	0.7081
36	0.6188	0.7093	0.6989
35	0.6092	0.6997	0.6893

This schedule and the one listed above, therefore, summarize the historical data on individual annuities which are relevant to the pension current equivalent computations.

APPENDIX L

PROFESSIONAL INCOMES ANALYSIS

In Chapter 9, a comparison was made of the rate of growth since 1940 of the total after-tax compensation of top executives and the after-tax earnings of "successful" physicians, lawyers, and dentists. As a means of estimating the likely impact of progressive personal income taxes on the last three groups, the assumption was that their earnings in 1962— the most recent year for which data are available—were of the same order of magnitude as the before-tax salaries and bonuses received by the executives in the sample studied. An assumption of this sort was necessary because published information on professional incomes exists only in the form of averages for the various occupational categories, and it is therefore impossible to identify the earnings of just that upper end of each which would seem to be the most logical focus for a comparison with senior executives. The objective here is to test the effects on such a comparison of some alternative income level choices.

The assumption made in Chapter 9 was that the before-tax earnings of the most successful men in the highest-paid of the three professions in 1962, i.e., medicine, were equal to the average before-tax direct current remuneration received during recent years by top executives. This implied a figure of $143,548 for physicians. The before-tax earnings of lawyers and dentists were then set equal to $97,439 and $99,984, respectively, these figures being in the same proportion to $143,548 as the reported averages for all lawyers and dentists were in 1962 to the average for all physicians. From the historical record of growth rates in before-tax earnings for the three groups, their incomes were projected back to 1940 and the relevant after-tax figures obtained.

As alternatives, the following assumptions will be tested here:

1. The before-tax earnings of the upper end of *all three* professions in 1962 equal to $143,548.

2. The before-tax earnings of the *lowest*-paid of the three—lawyers —set equal to $143,548 in 1962 and those of physicians and dentists raised proportionately to $211,450 and $147,295.

Developments back to 1940 may then be reproduced on these assumptions and new after-tax time series created. The results are summarized in the attached table and compared with executives' after-tax histories.

TABLE L-1

After-Tax Earnings Histories
(1940 = 1.00)

	Under Assumption 1 Above:			Under Assumption 2 Above:			Top Executives
Year	Physicians	Lawyers	Dentists	Physicians	Lawyers	Dentists	
1940	1.00	1.00	1.00	1.00	1.00	1.00	1.00
1941	0.94	0.86	0.94	0.91	0.86	0.93	0.95
1942	1.03	0.85	0.97	0.98	0.85	0.97	0.74
1943	1.09	0.80	1.02	1.00	0.80	1.01	0.65
1944	1.20	0.85	1.12	1.09	0.85	1.11	0.70
1945	1.29	0.88	1.14	1.15	0.88	1.14	0.69
1946	1.38	0.99	1.21	1.28	0.99	1.21	0.80
1947	1.42	1.03	1.24	1.32	1.03	1.23	0.84
1948	1.92	1.42	1.66	1.85	1.42	1.66	1.13
1949	1.97	1.41	1.68	1.90	1.41	1.68	1.19
1950	2.05	1.46	1.73	1.97	1.46	1.73	1.32
1951	2.11	1.48	1.75	2.00	1.48	1.74	1.29
1952	–	1.40	–	–	1.40	–	1.33
1953	–	1.44	–	–	1.44	–	1.44
1954	–	1.64	–	–	1.64	–	1.56
1955	–	–	–	–	–	–	2.15
1956	–	–	–	–	–	–	2.17
1957	–	–	–	–	–	–	2.20
1958	–	–	–	–	–	–	2.10
1959	2.90	2.06	2.60	2.70	2.06	2.60	2.16
1960	2.94	2.08	2.68	2.73	2.08	2.67	2.14
1961	3.01	2.21	2.79	2.79	2.21	2.78	2.16
1962	3.13	2.24	2.95	2.88	2.24	2.94	2.18
1963	–	–	–	–	–	–	2.16

As is evident, the conclusion reached in Chapter 9 that top executives have not fared as well as the professions in terms of rates of after-tax earnings growth still holds. The gap narrows the higher the pretax figures assumed for other occupations, but the range of estimates specified encompasses a fairly broad range of possibilities and should suffice for our purposes here.

APPENDIX M

COMPENSATION COST ANALYSIS

The question as to the relationship between the cost to the employer corporation of the various rewards in its executive pay package and the cost of the "current income equivalents" proposed for those rewards was raised at several points in the study. The answer to that question for each of the major components of the package is, given the appropriate framework by which to view the compensation transaction, quite clear-cut. The objective of this appendix is to spell out such a framework.

Pension Plans

Consider the case of an executive, now age x, who is promised K dollars per year in retirement under his firm's pension plan.[1] If we assume initially that there are no corporate or personal income taxes —which assumption will very shortly be relaxed—we may express the present value to him of that promise as

$$PV_P = (K) \left(\frac{N_{65}}{D_x} \right)$$

where N_{65} and D_x are the actuarial symbols defined in Appendix D and employed in developing the present value formulas in most subsequent appendixes. The annual cost to the corporation of providing the indicated pension is simply the annual premium it must pay for this

[1] For convenience, the discussion will be cast in terms of a *non*contributory pension and its current income equivalent. Nothing essential to the analysis is sacrificed by doing so, and the present value expressions necessary for the cost comparisons are much less complicated than would be the case for a contributory arrangement. The arguments developed and the conclusions reached will, however, apply equally to the latter.

346

executive to the insurance company from which it has purchased its group annuity contract.[2] If that premium is of size P_P per dollar of pension, the total annual cost to the firm for the executive in question is

$$C_P = (K)(P_P),$$

which cost it will incur each year until the man retires.

Now, according to the reasoning suggested in Chapter 2, the "current income equivalent" of an employee's pension is the increment to his annual after-tax salary which would permit him to purchase an individual retirement annuity having the same present value. In the absence of taxes, of course, a straight life annuity of precisely K dollars to begin at age 65 would be as valuable to our hypothetical executive as his pension, since its present value would also be

$$PV_A = (K)\left(\frac{N_{65}}{D_x}\right)$$

as of age x.[3] If we then let P_A denote the annual premium charged by an insurance company for a \$1 annuity of this type, the total annual premium that would be required of the executive beginning at age x and continuing through age 64 is

$$C_A = (K)(P_A)$$

and a salary increase of the same amount would be an appropriate substitute for his pension; he could acquire the annuity with that increase and be as well off in terms of present value.

The issue for our attention, therefore, is whether, given indifference from the executive's standpoint, the salary increase or the pension

---

[2] Or, alternatively, the amount the firm must set aside on the executive's behalf in its own pension fund if it has chosen to manage that fund itself.

[3] Again, for convenience and ease of comparison, the preretirement death benefits payable under such an arrangement will be ignored. The analysis should be affected very little by this simplification, however, since the present value of those prospective payments is in all cases quite small in relation to that of the retirement benefits themselves. For example, according to the mortality table used in the empirical portion of the current study, and assuming a 2½ per cent discount rate, the present value to an executive, age 40, of a \$1 per year retirement benefit to begin at age 65 is \$5.113. The present value of the preretirement death benefits associated with an individual annuity contract of that size is only about \$0.732. For a man, age 50, the corresponding figures are \$6.784 and \$0.735.

promise is more costly to the company. Since both costs have been put in the form of an annual outlay extending over the same future period, the relevant comparison is simply

$$C_P = (K)(P_P) \lessgtr (K)(P_A) = C_A.$$

Clearly, if $P_P = P_A$, i.e., if the premiums charged per dollar of prospective retirement benefit are the same for group annuity contracts as for individual annuities, the cost to the corporation of the current income equivalent of each of its employees' pensions will be equal to that of the pension itself.

It is worth noting that this assertion is completely independent of not only the executive's but the firm's opportunity costs. Whatever discount rate is chosen for the individual, the present value of the payments due under both his pension and its individual annuity counterpart are calculated using the same rate, which is built into the actuarial symbols N_x and D_x in the formulation above and thus is neutral in its impact on the comparisons. Similarly, if the costs to the firm of the two alternatives were expressed more fully as the *present values* of the indicated *series* of required annual outlays, the relationship between those present values would obviously be nothing more than a restatement of that between the annual figures themselves. This conclusion will be seen to apply to subsequent comparisons as well, since the analytical framework will be the same in each case.

Now, because group annuity premium rates are typically lower than those quoted for individual annuities, it would almost certainly turn out in practice that even if—as in the situation depicted—there were no corporate or personal income taxes, it would be less expensive for the business firm to provide pensions for its employees than to award them salary increases of equivalent value. In other words, we would expect to find that

$$P_P = (1 - a)(P_A)$$

where $0 < a < 1$. If so, then,

$$C_P < C_A,$$

since

$$(K)(P_P) = (K)(1 - a)(P_A) < (K)(P_A).$$

Thus, our first move toward a more realistic description of the relevant environment suggests that, for the corporation, the pension is the more "efficient" of the two alternatives proposed.

Introduction of the corporate income tax to the comparison leaves this relationship unchanged. Both the firm's contributions to its pension fund and any salary payments to its executives are tax-deductible. Hence the annual after-tax cost of the pension becomes

$$(K)(1 - a)(P_A)(1 - t_c)$$

where t_c denotes the corporate tax rate. Similarly, the annual cost of the salary equivalent is now

$$(K)(P_A)(1 - t_c).$$

Therefore, the conclusion remains that $C_P < C_A$ as long as group annuity premium rates—or funding obligations—are less per dollar of prospective benefit than those for individual annuity policies.

Consider next the impact of the personal income tax, assuming for the moment that the effective rate for the employee in question is expected to be the same after retirement as before and that both individual annuity benefits and any pension receipts are taxable in full at that rate. Under those conditions the present value to the employee of his pension now falls to

$$PV_P = (K)\left(\frac{N_{65}}{D_x}\right)(1 - t_p)$$

where t_p is the applicable personal tax rate. On the other hand, a matching decline in value is also associated with the K-dollar individual annuity which was, in the absence of taxes, as valuable to him as the indicated pension. Thus,

$$PV_A = (K)\left(\frac{N_{65}}{D_x}\right)(1 - t_p) = PV_P.$$

Accordingly, an annual premium of $(P_A)(K)$ dollars will *still* permit the purchase from an insurance company of an annuity of the proper size, and therefore $(K)(P_A)$ continues to define the amount of the "after-tax current income equivalent" at issue. In order to provide the executive with that much additional take-home pay each year, however, the corporation would have to raise his *before-tax* salary by $(K)(P_A)/(1 - t_p)$ dollars, thereby incurring a net annual cost of

$$C_A = \frac{(K)(P_A)(1 - t_c)}{(1 - t_p)}.$$

This obviously would be rather substantially in excess of the cost of the pension itself, since

$$C_P = (K)(1 - a)(P_A)(1 - t_c) < \frac{(K)(P_A)(1 - t_c)}{(1 - t_p)} = C_A.$$

The factor $1/(1 - t_p)$ represents, in effect, the tax advantage which results from the fact that employees need not, under present law, include in their taxable income the contributions made on their behalf to qualified corporate retirement plans by their employers. If such contributions *were* taxable—or if it were possible for the employee to opt instead for a salary increase which would be considered tax-free by the IRS as long as it were used for the purchase of an individual retirement annuity to replace his pension—the relationship between the cost to the firm of the two alternatives would revert to that wherein the only difference was attributable to a difference in group annuity and individual annuity premium rates.

The conclusion that the pension is less expensive than its current equivalent holds, therefore, even under the assumption that the employee's tax rate in retirement is as high as that which he confronts while still working. A more likely circumstance, of course, would be a lower over-all effective rate past age 65, since the man's income is almost certain to diminish when he retires. Nonetheless, if we let t_r denote the anticipated postretirement personal tax rate, where $t_r < t_p$, we simply substitute the term $(1 - t_r)$ for $(1 - t_p)$ in the expressions above for the present values of both the pension and the individual annuity, and we establish once again that

$$PV_P = PV_A,$$

since both are equal to

$$(K)\left(\frac{N_{65}}{D_x}\right)(1 - t_r).$$

Therefore, P_A and P_P are still the relevant annual pension and annuity premiums, and the resulting cost comparison from the standpoint of the firm remains

$$C_P = (K)(P_P)(1 - t_c) < \frac{(K)(P_A)(1 - t_c)}{(1 - t_p)} = C_A$$

where, as before, $P_P = (1 - a)(P_A)$.

Let us then remove the final constraint imposed on the analysis and recognize that in fact the retirement benefits received under an individual annuity policy are taxed less heavily than those received under a corporate pension plan. As indicated in Chapter 2, a portion of the annuity benefits are considered by the IRS to constitute a return of the policyholder's premiums and, as such, are exempt from tax. In particular, the fraction

$$F = \frac{(P_A)(65 - x)}{15}$$

of each payment received by the annuitant in retirement will be tax-free.[4] Accordingly, the present value, as of age x, of a K-dollar individual annuity is in reality

$$PV_A = (K)\left(\frac{N_{65}}{D_x}\right)[1 - t_r(1 - F)],$$

which is necessarily a somewhat larger present value than that implied by the prospect of a K-dollar pension benefit. As a result, the corporation, in order to permit the employee concerned to obtain an adequate replacement for that pension, need only raise his annual take-home pay by an amount equal to the premiums on an individual annuity of size $(K)(1 - b)$, where

$$PV_P = (K)\left(\frac{N_{65}}{D_x}\right)(1 - t_r) = (K)\left(\frac{N_{65}}{D_x}\right)[1 - t_r(1 - F)](1 - b) = PV_A'$$

and, of course, $0 < b < 1$. In short, a smaller annuity than that sug-

---

[4] Thus, $(P_A)(65 - x)$ represents the aggregate premiums per dollar of prospective annuity which will be paid between age x and age 65 by the policyholder, and fifteen years is specified by the IRS as his life expectancy at age 65, i.e., the aggregate annuity payments he is expected to receive under the contract.

gested by the simpler comparisons above will suffice to define the pension's current equivalent. Solving for $(1 - b)$, we find that

$$(1 - b) = \frac{1 - t_r}{1 - t_r(1 - F)}$$

and the annual individual annuity premium the employee would have to be able to meet out of any salary increase is just $(K)(P_A)(1 - b)$.

The cost to the firm of providing that increase would be

$$C_A = \frac{(K)(P_A)(1 - b)(1 - t_c)}{(1 - t_p)}$$

as compared with a pension cost of

$$C_P = (K)(P_A)(1 - a)(1 - t_c).$$

Therefore, if

$$(K)(P_A)(1 - a)(1 - t_c) < \frac{(K)(P_A)(1 - b)(1 - t_c)}{(1 - t_p)}$$

the pension will, after all, be less expensive than its current equivalent.

Assuming temporarily that $a = 0$, i.e., that there is no difference between group annuity and individual annuity premium rates, we may state the necessary condition as

$$1 < \frac{1 - b}{1 - t_p}$$

or

$$1 - t_p < 1 - b.$$

Substituting for $(1 - b)$

$$1 - t_p < \frac{(1 - t_r)}{1 - t_r(1 - F)}.$$

Clearly, even if F were equal to its maximum possible value of unity (the annuity benefits being completely tax-free), the inequality would hold, since we have established that $t_r < t_p$.[5] Any smaller F would then

[5] This result may be interpreted as follows: The tax saving in retirement occasioned by the employee's not having to pay taxes on his annuity benefits is necessarily less than the tax disadvantage involved in raising his salary during his active working life by enough to enable him to pay the taxes thereon and still end up with sufficient funds to purchase that annuity.

imply a larger value for the quotient on the right-hand side of the inequality and reinforce that relationship.

Finally, if we permit a to take on a positive value, the question becomes whether

$$(1 - a)(1 - t_p) < 1 - b,$$

the answer to which is obvious, given that $(1 - t_p) < (1 - b)$.

Our conclusion, therefore, is that under almost any conceivable set of circumstances, the cost of the pension to the employer corporation will be smaller than the cost of the salary increase which would provide the executive with the same level of after-tax remuneration. Only if the executive were expecting a higher total annual income after retirement than before, or if group annuity premium rates exceeded those quoted for individual annuities, could this conclusion be reversed. Both situations, of course, are extremely unlikely to occur in practice.[6]

Deferred Compensation

A similar story emerges from an examination of the costs of deferred compensation arrangements and their current equivalents. Consider an executive, now age x, who is promised K dollars per year for a total of m years upon his retirement at age 65. If we start out once again assuming that neither personal nor corporate income taxes are imposed, the present value to him of that promise as of age x may be written as

$$PVDC = (K) \left(\frac{N_{65} - N_{65+m}}{D_x} \right)$$

and the present value of the cost of those payments to the firm as

$$C_{dc} = (K) \left(\frac{N'_{65} - N'_{65+m}}{D'_x} \right).$$

[6] The preretirement vs. postretirement income issue does, however, illustrate why it would be inappropriate for a firm to attempt to minimize its compensation costs by paying only nominal salaries and utilizing pension benefits as the major component of the pay package. Even if its employees would accept such a strategy and the government would sanction it (corporate tax deductions for pension fund contributions are limited by law to 15 per cent of employee wage costs), at some point it would turn out that prospective pension receipts exceeded current salary payments and the tax advantage would disappear (in the formulation above, this would imply $t_r > t_p$).

The notation N'_i and D'_i indicates that the discount rates built into the actuarial symbols may not be the same for the executive and the corporation and therefore that the present value of exactly the same series of payments may differ depending on which one is doing the evaluating. Thus the relevant definitions are

$$D_x = l_x v^x = l_x \left(\frac{1}{1 + r_e}\right)^x$$

$$N_{65} - N_{65+m} = D_{65} + D_{66} + \cdots + D_{65+m-1}$$

$$D'_x = l_x (v')^x = l_x \left(\frac{1}{1 + r_c}\right)^x$$

$$N'_{65} - N'_{65+m} = D'_{65} + D'_{66} + \cdots + D'_{65+m-1}$$

where r_e represents the executive's opportunity cost and r_c the corporation's.[7] Clearly, if $r_c > r_e$, then $D'_x < D_x$ and $(N'_{65} - N'_{65+m}) < (N_{65} - N_{65+m})$; i.e., the present value of the cost of the arrangement to the corporation is less than the present value of the reward it implies for the executive.

Now, the "current income equivalent" of such a series of payments is taken to be that increase in the executive's salary which, if maintained from age x through age 64, would have the same present value to him. Denoting this increase by S, we have

$$(S) \left(\frac{N_x - N_{65}}{D_x}\right) = PVDC,$$

since, of course, the executive must remain alive up to retirement in order to claim all those additional payments. Substituting and solving for S

$$S = \frac{(PVDC)(D_x)}{(N_x - N_{65})}$$

$$S = (K) \frac{(N_{65} - N_{65+m})}{(N_x - N_{65})}.$$

[7] As in the case of pension plans, any death benefits payable under the deferred compensation contract will be ignored in order to simplify the analysis. Such a step will not affect our conclusions, however, since the present value of those benefits would appear in both the executive's and the firm's appraisal of the contract in question and—except for the same sort of effect of possible differences in discount rates which will be pinpointed in the discussion that follows—would thereby raise both to the same extent.

The question, then, is whether the cost to the firm of a salary increase of this magnitude differs from the cost of the deferred pay contract itself. That is, whether

$$C_s = (S)\left(\frac{N'_x - N'_{65}}{D'_x}\right) \lessgtr (K)\left(\frac{N'_{65} - N'_{65+m}}{D'_x}\right) = C_{dc}.$$

Substituting now for S and rearranging, the issue reduces to

$$\frac{(N'_x - N'_{65})}{(N_x - N_{65})} \lessgtr \frac{(N'_{65} - N'_{65+m})}{(N_{65} - N_{65+m})}.$$

If the same discount rate applies to both the executive and the corporation $(r_e = r_c)$, it will be true for all i that $N_i = N'_i$. In that case, the quotients on either side of this expression will be equal to one, and we may conclude that $C_s = C_{dc}$.

If, on the other hand, the corporation's opportunity cost exceeds that of the executive, it turns out that [8]

$$\frac{(N'_x - N'_{65})}{(N_x - N_{65})} > \frac{(N'_{65} - N'_{65+m})}{(N_{65} - N_{65+m})}$$

and therefore:

$$C_s > C_{dc}$$

which is, of course, what our intuition would lead us to expect. Thus, if a firm has available to it better investment opportunities than do its employees, it is not surprising to discover that, in effect, the advantage to it of being able to defer a portion of their wages is greater than the accompanying disadvantage that deferment entails for them. If, however, the firm can do no better with the funds than can the employees involved, neither party stands to gain through a deferred pay arrangement, and the current equivalent of such a contract would, at least in the absence of taxes, be precisely as expensive as the contract itself. If the firm cannot do as well, the current equivalent is cheaper. The consensus would probably be that, in practice, the first of the three situations is the most likely.[9]

---

[8] The difference in discount rates makes itself felt more strongly the farther in the future are the payments being considered. Thus, the ratio of any N'_i to the corresponding N_i or D'_i to D_i becomes smaller as i increases.

[9] It is important to recognize in this connection that, in speaking of potential investment returns, care must be taken to compare alternatives in which the

The presence of a corporate income tax does not alter these conclusions, since both immediate salary payments and any eventual outlays for deferred compensation awards are tax-deductible at the time they are made. Thus the present value, as of age x, of the net cost to the firm of the deferred payments described above is

$$C_{dc} = (K)(1 - t_c)\left(\frac{N'_{65} - N'_{65+m}}{D'_x}\right)$$

where t_c denotes the corporate tax rate. The cost of the current equivalent thereof is

$$C_s = (S)(1 - t_c)\left(\frac{N'_x - N'_{65}}{D'_x}\right)$$

and a comparison of the two produces exactly the same result as in the no tax case; i.e., if

$$\frac{(N'_x - N'_{65})}{(N_x - N_{65})} > \frac{(N'_{65} - N'_{65+m})}{(N_{65} - N_{65+m})}$$

then $C_s > C_{dc}$, the particular corporate tax rate levied being quite irrelevant.

The personal income tax is similarly neutral in its impact on the analysis as long as the executive in question is subject to the same overall effective rate after retirement as before. Under those conditions the present value to him, as of age x, of a series of m payments of K dollars each beginning at age 65 is

$$PVDC = (K)(1 - t_p)\left(\frac{N_{65} - N_{65+m}}{D_x}\right)$$

where t_p represents the applicable personal tax rate. It would therefore require an increase in his annual after-tax salary of only

$$S' = \frac{(PVDC)(D_x)}{(N_x - N_{65})}$$

$$S' = (K)(1 - t_p)\left(\frac{N_{65} - N_{65+m}}{(N_x - N_{65})}\right)$$

risks incurred are similar. Thus a corporation may indeed have available opportunities for employing its funds which hold out the promise of a rather higher rate of return than those effectively open to its executives as individuals, but such opportunities may also subject the firm to the possibility of more substantial losses if they do not work out as planned. Only if the corporation has differentially better investment prospects within given "risk classes" can we legitimately credit it with an advantage over its employees.

dollars in order to provide him with an equivalent reward. Before taxes, of course, this would mean a salary increase of $S'/(1 - t_p)$ dollars, having a net cost to the employer corporation of

$$C_s = (S') \frac{(1 - t_c)}{(1 - t_p)} \left[\frac{(N'_x - N'_{65})}{D'_x} \right].$$

This, conveniently, simplifies to

$$C_s = (S)(1 - t_c) \left(\frac{N'_x - N'_{65}}{D'_x} \right)$$

as in the situation where there were no personal income taxes. In effect, the reduction in the size of the computed equivalent salary increase which results from taking into account the taxes inevitably due on post-retirement income is precisely offset by the requirement that sufficient before-tax salary be paid to enable the executive to meet the taxes thereon while still an active employee. The cost to the firm of the deferred payments remains

$$C_{dc} = (K)(1 - t_c) \left(\frac{N'_{65} - N'_{65+m}}{D'_x} \right)$$

and the relationship between the two costs continues to be as expressed above.

If, however—as seems more likely—the executive's income falls when he retires and therefore his personal tax rate in retirement is expected to be lower than that applicable to his present salary, there is a clear cost advantage to deferred compensation arrangements. Letting t_r again denote the relevant postretirement tax rate, we have

$$PVDC = (K)(1 - t_r) \left(\frac{N_{65} - N_{65+m}}{D_x} \right)$$

for the after-tax present value to the executive of the deferred payments. An after-tax salary increase of size

$$S'' = \frac{(PVDC)(D_x)}{(N_x - N_{65})}$$

extending from age x through age 64 would be as valuable. The necessary before-tax increase then is $S''/(1 - t_p)$, and the present value of its cost to the corporation becomes

$$C_s = \frac{(S'')(1 - t_c)(N'_x - N'_{65})}{(1 - t_p)(D'_x)}$$

$$C_s = \frac{(K)(1 - t_r)(1 - t_c)(N'_x - N'_{65})(N_{65} - N_{65+m})}{(N_x - N_{65})(1 - t_p)(D'_x)} .$$

This compares with a cost of

$$C_{dc} = \frac{(K)(1 - t_c)(N'_{65} - N'_{65+m})}{D'_x}$$

for the deferred payments, and leads to the conclusion that if

$$\frac{(1 - t_r)(N'_x - N'_{65})}{(1 - t_p)(N_x - N_{65})} > \frac{(N'_{65} - N'_{65+m})}{(N_{65} - N_{65+m})} ,$$

the cost of the current equivalent of those payments is greater than that of the payments themselves. Accordingly, even in the situation where the corporation's and the executive's discount rates are identical, it will be true in the reduced expression that

$$\frac{1 - t_r}{1 - t_p} > 1$$

as long as $t_r < t_p$, and the current equivalent will be the more expensive reward. The existence of *either* of two conditions therefore is sufficient to establish a preference for deferred compensation over an immediate salary increase of comparable value: the firm has better investment opportunities than do its employees, or the income of the latter is expected to fall upon retirement. The probabilities certainly seem to point in the direction of at least one of the two being fulfilled in virtually every instance.[10]

Stock Options

The conclusion in the case of stock options is no less precise, but the analysis suggests there is rather more room for the adjustment of com-

[10] The preceding discussion applies as well to deferred compensation plans under which payments are to be made in the form of shares of the corporation's common stock. Thus, it makes no difference to the arguments made whether the value for K in the various formulas is actually specified by the contract being considered or is estimated from stock price data. However the figure is obtained, the current equivalent format is the same; any increments in the value of the arrangement in subsequent years are treated separately as they occur; and the comparisons indicated hold without qualification. See Chapter 5.

pensation strategy to the circumstances of the individual employee. Consider an executive who exercises a stock option for m shares at a time when the market price of those shares is equal to P_m. Given an option price of P_o, his before-tax profit is $K = (m)(P_m - P_o)$. With a capital gains tax rate equal to t_g, his after-tax reward comes to $(K)(1 - t_g)$ dollars. The cost of that transaction to the employer corporation is measured simply by the dilution in the shareholders' equity occasioned by the sale of a portion of the ownership of the firm to the executive at a price less than its actual value—in short, by the same total price differential, K, which defines his before-tax reward. Since no deductions from taxable income are allowed the firm in connection with the granting or subsequent exercise of stock options, K also represents the *after-tax* cost to it of that instrument.

Now, in order to have provided the executive with the same level of remuneration, it would have been necessary to award him a bonus of $(K)(1 - t_g)/(1 - t_p)$ dollars in the year of exercise, where t_p is the personal tax rate he would be subject to on that increment.[11] The cost of this alternative scheme would have been

$$C_s = \frac{(K)(1 - t_c)(1 - t_g)}{(1 - t_p)}$$

given a corporate income tax rate of t_c. The question then is which of the two costs is the larger,

$$C_s = \frac{(K)(1 - t_c)(1 - t_g)}{(1 - t_p)} \lessgtr K = C_o$$

or, simply

$$\frac{(1 - t_c)(1 - t_g)}{(1 - t_p)} \lessgtr 1.$$

As it turns out, the inequality may run either way, depending on the tax rates applicable to the particular situation. If we assume a 50 percent corporate tax rate and adopt the 15 per cent figure for the "ad-

---

[11] More accurately, the proposal offered in the text was for a current equivalent in which the required payments would be spread over a period of years and have an after-tax *present value* equal to $(K)(1 - t_g)$. It is more convenient to deal here with only a single payment, however, and the conclusions reached are not affected by doing so.

justed" capital gains rate which was rationalized in Chapter 4,[12] we can solve for the marginal personal income tax bracket in which the cost of the option is just equal to the cost of its current equivalent:

$$(1 - .50)(1 - .15) = (1 - t_p^*)$$
$$t_p^* = 0.575.$$

Therefore, only if the executive under consideration must pay taxes on any additions to his current income at a rate greater than 57.5 per cent will the corporation find it less expensive to grant him stock options than to provide a salary increase of equivalent value.

According to the tax rates in effect during the last decade of the period studied here—1954 through 1963—this "breakeven" point was located at a salary level of approximately $77,700, a figure which is derived as follows: If we assume that deductions and exemptions from taxable income amount to about 15 per cent of gross income for the typical executive,[13] the critical marginal tax rate on *taxable* income is $57.5/.85 = 67.6$ per cent. Thus, an extra dollar of salary or bonus received by the executive will normally give rise to just 85 cents of additional taxable income, and it is not until he attains a level of reward such that taxes are assessed on the taxable portion thereof at a 67.6 per cent marginal rate that he in fact incurs a tax liability of 57.5 cents on the extra dollar. Until 1964 the taxable income bracket in which that rate was exceeded for a married taxpayer was $76,000-to-$88,000, implying in the view here a gross income of at least $76,000/.85, or $89,400, before the indicated percentage took effect. Now, if we further assume— as was suggested in Chapter 2—that the executive is likely to have income from sources other than salary and bonus equal to 15 per cent of the latter, an annual direct current remuneration figure of $89,400/1.15, or $77,700, would have been sufficient to generate a total taxable income of $76,000 and therefore represents the point beyond which stock options were less costly to the employer corporation than matching increases in its executives' salaries and bonuses. A similar analysis

---

[12] Adjusted to reflect the impact of the additional deductions and exemptions from ordinary income likely to be generated by stock option profits and also the possibility that the optionee might not resell the shares involved before his death, thereby avoiding the capital gains tax entirely.

[13] See Chapter 2 and Appendix A.

using the lower personal tax rates introduced in 1964 [14] reveals that nowadays only those executives with salaries and bonuses in excess of fully $163,700 should be granted options. For the rest—and that category obviously includes all but a very few individuals even in the largest firms—salary increases tied to the price of the corporation's stock are a less expensive form of reward.

[14] That is, the rates applicable to the years 1965 and thereafter, these being the end product of a two-step reduction begun in 1964.

BIBLIOGRAPHY

A. Books

Baker, John C., *Executive Salaries and Bonus Plans,* New York: McGraw-Hill, 1938

Burgess, Leonard R., *Top Executive Pay Package,* New York, Free Press, 1963

Cootner, Paul H. (ed.), *The Random Character of Stock Market Prices,* Cambridge, Mass.: The M.I.T. Press, 1964

Fetter, Robert B., and Johnson, Donald C., *Compensation and Incentives for Industrial Executives,* Bloomington, Ind.: Indiana University Press, 1952

Gordon, Robert A., *Business Leadership in the Large Corporation,* Berkeley: University of California Press, 1961

Hall, Challis A., *Effects of Taxation on Executive Compensation and Retirement Plans,* Cambridge, Mass.: Riverside Press, 1951

Hamilton, James A., and Bronson, Dorrance ˜., *Pensions,* New York: McGraw-Hill, 1958

Industrial Union Department, AFL-CIO, *The Stock Option Scandal,* Washington, D.C., 1960

Lampman, Robert J., *The Share of Top Wealth-Holders in National Wealth: 1922–1956,* Princeton University Press for NBER, 1962

Marris, Robin, *The Economic Theory of Managerial Capitalism,* New York: Free Press, 1964

Patton, Arch, *Men, Money, and Motivation,* New York: McGraw-Hill, 1961

Poston, Charles F., *Restricted Stock Options for Management,* Research Paper 2, School of Business Administration, University of North Carolina, Chapel Hill, 1960

Roberts, David R., *Executive Compensation,* Glencoe, Ill.: Free Press, 1959

Sanders, Thomas H., *Effects of Taxation on Executives,* Cambridge, Mass.: Riverside Press, 1951

Siegel, Sidney, *Nonparametric Statistics for the Behavioral Sciences,* New York: McGraw-Hill, 1956

Smyth, Richard C., *Financial Incentives for Management,* New York: McGraw-Hill, 1960

Sweeney, Daniel L., *Accounting for Stock Options,* Bureau of Business Research, School of Business Administration, University of Michigan, Ann Arbor, 1960

Washington, George T., and Rothschild, V. Henry, *Corporate Executives' Compensation,* New York, Ronald Press, 1942 (title changed to *Compensating the Corporate Executive* for 2nd and 3rd eds., 1951 and 1962)

B. Publications of the Government

U.S. Bureau of the Census, *U.S. Census of Population: 1950, Volume IV, Special Reports,* Part I, Chapter B, "Ocupational Characteristics," Washington: U.S. Government Printing Office, 1956

U.S. Bureau of the Census, *U.S. Census of Population: 1960, Subject Reports, Occupational Characteristics,* Final Report PC(2)-7A, Washington: U.S. Government Printing Office, 1963

U.S. Bureau of the Census, *Statistical Abstract of the United States: 1965,* Washington: U.S. Government Printing Office, 1965

U.S. Committee on Ways and Means, *Tax Revision Compendium,* Vol. 4, Part 1. Washington: U.S. Government Printing Office, 1951

U.S. Department of Commerce, *Survey of Current Business,* Washington: U.S. Government Printing Office: August 1949; January 1950; July 1950; July 1951; July 1952; December 1956; May 1965

U.S. Department of Health, Education, and Welfare, Social Security Administration, Division of Research and Statistics, Research Note #13-1965, *Incomes of Physicians and Dentists from Private Self-Employment Practice: 1960–1962,* Washington: U.S. Government Printing Office, 1965

U.S. Department of Labor, Bureau of Labor Statistics, *Employment and Earnings Statistics for the United States: 1909–1964* (Bulletin No. 1312-2), Washington: U.S. Government Printing Office, 1964

U.S. Joint Committee on the Economic Report, *Federal Tax Policy for Economic Growth and Stability: Hearings Before the Subcommittee on Tax Policy,* 84 Cong., 1st Sess., Washington: U.S. Government Printing Office, 1955

U.S. Joint Economic Committee, *The Federal Revenue System: Facts and Problems,* Washington: U.S. Government Printing Office, 1960 and 1964

U.S. Joint Economic Committee, *The Federal Tax System: Facts and Problems,* Washington: U.S. Government Printing Office, 1964

U.S. Securities and Exchange Commission, *Official Summary of Security Transactions and Holdings,* Vols. 16–30, Washington: U.S. Government Printing Office, 1950–1964

U.S. Statutes at Large, 81st Cong., 2d Sess., Vol. 64, Part 1, Washington: U.S. Government Printing Office, 1951

U.S. Statutes at Large, 83d Cong., 2d Sess., Vol. 68A, Part 1, Washington: U.S. Government Printing Office, 1954

U.S. Treasury Department, Internal Revenue Service, *Statistics of Income, Business Tax Returns,* Washington: U.S. Government Printing Office, 1959–1962

U.S. Treasury Department, Internal Revenue Service, *Statistics of Income, Individual Tax Returns,* Washington: U.S. Government Printing Office, 1944, 1947, 1950, 1953, 1956, and 1959

C. Periodicals

Baumol, William J., "On the Theory of the Expansion of the Firm," *American Economic Review,* December 1962, pp. 1078–1087

Boness, A. James, "Elements of a Theory of Stock Option Value," *Journal of Political Economy,* April 1964, pp. 163–175

Business Week, "Executive Pay Rides Profit Tide," May 15, 1965, pp. 88–118

Chamber of Commerce of the United States, *Fringe Benefits 1963,* Washington, D.C., 1964

Commerce Clearing House, *Standard Federal Tax Reporter,* New York, 1960–1965

Fisher, Lawrence, and Lorie, James H., "Rates of Return on Investments in Common Stocks," *Journal of Business,* January 1964, pp. 1–21

Ford, Henry, II, "Stock Options Are in the Public Interest," *Harvard Business Review,* July–August 1961, pp. 45–51

Fortune, "The Fortune Directory," July 1964, pp. 179–198

Friedman, Milton, and Savage, Leonard J., "The Utility Analysis of Choices Involving Risk," *Journal of Political Economy,* August 1948, pp. 279–304

Giguere, G., "Warrants: A Mathematical Method of Evaluation," *Analysts Journal,* 14(1958), pp. 17–25

Griswold, Erwin N., "Are Stock Options Getting Out of Hand?", *Harvard Business Review,* November–December 1960, pp. 44–55

Holland, Daniel M., "Review" of Leonard R. Burgess, *Top Executive Pay Package,* in *Political Science Quarterly,* March 1964, pp. 129–133.

Holland, Daniel M., and Lewellen, Wilbur G., "Probing the Record of Stock Options," *Harvard Business Review,* March–April 1962, pp. 132–150

Ivins, James S. Y., "What Is New in Employee Stock Options," *Proceedings: New York University Tenth Annual Institute on Federal Taxation,* New York, Bender & Company, 1952, pp. 121–149

Lent, George E., and Menge, John A., "The Importance of Restricted Stock Options in Executive Compensation," *Management Record,* June 1962

Lentz, Bernard V., "Restricted Stock Options—Problems of the Executive," *Proceedings: New York University Fifteenth Annual Institute on Federal Taxation,* New York, Bender & Company, 1957, pp. 1117–1146

Lurie, Alvin D.,"Case History of a Stock Option Plan," *Proceedings: New York University Fourteenth Annual Institute on Federal Taxation,* New York, Bender & Company, 1956, pp. 1095–1122

McGuire, Joseph W., Chiu, John S. Y., and Elbing, Alvar O., "Executive Incomes, Sales, and Profits," *American Economic Review,* September 1962, pp. 753–761

Moody's Industrial Manual, 1941–1964, New York: Moody's Investors Service, Inc.

Patton, Arch., "Deterioration in Top Executive Pay," *Harvard Business Review,* November–December 1965, pp. 106–118

Poor's Register of Corporations, Directors, and Executives, 1952–1964, New York: Standard & Poor's Corporation, 1952–1964

Rayack, Elton, "The Supply of Physicians' Services," *Industrial and Labor Relations Review,* January 1964, pp. 221–237

Samuelson, Paul A., "Rational Theory of Warrant Pricing," *Industrial Management Review,* Spring 1965, pp. 13–32

Simon, Herbert A., "The Compensation of Executives," *Sociometry,* March 1957, pp. 32–35

Who's Who in America, Vols. 21–33, Chicago: Marquis-Who's Who, Inc., 1940–1964

Williamson, Oliver E., "Managerial Discretion and Business Behavior," *American Economic Review,* December 1963, pp. 1032–1057

World Who's Who in Commerce and Industry, Vols. 3–13, Chicago: Marquis-Who's Who, Inc., 1940–1965

INDEX